ENGLISH SEAMEN AND THE COLONIZATION OF AMERICA

Sir John Hawkins

ENGLISH SEAMEN AND THE COLONIZATION OF AMERICA

BY

EDWARD KEBLE CHATTERTON

WITH 26 ILLUSTRATIONS

BOOKS FOR LIBRARIES PRESS
FREEPORT, NEW YORK

First Published 1930
Reprinted 1971

INTERNATIONAL STANDARD BOOK NUMBER:
0-8369-6679-1

LIBRARY OF CONGRESS CATALOG CARD NUMBER:
74-37332

PRINTED IN THE UNITED STATES OF AMERICA
BY
NEW WORLD BOOK MANUFACTURING CO., INC.
HALLANDALE, FLORIDA 33009

In Honour of the Pioneers
Who Sailed the Seas
Cleared the Ground and
Planted Colonies for the
Coming of a Great Nation

" God gave a new light of a new world by the discovery of America, now daily known and frequented by us of Europe, and whose soil yields benefit to the Christian world."

(SIR WILLIAM MONSON, 1568–1643.)

PREFACE

I HAVE endeavoured in the following chapters to show how in the long process of colonizing America the very seeds of liberty were simultaneously being sown, so that the idea of independence was to develop not as a surprising phenomenon, but as an inevitable and natural harvest.

This is one long drama of ships and exploration, plantations and policies, plots and rebellions, follies and fatalities ; but above all it is a study of human endeavour amid every conceivable kind of obstacle, and a final triumph of liberty. No fiction could be more heroic than the real-life characters whose fears and jealousies, hatreds and suspicions, disappointments and sufferings, were part of their fight against Fate, against Nature, against the stupidity of ruling forces.

On the continent of North America was to be decided the last struggle of medieval ideas in regard to monarchy, and the first great principle essential to correct relations with a mother country. History is wasted if it does not hold out for us concentrated lessons for future guidance in avoiding old mistakes. No narrative could be more illuminating than that which in such few centuries gives us so clearly the results of certain actions and attitudes. And in these pages my aim has been not merely to assemble many apparently trivial and insignificant details which make up the mosaics and composite pictures, but to trace big events from their motives through environment to their inevitable and far-reaching conclusions.

In trying to get down to the very heart and mind of the man at the back of each great adventure, and indicating what influences were contemporary, the American pageant loses none of its brilliance and becomes more easy to comprehend. And I have found it well to stress the somewhat neglected but extremely important destiny which was occasioned by ocean, hulls and mariners.

E. KEBLE CHATTERTON.

CONTENTS

9

ILLUSTRATIONS

ENGLISH SEAMEN AND THE COLONIZATION OF AMERICA

CHAPTER I

THE SCHOOL FOR ADVENTURERS

A MERICAN history begins not with the bodily arrival on her continent of the first visitors from Europe, but with the birth of an idea that primarily had nothing whatever to do with colonization, still less with the founding of a great nation.

The story of the United States is one long drama, rich in characterization, suspense, crisis, human disappointment, high hope, sterling courage ; and like all great dramas there is at the back of this an inspiration, a motive. The inspiration was unquestionably the sea, the motive was that deep-seated instinct of eager curiosity which is thinly separated from that other wild yearning for liberty. Indeed, as the drama develops, we find that there is a distinct and repeating theme as noticeable as the leit-motif in a Wagnerian opera ; over and over again, in every generation, this liberty-melody comes singing up, then fades away amid the clash of discordant notes, till it rises like the triumphal chant in the final attainment of independence.

Accurately speaking, the first figure in this drama is that unknown man who left the shelter of his river and began running before the wind in a rude craft with a primitive square-sail. In the truest sense of the word he thus learned the freedom of the sea, and that there was here a means of gratifying his curiosity for observing what was hidden beyond that next headland ; what lay the other side of another wide bight. Few forces in the world have been so seductive as the sea, and the briefest cruises led him on to desire ardently those long, satisfying voyages. But the zest for travel was one thing ; the practicability of traversing wide oceans was something quite different. In a word, then, it was not till ships became more than boats, not till Europe knew how to build big-bellied, multiple-masted vessels, that this dream of crossing wide oceans could possibly come true.

That is to say, the period must be subsequent to one which relied chiefly on the galley type, and could not keep the sea for longer than a few days at a time. Relying for its propulsive power chiefly, though not exclusively, on its oars, the galley was thus committed to a very large crew, which in turn demanded considerable supplies of food and water. And these required additional space which could not be afforded. Again, even for long-suffering slaves, there comes a time every twenty-four hours when they must sleep and rest. Now a long, open, oared craft such as belonged to the classical Mediterranean of Greece and Rome, as handed down to them from the Egyptians through the Phœnicians, could and did make occasional lengthy passages when compelled, but normally she was hauled ashore every night ; the crew bivouacked on the beach, cooked their food and went to sleep. The story of the Phœnicians who, obeying the orders of the Egyptian ruler Neco, circumnavigated Africa about the beginning of the sixth century B.C., need not worry us ; for they were able to land, sow their corn, which rapidly became a crop, and then go on with short bursts of coasting. It would also have been not too strenuous (though distinctly unpleasant) for those Phœnician long, open galleys which came up the Bay of Biscay to the tin mines of Cornwall, just as the later Spanish galleys of the sixteenth century used to reach even Holland.

Now the Mediterranean seamen, with the most obstinate conservatism, encouraged the galley in spite of other ship developments for hundreds of years. True it is that these were primarily for fighting, and that even Rome had her beamy, deeper-draught, sail-driven vessels in which she fetched her corn from Egypt, but it took centuries before these grew into such a size that they could be satisfactorily adopted for use outside the Mediterranean. And when the hull was made bigger, more sail spread was needed, and this meant that for ease in handling the area must needs be split up. Thus, by the time a reliable ocean-keeping ship was evolved, she was a three-master with square-sails on the fore- and main-masts, but a typical Mediterranean triangular lateen sail on the mizzen- or after-mast.

Not till such a craft was being built could the trans-Atlantic crossing be seriously contemplated. Compared with the galley she needed few men, she could stand heavier weather, she could remain independent of the shore just as long as supplies lasted, and she was able to harness the wind even if death should decimate her crew.

But in some strange manner the ancient mind seemed to have a vague yet firm intuition that there was land right away west of the Mediterranean, and literature kept alive this belief. What Solon learned from the Egyptian priests was handed down to the late fifteenth century. All sorts of rumours and unproved theories went on through the ages, but the claim that the Chinese were the first to discover the American continent is by no means improbable, seeing that from such early days they were able to build ocean-going craft and thus cross the Pacific. Possibly the mysterious island of Atlantis is identifiable with the Azores or the Canaries, though it has been quoted as indicating that the ancients considered the existence of the Western Hemisphere to be a fact. Human inquisitiveness and a fair wind have accounted for an amazingly long list of discoveries, and it is a justifiable assumption that the Phœnicians were the first to find those islands rising out of the sea. The Atlantis legend may thus have first originated.

For the reasons already stated it is to me impossible of belief that any Mediterranean vessel had ever crossed the Atlantic before the time of Columbus. The history of sea discovery, like the history of scientific discovery, is along the lines of gradual evolution. Columbus had made voyages to Madeira and the Azores long before he had made the longer crossing to the West Indies. In the same way a sea route to India was not found by one lucky effort at rounding the Cape of Good Hope, but by voyages gradually extended farther and farther south down the west African coast, feeling a path and experimenting, rather than making a blind dash into a black void. Still, here again, some curious geographical instinct manifests itself; for a portolano (of which there is a reproduction in the Map Room of the British Museum) belonging to 1351 shows the shape of the whole African continent with a correctness that is remarkable, seeing that Good Hope was not rounded till a hundred and thirty-five years later. Malocello had found the Canaries as far back as the year 1270, but it needed some grand dominating motive and a great organizing genius to focus existing maritime ability into one profitable synthesis. It was Prince Henry the Navigator to whom under God must be assigned the credit for the birth of the American nation ; but for his energy, vision and enterprise, the full possibilities of ocean travel would have been delayed inevitably.

But what setting was there for this inadequately appraised personality ? Let us take a look around that cradle of civilization, the northern Mediterranean shores. There had always been a particular glamour over the Orient, and so long as the main routes thither were by land, the states of Genoa and Venice held the keys of that traffic which brought into Europe silks, purple garments, perfumes and spices that could be sold at high prices. But the very rivalry of these two states considerably helped the development of the seaman's art both generally and in particular. It was Genoa which gave birth to Columbus at a later date, generations after she had sent out squadrons to destroy pirates, and had established a lucrative trans-Mediterranean commerce. Venice, too, carried on a big trade as importer of Oriental produce, and must needs bring a fighting navy into being to protect her merchant ships. The power of Genoa was broken in 1380 by the surrender of her fleet at Chiozza, but the discovery of a road to India without having to make a land journey was destined to wrest from Venetian prosperity the very basis of her primacy. That the Italians had long been thinking of finding a means of reaching India by water is illustrated by Vivaldi's courageous but fruitless effort in 1281, when he set forth from Genoa and made for the west African coast.

Now it is requisite for a ship of discovery that she have something more than a seaworthy hull and sails : she must know how she is heading, and for this she requires a special instrument. It is probable that from early times the Chinese sailors were using some sort of compass ; and it is equally probable that the Arabs, obtaining from them this novelty, thus introduced it to the Mediterranean mariners via India and the Red Sea. What remains certain is that not till the year 1190 is the compass mentioned in Europe, where a French ballad distinctly makes reference to the needle which floated on a straw in water. It has been claimed that a Neapolitan pilot of the fourteenth century was the first to suspend the needle on a fixed pivot in a box.

Generally the Italians gave to maritime progress the basic elements on which the right master-mind could build securely, and this lesson in nautics echoed down the Middle Sea till it was heard on the Iberian peninsula. There was, too, a kind of intellectual spring beginning on its shores, which was presently to spread through northern Europe ; for that wonderful period which includes the fourteenth to the sixteenth centuries and is known as the Renaissance was in effect the greatest movement in the direction of liberty since the dawn of Christianity. There came an exhilaration, a fresh impulse, which set men's minds and imaginations working as they had never moved before. And while Italy was concentrating that new force on art as well as literature, Portugal was thinking in terms of big ships, charts, islands, astrolabes, capes, rigging, ocean commerce, astronomy and golden treasure. In other words, a new competition was about to begin for maritime trade, sea supremacy and in particular the Oriental traffic. The Portuguese were to learn everything which Italian experience could teach, but there was needed one controlling and centralizing intellect to collect, sift, choose and inaugurate.

Prince Henry, third son of King John I of Portugal, and nephew of the English Henry IV, saw such an opportunity as rarely comes in a thousand years. There was in him that ability which to-day we respect in a great merchant prince who founds a vast business by recognizing the world's market potentiality, creating the right machinery and selecting the best departmental heads. But that was not all. To this must be allied the acute mentality of a university's vice-chancellor, and of a scientist, together with the broad outlook of a consummate statesman and the ardour of a patriot.

It is noticeable in the lives of great philosophers, inventors and many who have left their indelible mark on the world, that the critical period of their existence has been spent in a kind of monastic seclusion in order the better to devote themselves

B

wholly to their vocational labours. Prince Henry the Navigator, as he became to history, withdrew himself from the attractions of court life that he might entirely change the whole current of human energy. In the year 1415 he retired to the cold, dreary promontory of Cape St. Vincent and settled at Sagres, with the Atlantic sweeping uninterruptedly right across from the New but still unknown World.

Here he founded the first great naval college, not far from the naval arsenal of Lagos, over which he was also Governor. He erected a palace, an observatory, a study for himself and a chapel for God, since the whole institution was run on a strong religious basis. Sagres became the most nautical cosmopolis in the whole of Europe, and a hive of activity. You would have met here the best practical navigators and shipbuilders from all Italy. Travellers and merchants brought all the international gossip of Bruges and London and Spain. Others added the latest facts concerning the trade with India. Jews and Arabs were sent for because they could impart a knowledge of mathematics and astronomy. Old pilots, rugged and tanned, brought their self-made charts, compared their experiences of seafaring and collated essential data. All available geographical knowledge was studied, and while caravels were being built by the shipbuilders of Lagos, the future ship-masters were learning from the instrument-makers how to use an astrolabe, how to make a map or read the compass. Little did Henry, or his own brother Pedro, who acted as chief-of-staff and contributed the result of his own travels, realize how deeply this busy hive was to impress all future generations.

What was the direct objective of all this? Henry's idea was twofold; and it is worth noting inasmuch as it was subsequently followed when the English ideal was expressed : he was set on finding a sea lane to India, there to establish a valuable trade, but at the same time to bring Christianity wherever ships did business. With the exception of short intervals Henry remained at Sagres for forty-five years, and was able to see some of the direct as well as indirect results of his work, though by no means the most important. Thus in 1419 Madeira was discovered, thirty years later Cape Bojador (the north-west shoulder of Africa) was rounded ; seven years more saw Cape Verde, still farther south ; in 1448 ships were using the Azores, in 1487 Diaz doubled the Cape of Good Hope, and in 1498 Vasco da Gama, having sailed from Lisbon, crossed the Indian Ocean. Thus the Portuguese had learned the secret route to that wealthy Orient, and there had been opened a way beyond India to China and Japan. Ceylon, the Sunda Islands, Malacca and Ormuz in the Persian Gulf were Portuguese, too, merely for the asking.

But there was another dreamer of dreams, and in him we see where the old eastern Mediterranean and the new western seamanhood unite. Here was another who made a tremendous bid for freedom from the conventional outlook. Cristofero Colombo, as his name was in the Italian, came into the world not till 1435 ; but at the age of fourteen he first went afloat and learned the grammar of his art from the Mediterranean Sea. His subsequent voyages as far north as Iceland, as far south as Madeira, and as far west as the Azores gave him the finest possible training which any mariner at that period could obtain. The crisis in his life was in 1470, when he was wrecked during a sea-fight with some Venetian galleys off the coast of Portugal. He settled at Lisbon, and by 1474 his mind was already working on the belief that India could be reached by sailing to the westward. This date, be it noted, was fourteen years after the death of Prince Henry, and thirteen years before Diaz got round the Cape of Good Hope. Henceforth Columbus was dominated by a great idea which was too broad for others to accept. To his native Genoa he appealed for assistance in vain, his overtures to King John II of Portugal came to nothing. For notwithstanding the high navigational achievements of that country's seafarers, somehow Columbus failed to create the right atmosphere of confidence. John certainly referred the matter to a committee of learned men, but only some of these were impressed. At the instigation of the Bishop of Ceuta a caravel was surreptitiously fitted out and sent to attempt this venture. But the seamen lost heart, the scheme failed, and when Columbus learned of this bit of sharp practice he quitted Portugal in 1484.

Four years later he sent his brother Bartholomew to lay a proposition before Henry VII of England, and here enters one of those small incidents which sometimes decide the course of the world's events for centuries. Bartholomew was delayed on his journey through falling into the hands of pirates, but was able to return with the joyful news that Henry had accepted the offer. It was too late. For in the meantime Christopher had secured, on religious grounds, the whole-hearted support of Isabella of Spain in April of 1492 ; in the following August he set sail with the *Santa Maria* and the two smaller vessels, *Niña* and *Pinta,* though it was not till after the Canaries were left astern on 6th September that his voyage became actually one of sailing in unknown seas.

Except for the chance interference by Bartholomew's pirates, the New World would have been discovered not on behalf of Spain but in the name of England, and the history of Tudor times would have been given a different destiny altogether. Nor is it too much to claim that the seventeenth-century emigration from England might thus have concentrated on the West Indies and South America, leaving North America to the Spanish and Portuguese. In that case the whole of the United States' future would seem to have been determined by the casual exploits of some rude corsairs out for what they could steal.

It was on 12th October that Columbus landed on one of the Bahama group which is now generally identified with Watling Island, but named by him San Salvador. After exploring other islands, including Cuba and Haiti (which he named Hispaniola), he had the misfortune to lose the *Santa Maria* on a sand-bank off Hispaniola on Christmas Day. The wind was very light at the time, Columbus had been without rest for two whole days, and went below at 11.0 p.m. The sea was so calm, the night air so drowsy, that the steersman also thought he would have a nap. So, handing over the helm to a boy, the mariner shut his eyes and dozed off. It had been expressly forbidden by Columbus that any boy should touch the helm, and the result of this disobedience was that the current imperceptibly, but gently, carried the flagship on to the bank. The boy at length noticing that the helm would no longer move, but that the tide was rushing by the ship over the shoal, cried out in alarm. This caused Columbus to tumble out, and he

The Dream of Columbus

An allegorical but unseamanlike engraving by Theodore de Bry (1594)

ordered a boat to be lowered and the crew to lay out an anchor astern. These stricken men, however, preferred to row off to the next ship. Finally, in spite of cutting away masts and lightening her, the *Santa Maria* was definitely doomed, the sea poured in through her hull, and she had to be abandoned. The journey home was continued aboard the two other ships, and after bad weather they were back at Palos, Andalusia, whence they had originally set out. It was now 15th March, 1493, and for the first time the New World had been brought to the knowledge of Europe.

The political results were that Spain was to colonize the West Indies and enter upon the ambitious career of seeking world supremacy. But power will always create the reaction of jealousy-inspired opposition. How would the ambitious and successful Portugal regard the dangerous possibilities of the newly-discovered western lands ? What was to happen if her navigators and mariners continued their explorations afloat ? There was no League of Nations to exercise some neutral influence, but there was the authority of the Pope, which was the final court of appeal in a world of Catholics. Fifty years previously, in 1444, but at a date when no one could foresee what marvellous achievements ships could accomplish, the Papal Bull of Martin V granted to the Portuguese the right to the lands which they claimed. And now, in this momentous year of 1493, Pope Alexander VI issued the famous Bull which divided the world into half by a line running north and south one hundred miles west of the Azores, all newly-discovered lands to the east of this demarcation being assigned to Portugal and those to the west being allotted to Spain. If Alexander showed any bias in this decision it may be attributed to the fact that he was a Spaniard by birth.

During the next half century both Spain and Portugal were busily engaged consolidating and extending their overseas dominions. In 1493, also, was translated Columbus' famous *Epistola de insulis nuper repertis*, and various editions were printed at Basel as well as in other towns of Europe. Thus was being spread in a slow-moving age the wonderful news of what lay beyond the Atlantic ; yet it seems a pity that the Genoese pilot should ever have been employed by Spain. For,

whatever may be said of her national characteristics, she never
had the genius for governing. Her treatment of the natives
in her initial Hispaniola colony was harsh to the point of
extermination, her policy being ruthless in government rather
than constructive and tolerant. And there is a pathetic
injustice that Italy, which had done so much for the Old
World in art, literature, navigation, the spread of ancient
learning and the propagation of fresh ideas, should have been,
while indirectly responsible for finding the New World, yet
directly unable thereby to profit.

The fifteenth century had inaugurated a quite different
conception of the universe, for during thirteen hundred years
the study of geography had been as dead as the Greek deities.
In the ancient times there had been such cartographers as
Posidonius, Hipparchus, Strabo and Claudius Ptolemæus. The
last named made astronomical observations at Alexandria
during the first half of the second century of the Christian era,
and his system of geography continued as the unquestioned
authority right down till this fifteenth century. It was not until
1478 that the earliest printed maps engraved on copper
appeared, when Arnold Bukinck at Rome issued an edition of
Ptolemy's *Cosmography* in answer to the awakened interest
caused by more frequent travels.

The voyages of Columbus were directly responsible for
the encouragement of all cartography, but the earliest known
map printed and showing any portion of America is one of
the world, dated 1506, by Joannes Matheus Contarenus and
Franciscus Rosellus. Not long since there was acquired by the
British Museum a unique copy of this rarity which indicates,
though crudely, the West Indies and part of the American coast.
But it is not without interest that we find the New World
shown to the eyes so quickly after its first discovery. And
when we come to the end of the century there is in Theodore
de Bry's map of the West Indies and the Caribbean, which he
engraved during 1594, a highly informative detailed record of
those parts which Columbus and others revealed.

Columbus remained but a little while ashore immediately
following the return from his first voyage, and sailed again
on 25th September, reaching Dominica (Lesser Antilles) on

3rd November, 1493, but did not get back till 1496. Two years later he set out on his third voyage, which resulted in his discovery of the South American mainland ; and in 1502 he started on his last voyage that concluded in 1504, during which he explored along the Gulf of Mexico. His death came in 1506, so here was a septuagenarian who carried on his great work till the end. He was thus able to connect that fateful sixteenth century with what may be termed the experimental fifteenth.

It is difficult to think of his achievements without emotion. Here was a man who had that rare combination of imaginative ability and practical sense ; one who believed in his mission and possessed both moral and physical courage to carry out his convinced duty. To him this western project was crystal clear, so that neither scoffers nor false witnesses, neither the terrors of the untracked Atlantic nor the disheartedness of his depressing crews, neither the difficulties of navigation nor the risk of pirates, could ever turn him aside from his definite vocation. Few pioneers receive the rewards of their dauntless persistence, but this Italian gave to awakening Europe an immense hope, and even a proof that the Atlantic wastes were but a pathway to another world.

It is fairly well established that Leif, son of Eric the Red, discovered North America in the year A.D. 1000, and it was unquestionably by a series of fine performances that the Viking single square sail craft should gradually have felt their way first by the guidance of Iceland and Greenland through areas notorious for vile weather. But there is something of grandeur when we recall the effective linking by Columbus of the Middle Ages' development with an entirely undeveloped sphere. It was to be no mere adventure, isolated, interesting, ephemeral, but the founding of new nations, other ideals, vast riches and unthought-of power which would all make themselves felt in the Old World after but a few generations. There is something peculiarly fitting that Italy, which, so to speak, had brought up and educated Europe, should at the passing of parental usefulness reveal to her family a new home with a final gesture of benediction. And it was a second Italian, John Cabot, who was to do for England in North American waters what Columbus had performed on Spain's behalf to the southward. It is always the first step which needs so much impelling energy and faith. When once the English seamen knew that, even if they sailed for months across the Western Ocean, they would still find land, then long Atlantic voyages were worth all that had to be endured. What Columbus and Cabot had done could be repeated by other mariners and improved upon.

Before we proceed further it is well that we should acquire a mental picture of the ocean-going ships at this time. Too little has been made of the maritime conditions under which the American discoveries and colonizations were effected. If we understand the life on board these vessels, we appreciate those apparently inexplicable mutinies and the epidemics which broke out so frequently. The matter of delay caused by the wide Atlantic, the prevailing winds, the methods of navigation and the rig of the ships has played an important part in the political history of America. Unless we know these reasons, and can by imagination travel as one of the passengers or crew, how can we enter into all their sorrows, their joys, their surprises ? How else shall we be able to get deep down into that human heart of events, a thing more vital than dates and far more intriguing than an unconnected category of facts ?

As to what the *Santa Maria* looked like we can gain a pretty good idea from a model that was presented by the Spanish Government to the British in 1923, and is preserved in the South Kensington Museum. Built under the direction of Captain Don Antonio de la Reyna y Pidal, Director of the Naval Museum in Madrid, the requisite information was obtained from historical documents, the diary of Columbus, tide maps, drawings and paintings found in archives and churches. This model is not strictly accurate in certain details, for there should be no bobstay, no ratlines, and the mainstay should be undivided ; there are even inaccuracies in such items as the forecastle and stern.

On the other hand, this representation enables us to visualize the point in ship development which made ocean going from now onward a regular undertaking. Continually we find stupid remarks made by the uninformed that Columbus' flagship was a mere cockle-shell, totally unfit for the open sea. On the contrary, she measured in extreme length over-all 128.25 ft. ;

extreme beam, 25.71 ft.; depth of hold, 12.46 ft.; with a displacement of 233 tons when fully laden. She was armed with eight pieces, two lombards firing stone shot of two pounds, and six wrought-iron falconets firing thirteen-ounce stones. Carrying a crew of fifty-two, she was not specially built for the job of exploration, but was just a typical trader which used to sail backward and forward between Spain and Flanders, with strong rubbing-strakes for lying alongside quays, a high poop and forecastle, and the general characteristics of the best contemporary merchantmen. Carvel-built, with full lines, round bow and square stern, three masts and bowsprit, she carried a square spritsail below the bowsprit, and one squaresail on the foremast. The mainmast set a squaresail and a square topsail above, detachable additional sail being carried in the bonnet, and drabbler which could be laced to the squaresail's foot. The mizzen-mast set the native Mediterranean triangular, fore-and-aft lateen sail, and this was hauled flat or slacked out by its sheet at the end of a projecting spar called an outrigger. "I remained thus with little wind until the afternoon, when it began to blow fresh," writes Columbus in his diary under date of Wednesday, 24th October. "I set all the sails in the ship, the mainsail with two bonnets, the foresail, spritsail, mizzen, maintopsail, and the boat's sail on the poop."

The time was kept by means of hour-glasses, which had to be capsized every half or full hour. His sailors were bad helmsmen and annoyed him by letting her fall off from her course, and it worried him when the compass exhibited such an alarming fact as variation of the needle. True, he had long ago studied cosmography and astrology at the University of Pavia, and he knew as much about navigation as any mariner, but that was little enough. It was his practice at sea to let the pilots of his two other ships, *Niña* and *Pinta*, work out their own positions, and then he would bring the *Santa Maria* close enough for the *Pinta* to pass aboard, at the end of a rope, her chart with the estimated position marked thereon.

The *Santa Maria* was not sea-kindly, and off Teneriffe she "took in much sea over the bows." This can well be credited by some interesting testimony. Toward the close of the nineteenth century, when preparations were being made for the Chicago

Exhibition, the United States sent over to inquire of the Spanish Government if by chance the plans and specifications of this ship were still in existence. As a result of research among the archives in Cadiz dockyard, a replica was built, timber for timber, bolt for bolt, spar for spar ; and thus in 1893, after four centuries, the *Santa Maria* again set forth and sailed across the Atlantic, under the command this time of Captain Concas. His report was that she pitched abominably. Just before she started out there happened to be lying half a cable's distance away from her a British gunboat, whose commanding officer, Commander Hamilton Currey, R.N., informed me that she appeared hardly fit for Atlantic work. " I may say," he wrote, " that great as my respect for Columbus had always been, it was greatly enhanced when I saw the thing, like half a man's tall-hat case, in which he sailed out into the unknown."

In bad weather such vessels used to heave-to under mainsail, or when waiting off the land for daylight. They were built roughly and iron-fastened, the hull being painted with tar, but sometimes greased below water-line to lessen friction through the sea. Of course, they " worked " and leaked badly ; the masts and yards were but rudely fashioned, and there was none of the finish which modern ship-building produces with pride. " I departed in the name of the Holy Trinity, on Easter night," writes Columbus concerning his fourth voyage, " with the ships rotten, worm-eaten, and full of holes." " My ships were pierced with worm-holes, like a bee-hive." " With three pumps, and the use of pots and kettles, we could scarcely with all hands clear the water that came into the ship, there being no remedy but this for the mischief done by the ship worm."

There was little enough ornamentation aboard the *Santa Maria*, but by the door to the cabin of the " Admiral " (as Columbus was called), on the starboard side of the poop, there was a standard, emblem of the royal powers conferred on him, and this he always carried ashore when about to take possession of any newly-discovered land. His quarters were on the poop deck, because he was thus in the best position for overlooking the ship, quelling mutiny, and within hail of the helmsman. In his cabin Columbus had a bed with red draperies, and there was sufficient room in the cabin for several persons to be seated. A stool, a couple of chairs, a dining-table for two, a press for his clothes, an astrolabe, charts and books completed the inventory. Cooking in these ships was done in a galley made of brick and placed below ; but the food of salt fish, cheese, bread, bacon, beans and wine became often inedible owing to heat and damp.

The astrolabe was an instrument used for ascertaining the altitude of the sun and stars, consisting of a flat brass ring, fifteen inches in diameter, graduated along the rim in degrees and minutes, fitted with two sights. The word was derived from the two Greek words signifying " to take a star." This instrument, which was to mean everything to the fifteenth- and sixteenth-century mariners in finding their latitude, cannot be over-estimated for its historical importance. It was the link between theoretical shore sages, learned in mathematics or astronomy, and those who were practical seamen. It was the Arab sailors who had been using it for two hundred years before the Mediterranean pilots, and the Arabic " asthar-lab " soon passed thereafter into nautical language, just as the word " Admiral " also was an Arabic word, of no essentially naval origin but used generally to signify the senior officer, and sometimes the senior ship, of any overseas undertaking.

Chaucer, who died in the year 1400, left behind a treatise on the astrolabe, by which the mariner could " knowe the altitude of the sonne, or of other celestial bodies " ; but while this proves that even English seafarers understood something of navigation, yet as far back as the eighth century a learned Rabbi named Messahala had also written a treatise on this self-same subject. The distinguished cosmographer Martin Behaim came to Lisbon to co-operate with the learned men there assembled and bring about an improved *sea* astrolabe, just as there had so long been in existence a land astrolabe. Before the charts came the globes. The first ever to be made were for astronomical purposes. Such experts as Strabo and Ptolemy knew all about their construction, and the Arabs during the Middle Ages were accustomed to making celestial spheres in metal. But in 1492, the year Columbus first set out, Martin Behaim, a German who had been to sea as far south as the River Congo, made at Nuremberg his famous terrestrial globe, which was twenty-one inches in diameter. Other globes engraved on copper followed,

and were often taken to sea by ocean pilots. It was Behaim's
astrolabe which was used by Columbus, Vasco da Gama, Diaz
and others. But the first English globes do not enter until 1592.
The drawback to the astrolabe was that it was difficult to
use accurately, owing to the ship's rolling and pitching ; so an
instrument called the cross-staff was later introduced and could
be held in the hand more steadily ; and this *balla stella* (as the
Spaniards named it) was relied on by the Elizabethan pilots.
I make no apology for stressing these points ; for, while
Columbus and others when in the neighbourhood of land kept
careful watch for the flight of birds, bits of seaweed and other
manifestations, yet without some primitive kind of sextant no
proper navigation in its scientific meaning could have been
possible. Each and every voyage would have been a sheer
gamble, and there would have been no constructive geographical
progress. The prime essentials for the discovery of America, or
any other new land, were that sea-going ships should be able
to inform themselves on the passage as to how many leagues
they were north of the equator ; or as we should express it, they
must know their latitude. Then there gradually grew up a
body of knowledge which was increased by each subsequent
voyage till a book of pilotage was formed. " If," it amounted
to, " you wish to reach the West Indies, steer so far south till
you reach such-and-such latitude. You will then pick up the
north-east trade winds that will carry you with fair breezes
the whole way." Similarly, on the return journey, the Azores
could be sighted with justifiable expectation, and thus a new
departure taken for the European continent, provided the
latitude of the Azores were put down on globe or chart. But
the ability of finding longitude was a problem that puzzled the
mariner for many more generations.

The *Santa Maria* was a caravel or " carabela," a name given
to certain trading vessels of medium tonnage such as were used
for trading up the Bay of Biscay and English Channel to
Flanders ; and from this type the ocean-going vessels, which
revealed stage by stage the shores of North America, were
evolved. The *Niña* and *Pinta* were smaller craft, built for the
Mediterranean commerce, and the former had started out with
Columbus as a pure lateener on all masts, though on reaching

Grand Canary she was rigged with squaresail, which every seaman knows to be more suitable for ocean work.

The cordage in such a caravel as the *Santa Maria* was of hemp, the yards were each of two pieces, in accordance with the ancient Mediterranean practice which still obtains on that sea, and lashed together at the centre. The mainmast was two and one-half feet in diameter. Steering was done by means of a tiller which came in under the quarter-deck, a bar being attached to the tiller's forward end. In Elizabethan ships this tiller was controlled by a bar or whipstaff, the steersman receiving his orders from the master of the ship at sea or from the pilot when making land or entering port. It was Columbus who introduced hammocks on board ship, after contact with the Indians who already were using these.

Life on board was hardly tolerable even during the fine spells when ships ran before the trade winds in favourable weather. The crews were composed largely of the worst characters ashore. The utter discomfort, the bad food, the uncertainty of ever reaching their homes again, the necessarily harsh discipline, the annoyance of being cooped up in small space for weeks at a time, the ever-present determination to desert if chance offered, all created a spirit that was favourable to mutiny and murder. The Admiral would, however, take every precaution to begin well. The voyage had for its aim the glory of God, therefore such offences as blasphemy, excessive gambling, or the king's dishonour were forbidden. Daily the crew would muster before the statue of Our Lady—" Stella Maris "—and sing their *Salve*, while on festivals Columbus would dress ship. Before leaving Spain everyone made his will and went to confession and communion.

To encourage a vigilant look-out, a handsome reward was promised to him who should first sight land ; both this custom as well as the habits of prayers aboard ship, together with the rules for behaviour afloat and respect for the sovereign, were continued by the English ships of the sixteenth and seventeenth centuries. In this as well as in so many other respects English Tudor customs at sea followed closely those which Spanish usage had caused to be recognized favourable. As an instance, the *Santa Maria* used to tow a thirty-foot boat astern, and we know from literature as well as old engravings that Atlantic ships from England used to do the same. On entering a strange haven this boat would be sent ahead to take soundings.

We get an insight into the navigator's mind when Columbus writes of his third voyage outward-bound : " At the end of these days it pleased our Lord to give me a favourable east wind, and I steered to the west, but did not venture to move lower down toward the south, because I discovered a very great change in the sky and stars. . . . I resolved, therefore, to keep on the direct westward course in a line from Sierra Leone, and not to change it until I reached the point where I had thought I should find land." On the return voyage he used to watch the Polar Star with care and wonder, and it was this old, accumulated, stellar knowledge, handed down from the ancients through the Middle Ages, that had at last been put to practical use in the Western Hemisphere's revelation.

With this insight into that heroic school, which was to produce such historic adventurers, we are so situated that we can comprehend more adequately the motives and environment of the great English explorers, whose duty it was to show a New World to their own countrymen. And the work which now devolved on them was far more in the nature of an innovation than has been appreciated by some writers. Step by step, as we have seen, the Latin sailors had been cautiously feeling their way across the ocean until Columbus took the grand leap. But in northern Europe the conditions were different, and mental progress was more distant from the centre of things.

Since the time of Chaucer, whose shipman wore a gown of coarse cloth extending to the knee, with a dagger hanging from a lanyard ; a good fellow with a tanned face, who knew

> " .   .   . alle the havenes, as they were,
> From Gootlond to the Cape of Fynystere
> And every cryke in Britaigne and in Spayne,"

the English sailor had altered but little. In spite of occasionally crossing the Bay of Biscay for trade or taking pilgrims for Santiago de Compostela (thirty-three miles south of Corunna where the shrine of St. James was the attraction), these mariners were little better than coasters untouched by Time's hard hand. To the Spaniards (as Ferdinand's ambassador to Henry VII wrote) they were " generally savages."

They were mostly fishermen who got their living in the English Channel or the North Sea, with an occasional trip to Iceland. The Crusade of Richard I to the Mediterranean did something to open their eyes, and in the time of Richard III English ships were carrying merchandise to Genoa as well as Venice. Still, the people of England had at the beginning of the Tudor period scarcely got over two tremendous national crises, which had almost ruined her human and financial strength. That epidemic of plague, known as the Black Death, which visited England during 1348 – 49 was rendered additionally terrible because only just before its advent the country had gone through half a dozen similar visitations. Left in a state of low vitality, the nation was in no physical condition to resist the scourge which broke out in Dorsetshire, next spread by Bristol, Gloucester and Oxford eastward to London. The result was that of the total population in the whole of England (then numbering five million) over one-third were swept away by death, London alone losing one hundred thousand. And the Wars of the Roses were so long-drawn-out that everything seemed destined to perdition, till Henry VII came to the throne and exercised an immense interest concerning seafaring, which Henry VIII was to continue.

CHAPTER II

ENGLAND SEES DAY DAWN OVER THE SEA

IT was on this wise that the southern influence of Italy,
Portugal and Spain spread northward to England. Whereas
there existed good material among the fishermen and few sea
traders, there was extraordinarily little navigational knowledge.
This meant that if any capable pilot from Genoa or Venice
liked to find his way north and settle in some English port he
would probably have every encouragement.

So before the close of the fifteenth century we find John
Cabot, " citizen of Venes," well established in Bristol as a trader.
Shortly after the return of Columbus to Spain from his first
voyage to the New World, John Cabot and his sons petitioned
Henry VII to grant them letters-patent for the discovery of
islands and countries as yet unknown to Christians, and on
5th March, 1496, this request was conceded. We thus have the
immediate sequel, and a proposition similar, to Columbus'
undertaking. But the speed of enterprise in those days was
slow, and it was not till the spring of 1497 that Cabot with his
sons sailed from Bristol with a couple of ships. The net result
was that he discovered Labrador, Newfoundland, Cape Breton
Island and Nova Scotia. St. John's, Newfoundland, still retains
the name given to it because it was on the day of St. John the
Baptist that this coast was sighted.

The resultant effects of this voyage were, on return to
England, no more clear to our forefathers than are the likely
possibilities which may result from the expeditions to Polar
regions known to us. But it established a geographical fact
that in a certain northern latitude there was land many days
beyond the broad Atlantic. In other words, it presented
merchants, adventurers and fishermen with a new idea over
which to ponder. It might mean a great deal, or a very little ;

perhaps a much-needed route for trade with the East, as the Portuguese had found their new road to India ; or it might mean just new fishing grounds for the West of England men.

At any rate, another expedition was sent out in 1499, and either John Cabot or his son Sebastian sailed up the Labrador coast to Lat. 60° N., that is, about the entrance of what we call to-day the Hudson Straits, and returned along the coast of Newfoundland. Between the years 1501 and 1505 other expeditions were sent by the Bristol merchants to Newfoundland, assisted by the Portuguese. Bear in mind that there was still no thought of America being a vast continent ; no greater conception existed than that it was a chain of islands, and that along this direction there would be found a short cut to Cathay instead of going south, round the coast of Africa. What, in the minds of the financing merchants, was heartily to be desired may be summed up in one brief formula : a secret path to Oriental riches, north - about, obviating any collision with Portuguese or Spaniards.

Cathay was one of those mysterious magical words which had become a tradition and an inspiration. Its vagueness was in proportion to the ardour which it inflamed. As far back as the thirteenth century it had fascinated Europe, the next two centuries kept it well alive, and now it was persuading staid, cautious business men to invest their wealth in order to find a way thither. It all began with that Venetian Polo family. Nicolo Polo and his brother Maffeo were merchants who went to the East from Italy and had been received by the Great Mongol Khan of Cathay, or China. In 1271 they started out again, taking with them Nicolo's son Marco, then aged seventeen, and four years later were again at the Great Mongol's court, but were not back home until 1295. Three years later Marco was captured by the Genoese in a sea-fight, and it was during his captivity that he dictated his marvellous travels to a fellow-prisoner. Graphically, not without restraint, he related facts about geography, peoples and customs, just as he had observed them.

Cathay was the name which Marco gave to the Chinese Empire, and this word was the cause of geographical study as well as innumerable voyages by sea. It became also allied with the belief that here lay the earthly paradise of the poets.

c

Furthermore, that great religious revival of the thirteenth
century had its logical sequel in Far East missions ; and the
travellers' stories brought back by friars to Europe surpassed
anything which the poets had imagined. Thus, in short, the
quest for Cathay was never out of the minds of the Tudor and
early Stuart adventurers. Sebastian Cabot, for instance, always
longed to find a passage thither by the north or north-east.

Sebastian was a skilled cosmographer, and when Henry VIII
came to the throne in 1509 the King employed him making
maps of the French coast, until three years later Cabot entered
the pay of Spain, in whose service he remained (with the
exception of one brief interval) for thirty-six years. His
practical experience as a navigator, and his cartographical skill,
resulted in his being given the office of Chief Pilot, and he even
proceeded afloat during this period to discover eastern Cathay.
Henry VIII died in 1547, and two years later we find Cabot
returning to England, where he was appointed Grand Pilot of
England at a time when a fresh impulse was needed for English
enterprise at sea.

This office was, like so many other innovations among
English maritime methods, copied from the south. The great
Charles V founded at Seville a lectureship on the art of
navigation, but owing to what Hakluyt called " the rawnesse of
his seamen, and the manifolde shipwracks which they systeyned
in passing and repassing betweene Spaine and the West Indies,"
Charles established " a Pilote Major, for the examination of such
as sought to take chaıge of ships in that voyage." Henry VIII,
for the education of men in seamanship and navigation,
founded three guilds on similar lines in three separate English
ports, viz. Deptford - on - the -Thames, Kingston - on - Hull and
Newcastle-on-Tyne, that at Deptford being licensed in 1513.

While Sebastian Cabot was engaged at Seville examining
pilot candidates and compiling his mappemonde (of which there
is a copy in the Bibliothèque Nationale, Paris, that shows the
Cabot discoveries in North America, and which served as a
model for Ortelius' well-known map of the world), English
enterprise was not entirely dormant. Besides that unsuccessful
attempt of Sir Thomas Pert, assisted by Cabot, in 1517 to
discover a North-West Passage to Cathay, an expedition had

been made through the efforts of a wealthy and mathematical Canon of St. Paul's Cathedral, London, who had sent two ships to Labrador ten years later. And in 1536 a lawyer named Hore conducted to the same coast another company, which came back after their stores gave out.

But Cabot's return from Spain to Bristol, bringing with him no little information that Spain could ill afford to lose, continued the new era which he and his father had created in England ; he was the connecting-link between the business men and the mariners. The merchants consulted him as to where new trade might be opened, and they relied on his advice. Thus, with the Cathay complex still acute, he persuaded them to seek a north-east sea-route to that country, and so it was that on 18th December, 1551, there was formed the Company of Merchant Adventurers with Cabot himself as life Governor. There resulted from this the accidental discovery of Russia two years later.

As we think of this septuagenarian at Gravesend inspecting the ships with critical care before they were allowed to depart, we can realize something of that old enthusiasm which still burned within him. From Purchas we derive the definite reason for Sebastian's original zeal : " that upon occasion of the admiration of Columbus his voyage into the East, where the Spices grew, by the West, so rife then in the Court of King Henrie the seventh, there arose in his heart a great desire to attempt some notable thing. And understanding by the Sphere (saith he) that if I should saile by the North-West, I should by a shorter Tract come into India ; I thereupon caused the King to be advertised of my devise ; who immediately commanded two Carvels to bee furnished with all things appertayning to the Voyage. . . . I beganne therefore to saile toward the North-West, not thinking to find any other Land then that of Cathay, and from thence to turne toward India. But after certaine dayes I found that the Land turned toward the North, which was to me a great displeasure." Finally, " I turned back againe, and sayled downe by the Coast of that Land toward the Equinoctiall (ever with intent to finde the said passage to India) and came to that part of this firme land, which is now called Florida."

The first Americans that ever set foot in England were three men whom Cabot brought from Newfoundland, as a present to the King. " These were clothed in beasts skins, and did eate raw flesh, and spake such speech that none could understand them, and in their demeanour like to bruit beasts, whom the King kept a long time." This was proof enough of the new territory beyond the sea.

Sebastian Cabot died in 1557, but before his decease much had been done by the explorers of other nations, and this filled in a few of the many gaps which were still a matter of dispute. Firstly, the existence of the Pacific Ocean was established when Vasco Nuñez de Balboa at Darien sighted this other sea. It was in 1513, and seven years later the Portuguese Magellan went through the straits of his name and crossed the Pacific to the Philippines. This suggested, of course, that the journey to Cathay could still be made by the direct west route. In 1523 again an Italian helped to discover the east American coast : Giovanni Verazzano, a Florentine employed by King Francis I of France, explored northward from that land now called Georgia to Canada. Others followed, including Jacques Cartier of St. Malo, who sailed in 1534 with two small ships, called at Newfoundland, discovered New Brunswick ; and then in 1535–36 came up the St. Lawrence, discovered and named Montreal, and took possession of the land in the name of Francis I.

The position of England, before the middle of the sixteenth century had been reached, was one of curious strategic interest. The result of other nations' discoveries was that she was fain to experience a kind of distant blockade, which afforded but one outlet. Unless she was to come in collision with other powers through the overseas situation, and thus be hurled into war, she would have to be extraordinarily careful. It was this mad infatuation for the country of Cathay, and the great poverty then existing in England, which kept urging the shipmen on. And when the news filtered through from the Iberian peninsula that the Western World was rich in gold as well as spices, then it was difficult to restrain fiery mariners. But less than a hundred years ago there was only a land way to India ; now there were two sea-routes, one by South Africa and the other

Gerard Mercator

The famous cosmographer (1512–94)

by South America. The unfortunate fact raised itself that the Portuguese held the one and the Spaniards the other. The West Indies, Florida and Canada had been earmarked, so that if England wished to seek spices and gold she had only two alternatives : to find a way to Cathay north-about, or to explore and claim for herself that unknown territory lying between Florida and Canada.

The idea of the North-East Passage was soon dropped and forgotten, but the North-West Passage was very much alive. It continued to exercise men's minds through the ensuing centuries till Amundsen early in the twentieth settled the problem by taking the *Gjoa* that way from Christiania to San Francisco. The last of the north-eastern voyages was undertaken eight years before the coming of the Armada, and it was realized that the Cathay route could not be by that direction. But the Tudor mind was now widening. America in an English book was mentioned to our forefathers in 1511, but in 1553 and 1555 there were printed in London the translations and compilations of Richard Eden which had no little effect, for they narrated the achievements of the Spaniards and thus created an acute interest in the India of the West, as well as of the East. *A Treatyse of the Newe India*, and *The Decades of the New Worlde or West India*, became nothing less than an irresistible invitation for English mariners to leave their narrow seas and try their fortunes across the Atlantic. Before Drake first set eyes on the West Indies his mind had been fired by Eden's presentation of such wonderful possibilities. For a moment the Oriental spices could wait ; there were " mynes of golde," " mynes of silver," " fyshynge for perles," and every kind of " great rychesse " waiting for the adventurous. Surely what the men of Spain had found could be discovered also by the English !

England was handicapped by the fact that she was a century behind the European continent in the art of line-engraving ; indeed from 1550 till 1640 the home of that industry was not London but Antwerp, which was the great commercial centre. In 1570 Abraham Ortelius, that distinguished geographer and mathematician of Antwerp, published his famous atlas, *Theatrum Orbis Terrarum*, which was the first really important and comprehensive book on modern geography. It was Gerard

Mercator (whose real name was Kremer) that we have to thank for having perfected the maps for such as would travel by sea. This Fleming lived from 1512 till 1592, and his life thus covers the height of the Tudor sea-fever. But there was also Lucus Wagenaer, who in 1585 published at Leyden an atlas containing valuable plans of Dutch harbours, charts of the Thames estuary, and other European waters, with such information as soundings, sand banks and so on. Thus it was not long before an English version of Wagenaer was issued with a wonderful title-page entitled : " The Mariners Mirrour wherein may playnly be seen the courses, heights, distances, depths, soundings, flouds and ebs, risings of lands, rocks, sands and shoals, with the marks for th' entrings of the Harbouroughs, Havens and Ports of the greatest part of Europe."

This was an important beginning in the history of English cartography. True it is that a foreigner, Theodore de Bry, was employed to do the plates, but the time would come when the home-made charts of the American coast would be engraved by Englishmen from the work of English pilots. The importance of this cartographical development cannot be stressed too strongly ; for the absence of good charts, coupled with indifferent navigation, caused some of the early colonizing ships bound for Virginia to waste valuable days sailing up and down the North American coast looking for their objective. Such delays compelled them to get caught in bad weather at the end of a long, fatiguing voyage, and besides creating a general feeling on board of despondency and discontent, put the finishing and fatal touches to the invalid passengers who had suffered most of the way.

The Spaniards were at an advantage because they had not merely more numerous navigators of experience, but had already published such first-class manuals on navigation. One of the most important was that by Martin Cortes entitled *Breve Compendio de la Sphera y de la arte de nauegar*, which exercised considerable influence. In 1561 appeared an English translation by Richard Eden entitled *The Arte of Nauigation . . . wrytten in the Spanyshe tongue by Martin Curtes*. There is no mistaking the object for which it was compiled or translated. Eden's preface is addressed to the Aldermen of the City of

London, certain of the nobility and merchant-adventurers, " for
the discovery of Landes, Territories, Ilandes, and Seignories
unknowen." So also Cortes, in his epistolary introduction
draws attention to the sad existing ignorance of pilots :
" What," he writes, " can be more difficulte then to guyde a
shyppe engoulfed, where only water and heauen may be seene ? "
In these days, he adds, " we or none of the Pilotes can scarcely
reade," whereas " the gouernall or sterage ought to be committed
to expert men, and of good understanding."

Thus it was not merely the lack of ocean-going ships, but
ignorance of how to navigate them which continued, long after
Prince Henry's time, to keep America still unrevealed in its
fullness. It was, therefore, most important that Spaniards,
Portuguese and Englishmen should get ahead with their
schooling, for the world's progress was being seriously kept
back. So, besides teaching mariners about the sphere, planets,
sun, moon and winds, Cortes and Eden provided the necessary
instruction for " composition of Cardes for the Sea," in other
words chart-making. After the completed voyage these bits of
vellum were preserved with great secrecy lest the inquisitive
might steal a voyage and find their way to those places marked
so carefully. There was no common cartographical knowledge
as to-day, when the charts of Great Britain, the United States,
Holland, France and Germany can be bought by anyone.

If a pilot found his way to the West Indies, North America
or elsewhere, that was his own professional secret which he
confided to his financial backers, perhaps one or two of his
shipmates, but hardly anyone else. The result was that charts
were the most highly prized of any pilot's possessions, and were
occasionally stolen from him by unprincipled people anxious
to learn the route to overseas wealth. The very few men who
had ever taken ships across to the North American continent
were accordingly at a premium when merchants in the early
seventeenth century were about to send an expedition across to
colonize Virginia. Such expert navigators were regarded almost
as magicians and wizards held in the highest esteem.

They belonged to the closest of corporations, the most
exclusive of professions. And their technical skill was based on
rigid rules. Thus Eden instructs them how to make their sea-

charts in the following words : " With a small penne shall you descrybe in the carde all the places and names of the coast . . . and fyrst you must descrybe in red the portes, principall capes, famous Cities, with other notable thynges : and all the residue in blacke. Then shall you drawe or paynt Cities, shyppes, banners, and beastes. . . . Then with colours and golde shall you garnyshe and beautifie the Cities, Compasses, Shyppes, and other partes of the Carde. Then shall you set forth the coastes with greene . . . and make them fayre to syght with a little saffron." It is easy to understand how impressed would be the imagination of any adventurous-minded youth when he was shown by his grandfather in Devon such dull-yellow, sea-stained, crinkled documents illuminated with gorgeous splashes of green and gold, red and saffron, as he listened to the yarns about wondrous trees, fruits and plants, pearls, savages and precious metals. Who that was full-blooded would not sail off to the New World and get rich quickly ? Who could be restrained for ever by Spanish exclusiveness or the arbitrary division of a Papal Bull ?

It was the glitter of gold which dazzled the minds of the English nation from now on, and brought about American colonization as a means to obtaining such treasure ; though we shall find such materialistic aim tinged with religious and patriotic aspirations. Some new territory to equal, if not surpass, the rich quarries of the Spanish Main and Peru seemed to English merchants and mariners overdue. Such men as Martin Frobisher still believed in the North-West notion, and there was more than joy when the piece of black stone that was brought home was declared by an assayer to contain gold. But, truth to tell, it was the old case of the wish being father to the thought, for this was no better or more valuable than pyrites, a sulphide of iron and copper. Still, it was difficult to convince the inconvincible, and the magic gold fairly obsessed the Elizabethan minds during this last quarter of the sixteenth century. There are no greater simpletons (as the history of finance shows us) than normal business men bitten with some romantic scheme of the get-rich-quick type. All previous bankruptcies, pricked bubbles, wild-cat undertakings have no precautionary value when the emotions and imaginations have

come under some plausible spell. In our own age we marvel
that these should be possible among otherwise sane and cautious
investors, so we can scarcely be surprised that the equivalent
of what to-day would be one hundred thousand pounds was
subscribed by London merchants and others to send Frobisher
out again. Nothing less than a whole cargo of gold was
expected in return. But what the explorers found was no
better than black lead ; the merchant-adventurers had lost
their money and the North-West Passage lost some of its
reputation, though even in later years of the next century this
gold-dirt still flourished in Stuart minds.

Frobisher's three voyages are included in the period
1576–78. The three voyages of John Davis in 1585 and two
following years were the final Elizabethan effort to discover
this passage. The gain resulting from these six expensive
undertakings was geographical in the sense that the Hudson
Straits were discovered, but also it was proved that a road to
Cathay north-about was hardly worth the concentration of
further time, money or hope ; that is to say, these negative
consequences cleared the air of a wild theory, and it allowed a
later company of investigators to risk their money on a venture
which started the colonization of that country we call the
United States of America. It is on the stepping-stones of dead
schemes and failures that the successful have learned to tread
warily. It is by studying the misdirected efforts of others that
those who attain learn where to operate. And thus the time
was approaching slowly, though surely, when our ancestors
would find their way to the right and predestined region.

CHAPTER III

THE QUEST FOR A COUNTRY

THE sixteenth-century sea story, which began with exploration and was to find its logical expression in seventeenth-
century colonization, was not merely one expression of
Reformation Protestantism, as the historian Froude would
have us suppose, but rather an inevitable activity which dated
back through Columbus to Henry the Navigator. Had there
been no religious upheaval in England, there would still have
been aroused that desire to use the ocean as a great highway.
An island race with Viking blood in its veins, and separated from
all foreign trade only by means of water, must assuredly soon be
under the influence of all this talk about navigation and
discovery. Starvation or poverty are too impatient to listen to
abstract laws, and England was so poor that she must needs
find fresh opportunities for exchange of commodities. It is
unthinkable that she could, with all her undeveloped sea
instinct, stand aside indefinitely from the New World while
Spain was bringing into Europe real gold and silver. There
would have been unavoidable trouble over that geographical
Papal Bull, which might have created a crisis in the Church as
fierce as was brought about by Henry VIII's adulteries. To
stop national expansion and overseas aspirations is an almost
impossible task without the employment of brutal warfare, and
some modification must have been devised to allow the English
energy to show itself in distant waters. I would, therefore,
submit that most of these new post-Reformation voyages were
traceable back to the Renaissance in origin, though the anti-
Papal hatred exhibited in the sea-fights was not infrequently
little more than anti-Spanish.

Nevertheless, it is undeniable that the Reformation did
concede to the English seamen an additional sense of freedom,

and an infantile joy in going whither they had been forbidden to trespass. Every English sea victory resulting from the clashes and collisions that followed, still more, every injury that was received, stirred and stiffened the determination to go on with this wandering over oceans unknown, to territory unseen. Thus was the difference in national characteristics clearly denoted. The rude, stubborn, independent English spirit had nothing in common with the formal, courtly, decadent refinement of Spain. But, apart altogether from anything to do with religion, there were changes going on in England's social life which had nothing to do with shipping or exploration. " There are old men yet dwelling in the village," wrote William Harrison, an Essex parson in the latter part of Elizabeth's reign, " where I remain, which have noted three things to be marvellously altered in England within their sound remembrance. . . . One is the multitude of chimneys lately erected. . . . The second is the great (although not general) amendment of lodging. . . . The third thing they tell of is the exchange of vessel, as of treen [*i.e.* wooden] platters into pewter, and wooden spoons into silver or tin."

Discontent with conditions at home—religious, political, personal—have been the most fruitful causes for emigration from Europe to America. The first instance of this is found in the French leader René Laudonnière's ill-fated efforts to inaugurate a Huguenot colony in Florida during 1563–65, half a century before English Puritans crossed the sea for conscience' sake. Recent writers (including Mr. Lytton Strachey) have marvelled at the contradictions of the Elizabethan age, but this inconsistency is scarcely surprising, seeing that it was a period of transition which was half medieval and half modern, full of people who were reborn by the Renaissance in a world they could not understand, marching to a goal they had scarcely visualized. The one thing they comprehended was that there was spring in the sea air, that there was a strange movement instead of the old stagnation. Thoughts and personalities were in a fluid state continually. The Church, national policy, commerce, home life, art, education—everything was undergoing a change. No wonder that men's minds were puzzled and that they became dizzy amid all this wild whirl. Elizabeth herself, with her indecision, dissimulation, procrastination and unreliability, was the exact representation of an age that was made for adventure and new thrills.

On the Continent there existed a kind of training school, where those Englishmen could employ their surplus energy and try out their strength until their own country needed their services ; and through this seminary passed some of the greatest characters who were afterward to mould American history. It suited the policy of Elizabeth to render aid to the Huguenots in France, and during those religious wars of 1562–98 individuals would cross the English Channel to fight, not so much out of any real love for the anti-Catholics as for the opportunity of leading a gentleman's life amid martial surroundings. Captain John Smith, for example, went over to France for this object, but arrived just too late. So also in the Netherlands a suitable struggle was continuing till the year 1609, and Smith was in time for that. Sir Humphrey Gilbert also went to the Low Countries and led a band of volunteers against the power of Alva and Spain. Raleigh, too, learned something in that same warfare. However, this brief list does not include other names of Anglo-American interest that will have to be mentioned later. The effect of the Continental period on the lives of these historic characters was to develop self-reliance, personal courage, initiative and leadership, the very qualities which pioneers of colonization most require. "He is not worthy to live at all, that for fear or danger of death shunneth his Country's service and his own honour ; seeing death is inevitable, and the fame of virtue immortal," were Gilbert's own words to express his moral code.

Here was a man who was all afire with zeal for exploration, and it was his *Discourse of a Discovery for a New Passage to Cataia*, written in 1574 and printed two years later, that inspired the voyages of Frobisher and Davis. In that same year, 1574, a petition was made to Queen Elizabeth by certain prominent West of England gentlemen soliciting her to permit an enterprise for discovery of " sundry ritche and unknowen landes," the petitioners including such well-known names as Sir Humphrey Gilbert, Sir George Peckham, Sir Richard Grenville and Mr. Carlile. On behalf of the company that was

Martin Frobisher

to back this intended undertaking a committee was appointed
to confer with Mr. Carlile, and they were to examine this
suggestion of making a " discovery and attempt in the northern
parts of America." This committee, which also included
Alderman Hart, William Borough (an experienced master
mariner, who made charts and accompanied Frobisher toward
the North-West Passage) and eight others, finally recorded that
they were well persuaded this northern part of America was
very fruitful, inhabited with savage people of a mild and
tractable disposition, and of all other unfrequented places this
was " the only most fittest and most commodious for us to
intermeddle withal." They proposed that one hundred men
should be conveyed there and remain one year, who, by forming
friendships with the natives, might obtain a better knowledge
of the country and gather what commodities might hereafter
be expected of it. The cost would amount to four thousand
pounds, of which the city of Bristol had already offered one
thousand pounds, so the residue remained to be furnished
in London. Liberty was to be granted by the Queen to
transport thither all who cared to go, and these colonists
would be bound to remain at least ten years. None were
to go without license from the patentees, nor to inhabit,
nor traffic within two hundred leagues of the place
where " the General shall have first settled his being and
residence."

As a sequel to this petition Elizabeth, on 11th June, 1578,
granted letters-patent[1] to Sir Humphrey Gilbert in the
following words : " . . . free power and liberty to him, his
heirs and assigns for ever, to discover . . . all such remote,
heathen, and barbarous lands, countries, or territories as were
not actually possessed by any Christian prince or people ; and
thither to lead and carry with him, to travel thitherward, and
there inhabit, such and so many of her Majesty's subjects as
would willingly accompany and join in the enterprise." He
was further authorized to " hold, occupy and enjoy to himself,
his heirs and assigns for ever all such lands, countries and
territories . . . with full power to dispose thereof to her

---

[1] Letters-patent signified an open letter, or agreement, or authorization which conferred on the receiver the right to do a certain act.

Majesty's subjects," but " paying to the Queen, her heirs and
successors . . . the fifth part of all the ore of gold and silver
which should at any time there be gotten."

In the committee's accentuation of the word " intermeddle,"
and in the phrase of the letters-patent " not actually possessed
by any Christian prince or people," we see the nervousness lest
any complications should arise through impinging on Spanish
or French territory. Gilbert is certainly the father of North
American colonization, yet he was a mere lad when Richard
Eden had put forward the suggestion of England inhabiting
lands between Florida and Newfoundland. Thus, when at
length in the early seventeenth century Virginia was at last
colonized, it was not by chance that the ships brought the
emigrants to, roughly, where they expected to find the required
immunity from political complications.

There is, however, one colonial heresy which began as early
as Humphrey Gilbert, and it may well be brought forward
now because it was continued from the first through generations
of mistaken policy. " We might inhabit some part of those
countries," Gilbert suggested narrow - sightedly, " and settle
there such needy people of our country, which now trouble the
commonwealth, and through want here at home are forced to
commit outrageous offences, whereby they are daily consumed
with the gallows." He was neither the last to make this fatal
error in English colonial outlook, nor was he at the time singular
in such thoughts. Even Hakluyt knew no better. We thus
have the germ of an unfortunate idea that North America
was to be the dumping-ground for those people who were
not welcome in the mother country. The London Virginia
Company was presently to intensify that idea, and the Puritans
brought over their own unhappiness with them. Thus, from
the first colonial conception, there was a wrong principle
involved. That is why we find, throughout sixteenth- and
seventeenth - century North America, the red streak of
revolution always discernible and frequently prominent. For
the settling of new lands it is not the village scalawag, not the
town jail-bird nor the confirmed criminal who should be chosen
to build up a fine national tradition, but the hand-picked
families of good antecedents, healthy in mind and body, of

sound moral worth and happy disposition. It took years for
the good to overcome the bad emigrants.

A second mistake, in deed as well as intention, occurred
when Gilbert did set out in 1578 armed with that charter from
Elizabeth. Instead of proceeding on a genuine honest discovery,
he really meant to take a powerful fleet to the West Indies and
attack the Spaniards. It was a stupid scheme, and is well
typical of that contradictory, inexplicable character of the
Elizabethans. Eleven vessels were got ready, he had sunk his
fortune in the adventure—his own patrimony and the Kent
estates which had come to him through his wife. Many other
gentlemen of adventure had joined with him, but before
anchors were weighed a great discordance had broken out. The
gentlemen quarrelled fiercely among themselves, the crews
followed this example of dissension by acts of mutiny and
" raising hell " in the streets of Plymouth. It was a terribly
unfortunate beginning, and of the eleven ships four finally
refused to proceed. On 19th November the remaining seven set
forth, fell in with some ships of Spain, engaged in hostilities, and
returned to England having lost the fight and one vessel. Thus
time, money and effort had been expended to no purpose.

It seems fairly clear from the slender details of this
expedition that exist that there was no sharp-cut unified plan ;
some of these captains were minded for exploration, while the
rest contemplated piracy on a large scale. Sometimes, though
by no means always, the captain was a mariner ; but his
position in the ship was that of commanding officer, who took
charge when the fighting began, preserved discipline throughout
the voyage, and (when he was more of a soldier than a sailor)
simply ordered the master of the ship to take her whither she
was bound. The master and his mate were responsible that
the steersman kept her on the course as ordered, and it was
their duty to look after the trimming of the sails as well as
the really marine activities generally. The pilot, as we have
already observed, was the navigating specialist. This division
of authority between a landsman in supreme command (but
ignorant of nautical matters) and the master (who had spent his
life afloat) contained the very elements of trouble and disunity.

Associated with the captain, and in the latter's absence

carrying on his office, was a lieutenant, who supervised the duties of the marshal and the corporal, as well as assisting these two under-officers in the instruction of the soldiers. On going into action the lieutenant took charge of the forecastle, while the captain was aft on the half-deck, with the quarter-masters stationed amidships. The marshal corresponded to our modern master-at-arms, but also punished the offenders against discipline. The corporal saw that the watch was punctually set and relieved, that both soldiers and sailors kept their arms clean. In addition to these military officers there were carried the purser, master-gunner, carpenter and his mate, boatswain, surgeon, steward, cooper (who repaired all the casks for meat as well as the pipes and butts for wine, beer and cider or drinking water), the coxswain (who looked after the ship's boat), the cook, the swabber (who kept clean the ship and, curiously, the maps), the sailors (who were the experienced mariners and hoisted the sails, got the tacks aboard, hauled on the bow-lines when the ship was on a wind, and also did their tick at the helm), and finally the yonkers, who were the younger mariners. The latter were sent aloft when topsails had to be stowed, yards topped, and all lower canvas furled. They were sometimes allowed to steer.

But when the captain was able to unite in his person the ability of ship-master and pilot, then he was a genuine superman whose authority was unique. Often we find him graduating after an apprenticeship under some famous pioneer who went on voyages of discovery. So little was known of the North American waters that he who had crossed the Atlantic twice was regarded as a considerable authority. Such a man, for example, was Simon Ferdinando, who had the reputation of having sailed to North America and back in three months during the year 1579. Not all those post-Cabot early voyages to the East American coast have been handed down to us, for the good reason that the skippers were illiterate men who preferred to keep to themselves the secret of their fishing grounds, and the places whence they obtained furs from the natives. But they did keep alive the consciousness of the trans-oceanic land for their sons thereby to profit.

And it was wonderful to note all the strange tales that

reached England concerning this new America which was coming on to the maps. Among the Elizabethan State Papers of this time there is still preserved a fragment containing the report of David Ingram, who had already been to North America by 1580, and this document contains a marvellous account of the natives, their dispositions, dress ; how that the women wore great plates of gold which covered their whole bodies like armour. Amazing details are given of the habits, customs, religion, mode of warfare and the excellent soil. There were " great beasts as big as two of our oxen," by which doubtless were indicated the buffaloes, or more accurately bison. And then the traveller (perhaps knowing that no one dare call him a liar, and letting his imagination have full freedom) goes on to add that in every dwelling was to be found a pearl, and in some houses even a peck of them ; the banqueting houses being built of crystal with pillars of massive silver, and some even of gold. In certain rivers were pieces of gold as big as a man's fist. There was plenty of iron, and there was an abundance of silkworms.

Now we may smile at these yarns, but the sober fact is that they were accepted at the time as true, and they continued to dominate the minds of those stolid London merchants who financed the London Virginia Company during the next reign. The precious metals and the silkworms will all reappear when we see the early colonists trying to settle down. The voyage of 1579 was immortalized some years afterward in the English drama. In 1605 Ben Jonson, together with George Chapman and John Marston, wrote a play entitled *Eastward Ho*, in which (Act III) there is a scene that allows three rough characters " Seagull," " Scapethrift " and " Spendall " to discourse on North America. The date, be it noted, of this play was two years before Captain John Smith's party colonized Virginia. The following extract is representative of the American gossip that went on in the English taverns and streets :—

SEAGULL : A whole country of English is there, man, bred of those that were left there in '79. They have married with the Indians, and make 'em bring forth as beautiful faces as any we have in England ; and therefore the Indians are so in love with them that all the treasure they have they lay at their feet.

D

SCAPETHRIFT : But is there such treasure there, Captain, as I have heard ?

SEAGULL : I tell thee, gold is more plentiful there than copper is with us ; and for as much red copper as I can bring, I'll have thrice the weight in gold. Why, man, all their dripping-pans and their chamber-pots are pure gold ; and all the chains with which they chain up their streets are massy gold ; all the prisoners they take are fettered in gold ; and for rubies and diamonds, they go forth on holidays and gather 'em by the sea-shore to hang on their children's coats and stick in their children's caps, as commonly as our children wear saffron-gilt brooches and groats with holes in 'em. . . .

SPENDALL : God's me ! And how far is it thither ?

SEAGULL : Some six weeks' sail, no more, with any indifferent good wind. And if I get to any part of the coast of Africa, I'll sail thither with any wind. . . ."

There can be little doubt but that Ben Jonson got his inspiration here from the same set of facts which are contained in that fragmentary Elizabethan document. Simon Ferdinando is referred to as Walsingham's man, and his three months' voyage was done in " the little frigate " without any escort, according to this same State Paper. Jonson was in a position to pick up many of the true or exaggerated yarns touching voyages, and it will not be forgotten that at a later date he became tutor to Sir Walter Raleigh's son.

Now all this time, ever since that unhappy exploit with the Spaniards, Sir Humphrey Gilbert had still been thinking of the letters-patent granted him for the discovery of some remote territory not actually possessed by any Christian. But the commission of 1578 was to last only six years, if in that space of time he had not got full possession of such new land. Gilbert, having expended so much of his means on his first voyage, assigned his patent to Sir Thomas Gerrard and Sir George Peckham, who even went so far as to ask Secretary Walsingham for a licence to enable certain persons to leave England. But nothing was accomplished, and in another couple of years the patent would automatically lapse. Gilbert, therefore, having received the financial assistance of Sir George Peckham and other gentlemen, resolved to make the voyage himself, and he set off in 1583. It was impossible for this man of Devon, who had helped to put down rebellion in Ireland, had served five active years in the Netherlands, had fought the Spanish at sea, and now was only forty-four years old, to remain brooding in England ; he must be up and doing.

What were Gilbert's intentions ? What information was available ? He was attracted by the thought of North America, and he availed himself of (a) the information which had been brought back to Europe by Verrazano, and Jacques Cartier for the French ; (b) facts obtained from conversations which Gilbert himself had with Englishmen who had recently been to America, including John Walker, who claimed to have discovered in 1580 a silver mine within the river of Norumbega. He also conferred with André Thévet, who had published *Les Singularités de la France Antartique* in Paris during 1558. This book not merely described the author's South American sojourn, but devoted some chapters to Canada ; and in 1568 an English edition entitled *The New Found Worlde* was published in London. John Florio's *A Shorte and Briefe Narration of the Two Navigations and Discoveries to . . .Newe France*, which was published in London during 1580, contained material relative to Cartier's explorations.

Gilbert was not an illiterate sea-dog of the Frobisher type, but a man who had been educated at Eton and Oxford, the son of a Devonshire gentleman, and one of Elizabeth's courtiers and half-brother to Raleigh. He read, he moved about and met people, he possessed influence, he was in close touch with the development which was going on in English sea-life. Moreover, there was a certain wholesome rivalry inspired by the three voyages of Frobisher, and Drake's return in the latter part of 1580 as the first Englishman to circumnavigate the globe. Still, not one of his countrymen's travels had so far set going a colony.

" Many voyages," wrote Hakluyt, " have bene pretended, yet hitherto never any thorowly accomplished by our nation of exact discovery into the bowels of those maine, ample & vast countreys, neither hath a right way bene taken of planting a Christian habitation and regiment [*i.e.* rule] upon the same, as well may appeare both by the little we yet do actually possesse therein, & by our ignorance of the riches and secrets within those lands, which unto this day we know chiefly by the travell and report of other nations, and most of the French." It was this same writer who remarked pointedly that while Portugal and Spain had found employment for all their subjects, so that these two nations bred no pirates, " we and the French are most infamous for our outrageous, common, and daily piracies."

Gilbert himself as far back as 1576 in his *Discourse* was convinced that there were divers very rich countries, " where there is to be found great abundance of gold, silver, precious stones, cloth of gold, silks, all manner of spices, grocery wares, and other kinds of merchandise of an inestimable price, which both the Spaniard and the Portugal, through the length of their journeys, cannot well attain unto." Hakluyt emphasizes the fact that Gilbert had " buried onely in a preparation a great masse of substance, wherby his estate was impaired," but " at last he granted certaine assignments out of his commission to sundry persons of meane ability, desiring the privilege of his grant, to plant & fortifie in the North parts of America about the river of Canada, to whom if God gave good successe in the North parts (where then no matter of moment was expected) the same (he thought) would greatly advance the hope of the South, & be a furtherance unto his determination that way."

Thus, at length, having got over the Cathay complex, and letting the Spanish West Indies well alone, Gilbert had come back to the Cabot tradition such as the Bristol merchants had often considered with mixed feelings some eighty years previously. Five years before the coming of the Armada England had made up her mind as to the coast with which she must concern herself for the discovery of new territory still unclaimed, and in course of time she would concentrate her energies on one selected area.

Sir Humphrey Gilbert

CHAPTER IV

COLONIAL ENTERPRISE

ON the western side of Plymouth Sound lies Cawsand Bay, which affords excellent shelter except in easterly winds. There is deep water right close in to the shore ; it is easy to get in and out, with plenty of room, and it is most conveniently situated for vessels about to proceed seaward. The prevailing winds over the British Isles being from the west and south-west, and the presence of easterly breezes being usually accompanied by fine, settled weather, Cawsand Bay has always had the reputation of being a first-class anchorage. Even in this age of mammoth steamships it is no uncommon sight to find some four-funnelled fellow from America coming to anchor off here and landing her passengers with comfort, while a westerly winter's gale off Rame Head is kicking up an ugly smother of sea.

In the days of the old sailing ships it was no isolated practice for them to clear out of Plymouth, get the crews away from the bad influences of the shore, and proceed just three miles to the Cawsand bight to wait under the protection of the Cornish hills for a favourable slant before going foreign. To anyone with a sense of the beautiful this picture of rich, verdant foliage and sunlit rocks, with the water lapping lazily below the trees, has never failed to appeal. For many an old shell-back it was the last bit of peacefulness he ever should see for years, till he returned storm-tossed and tired of wandering over the ocean.

It was in Cawsand Bay that Sir Humphrey Gilbert assembled a squadron of five ships for a voyage across to North America in the summer of 1583. He himself was the " General " or " Admiral " of the undertaking, his flagship being the *Delight*, one hundred and twenty tons. His half-brother, Sir Walter Raleigh, joined him with the *Bark Raleigh*, two hundred tons, a vessel which must not be confused with the eight-hundred-ton *Ark Raleigh* that was built in 1587, sold while on the stocks to Queen Elizabeth for five thousand pounds, and was the English commander-in-chief's flagship in the naval operations against the Armada. Now this was not the first occasion that he had adventured afloat under Gilbert's command ; Raleigh, indeed, was in that ill-fated affair of 1578 when the Spaniards had dispersed the English fleet. The scattered squadron had returned to Plymouth as independent units, Raleigh's vessel having hardly any provisions left. The third vessel was the forty-ton *Golden Hind,* which of course was not the *Golden Hind* that had carried Drake home from his voyage round the world. The fourth unit was the *Swallow,* also of forty tons ; and the fifth was the small ten-tonner *Squirrel.*

Gilbert hoped by means of this expedition to found a self-supporting colony, and so get back to his wife and family some of the money previously lost. On 7th February of this same 1583 he had written to Elizabeth trusting that the Queen " will allow me to gett my livinge as well as I may, honestlye (which is every subjectts right) and not to constrayne me, by my idle abode at home, to begg my bred with my wife and children." Her Majesty not merely sent him permission, but her good wishes, and a token in the form of an anchor guided by a woman.

Aboard the ships were a rough, disorderly lot of artizans who were to settle in the American territory and get to work mining for metal. But they would be a difficult crowd to keep in check if the scheme miscarried. The squadron weighed from the bay on the eleventh of June and went round Rame Head down Channel. It was rather late in the season, they realized, to begin the North Atlantic trip, for they had lots of advice from the West-countrymen who had been fishing and trading in North American waters. But there was some uncertainty at the outset as to how they should proceed, " what way to shape our course, and to begin our intended discovery, either from the South Northward, or from the North Southward." They believed that from Cape Florida (which is shown marked at the south-eastern extremity of that peninsula on the map engraved by Theodore de Bry, printed in 1594) the current ran northward and would thus aid them toward Cape Breton. But they had been warned they must expect to find that the winds over the Atlantic in the direction of Newfoundland would be westerly, " whereby the course thither falleth out to be long and tedious after June," though the passage from England to Newfoundland had during the months of March, April and May at times been made in twenty-two days and even less.

Could these Elizabethan ships tack ? Were they able to do anything with a head wind ? The answer is that normally they could sail not nearer to the wind than seven points. We know that from a study of the many voyages which are available for examination. Mainwaring has left it on record that " a cross-sail ship in a sea cannot make her way nearer than 6 points unless there be tide or current which doth set to windward." That would be for the smartest ships. But there is other evidence that these craft, close-hauled, would not make good if brought closer than seven points. Thus, Essex writing to Cecil in July, 1597, remarked : " The wind is now W. by S., so as we stand close by the wind and the water is smooth, we make our way good S. at the least." The plain truth is that the old-time sailing ships were at their very worst when they were made to go against the wind ; for the squaresail rig was at its best only with the wind aft or on the quarter. Consequently, they would ordinarily wait days and even weeks for favourable conditions, just as one finds many a topsail schooner or ketch delaying her passage round the British Isles to-day. In the year 1719 two men-of-war were required to get away from Plymouth on a certain service across the Bay of Biscay, yet actually they waited in Plymouth Sound three months because of head winds.

But Gilbert was in a hurry, time was short, and he had all sorts of ill-luck. On the second day out the squadron was caught in a heavy thunderstorm, and on the following midnight his own half-brother deserted him when the *Bark Raleigh* turned back home on the plea of sickness. This aroused indignation and contempt, but the fact was that Raleigh was not the real sailorman, and he was never happy when serving in a subordinate capacity. This was to be a heart-breaking voyage of monotony. Because of the head winds it was necessary to go as far south as about Lat. 41° N., while on the other tack they stood up as far north as Lat. 51° N. Not till

after seven weeks did Gilbert sight the Newfoundland coast near
the Strait of Belle Isle.   This was 30th July, and on 3rd August
they reached that port which Cabot had named St. John's.
Two days later Gilbert made the first act in England's
colonization of North America, when he took possession of
St. John's harbour, and the territory extending two hundred
leagues in every direction " to the behalfe of the crowne of
England, and the advancement of Christian religion."

The squadron had encountered the usual fogs off the
Newfoundland Banks, where from April to July every year
about a hundred Portuguese, Biscayan and French fishing craft
used to work, just as the sailing craft still go out every year
thither from northern ports of France.   There were not a few
English fishermen whom Gilbert found at St. John's, and to
the fishing fleet's masters and owners he showed his royal
commission.   The next duty was to establish, " for a beginning,"
three laws for the future government of this first colony, which
may be summed up thus :—

1. The religion of Newfoundland was to be in accordance with
    that of the Church of England.
2. If anything were attempted that was prejudicial to the
    Queen's right, the person should suffer the penalty of
    execution.
3. If any person so much as uttered words " sounding to the
    dishonour of her Majestie, he should loose his eares, and
    have his ship and goods confiscate."

Rightly to appreciate this historic picture we must imagine
the effect of some distinguished courtier bursting into
Gloucester, U.S.A., or Great Yarmouth, England, and telling
these hardy fishing sailors that henceforth they would have to
obey certain regulations or be punished with death.   Fishermen
are a race apart, the whole world over, conservative in character,
little altered by the flying centuries.   They have scant interest
in politics ;   their thoughts are confined to nets, long lines,
suitable grounds, shipping, waves and weather.   The sea is
their whole sphere ;   they desire merely to be let alone.   So the
rugged, hardy crowd of English and foreigners rolled up and
listened to the speaker ;   obedience was promised " by generall

voyce and consent of the multitude," after which they all
ambled off again.

Lying at anchor were some of the fishing fleet. At the
waterside worked the shipowners dressing and drying the cod
which had been brought in and would fetch good prices in
Europe. But Gilbert now went through the formality of leasing
" divers parcels of land " adjacent to the shore, and determined
the rent. Trout, salmon, herring, lobsters, turbot, oysters and
even whales were being found in the neighbourhood, while
ashore was plenty of game. As to metals, there were iron, lead
and copper. He had been charged to inquire into the country's
minerals, and had brought out with him an expert metallurgist
and refiner, whose name was Daniel.

On the 8th August Gilbert sat down and wrote the following
letter to his friend and financier, Sir George Peckham :—

" Sir George, I departed from Plymouth on the eleventh of
June with five sailes, and on the thirteenth the Barke Rawley
ran from me in faire and cleere weather, having a large winde.
I pray you solicite my brother Rawley to make them an
example of all Knaves. On the third of August wee arrived at
a Port called Saint Johns, and will put to the Seas from thence
(God willing) so soone as our ships will be ready. Of the
New-found Land I will say nothing, untill my next Letters. Be
of good cheare, for if there were no better expectation, it were a
very rich demaynes, the Country being very good and full of all
sorts of victuall, as fish both of the fresh water and Seafish,
Deere, Pheasants, Partridges, Swannes, and divers Fowles else.
I am in haste, you shall by every Messenger heare more at large.
On the fifth of August, I entred here in the right of the Crowne
of England ; and have engraven the Armes of England, divers
Spaniards, Portugals and other strangers, witnessing the same.
I can stay no longer ; fare you well with my good Lady : and
be of good cheare, for I have comforted my selfe, answerable to
all my hopes. From Saint Johns in the New-found Land, the
8. of August, 1583.
    " Yours wholly to command, no man more,
                                    " HUM. GILBART."

But no permanent settlement of the island was made until
the year 1621, and Gilbert's men, after their miserable seven

weeks' beating up and down the Atlantic amid the greatest
discomfort, thought so little of Newfoundland with its fogs, its
raw climate and rocky loneliness that they soon gave great
trouble. " While the better sort of us were seriously occupied
in repairing our wants, and contriving of matters for the
commoditie of our voyage," wrote Edward Hayes who had come
out with them from Cawsand Bay, " others of another sort &
disposition were plotting of mischiefe." Some tried to steal the
ships away at night while the officers were ashore ; others stole
a fishing vessel and put the wretched fishermen on the beach.
But some, not surprisingly, fell sick of fluxes, and many died.
There were yet again some who deserted and ran off to hide in
the woods. The *Swallow*, after being employed by its crew in
piracy, was ultimately sent back to England with invalids ; the
Delight hit a rock, and was lost, together with men and a
mineral cargo.

On 20th August Gilbert left St. John's. The *Squirrel* had
been very useful to him for exploring the coast, but
unfortunately all the " cardes " and " plats " of harbours, bays
and capes were destined to perish. Having started for home
with his two remaining craft, he shipped himself aboard the
little *Squirrel*. It was typical of the man. " I will not forsake
my little company going homeward, with whom I have passed
so many storms and perils," he declared. On his return voyage
the North Atlantic was in a terrible humour. Vile weather
came on. Sunday, 8th September, saw the *Squirrel* and *Golden
Hind* in the greatest danger, but trying to survive a heavy gale.
The seas were " breaking short and high, pyramid-wise."
During the afternoon of Monday, the *Golden Hind* observed the
Squirrel almost oppressed by the waves, but she shook herself
free, " giving forth signs of joy." Gilbert, in this hour of peril,
set a perfect example of cool bravery which so exactly indicates
to us his character. He was sitting aft with a book in his hand,
and every time as the *Golden Hind* came running down the
green valleys and up to the white crests within hailing distance,
" the General " kept crying out across the waters : " We are
as neare to heaven by sea as by land."

During the dark hours the *Hind* followed the *Squirrel*, until
at midnight the latter's light suddenly disappeared. The ten-

tonner was never seen again, and that fine English gentleman, still aflame for colonization but doomed always to disappointment, went down to his death. Hakluyt refers to him as the "worthy gentleman our countryman Sir Humfrey Gilbert Knight, who was the first of our nation that caried people to erect an habitation and government in those Northerly countreys of America." This mixed personnel which he had taken out included raw adventurers of the worst types, disgruntled seamen and lazy landsmen, lousy, useless and undisciplined, and was ill-chosen as were so many of the later people who embarked on the early American voyages. Even before quitting Cawsand Bay Gilbert's party were at variance, "their dispositions were divers, which bred a jarre ; and made a division in the end."

But little time was lost in continuing Gilbert's idea toward a successful conclusion, and in Raleigh's active promptness we can notice a practical reparation for having forsaken his kinsman. Walter Raleigh, tall, handsome, proud, well-bred, always well and expensively dressed, had a presence and a plausibility that made him more than attractive to Elizabeth. Although in his youth he had chosen for his companions "boysterous blades," he had grown up into the ambitious man-of-affairs who knew the value of expediency in working out his destiny. His voice was small, he spoke with a broad Devonshire accent, but he was witty. His high forehead, long face, his beard that turned up naturally (on which he used to spend a long time daily combing), his "pig" eyes, gave him the appearance not of the man who likes roughing it and is a born explorer, but rather the courtier, the diplomatic negotiator, who cleverly arranges all the preliminaries of a big scheme, and then hands over the troublesome details to subordinates. He is not to be thought of as a sea-rover ; for the stench of leaky, ill-found ships, with their dark corners into which sunlight could never penetrate, and the life afloat were not suitable to his tastes. But in vision, statesman-like skill and organizing ability he was very much of a colonizer, the intellect at the back of the enterprise.

The result was that he petitioned the Queen, and received from her letters-patent on 25th March, 1584, to plant a colony on terms similar to those received by Gilbert. Instead of a large squadron setting out with a considerable number of settlers for the extreme north of North America, as had been the Gilbertian idea, Raleigh more cautiously and prudently decided to send out only two ships to examine that territory farther south, but not so far south as Florida. On the report of this preliminary reconnaissance would depend future plantation plans. With the co-operation of various gentlemen and merchants he was able to obtain a couple of vessels—a ship and a pinnace—which were fitted out and dispatched under the respective commands of Captain Philip Amidas and Captain Arthur Barlow. They sailed from the Thames on 27th April, 1584, passed down the English Channel, across the Bay of Biscay and down the Atlantic till they sighted the Canary Islands on 10th May ; then, having picked up the north-east trade winds, they struck westward right across the Atlantic, sighted the West Indies on 10th June, and on 2nd July " they felt a most delicate sweete smell, though they saw no land, which ere long they espied." They were now off Flo ida. Sailing on noithward, they could find no harbour till they reached the coast of what we know to-day by the name of North Carolina, with its sand-bars, behind which are the shallow Pamlico and Albemarle Sounds and the low marshy country. Cape Hatteras was thus a kind of natural landmark which attracted their hesitating attention and curiosity. With some difficulty they brought the two vessels inside by one of the inlets to Pamlico Sound and let go anchor. Next, having given thanks to God, they landed to examine the territory and to take possession " for the Queenes most excellent Maiestie."

It was one of the most historic occasions in the history of the world. At last, just ninety-two years since Columbus discovered the New World, Englishmen had set foot on Ocacock Island adjacent to the continent of North America. All the tempestuous voyages of Cabot, Frobisher, Gilbert and others had produced valuable but negative information. By the method of elimination the profitable way was learned to be not so far northerly ; Amidas and Barlow had now proved that. Instead of the bleak rawness of Newfoundland, here was an attractive climate ; they had reached, apparently, a country that was luxuriantly fertile down to the very water's edge, and an earthly paradise. " They found their first landing place very

sandy and low, but so full of grapes that the very surge of the
Sea sometimes over-flowed them : of which they found such
plenty in all places, both on the sand, the greene soyle and hils,
as in the plaines as well on euery little shrub, as also climbing
towardes the tops of high Cedars, that they did thinke in the
world were not the like abundance."

It was on the third day that they first saw the natives. One
was brought aboard and well entertained. Next day came other
boats, from which it was learned that this country was called
Wingandacoa, and that its king was Wingina. The travellers,
however, were not on the mainland but an island " twentie
myles in length, and six in breadth." Taking the ship's boat,
Amidas went with seven other Englishmen and discovered
Roanoke Island, which is separated from the mainland by
Croatan Sound. They calculated that this was distant " from
the harbour where we entred 7. leagues." Thus, by great good
fortune, these explorers had been able to bring their ships
without accident to a coast that is in itself tricky and dangerous,
where Cape Hatteras at the extremity of a low-lying sand-bank
is still dreaded by mariners as the region of heavy gales. But
ignorance for these Elizabethans was bliss ; they got inside the
Sound safely, and presently got out.

" Beyond this Ile," they realized, " is the maine land. . . .
Beyond Roanoak are many Iles full of fruits and other Naturall
increases. . . . Those Iles lye 200. myles in length, and
betweene them and the mayne a great long sea, in some places
20. 40. or 50. myles broad, in other more, somewhere lesse.
And in this sea are 100. Iles of diuers bignesses, but to get into
it, you haue but 3. passages and they are very dangerous."

They bartered pewter dishes and copper kettles with the
natives for skins ; received presents of venison, rabbits, hares,
fish, melons, cucumbers ; found the land well wooded with
cedar and oak, the natives gentle, hospitable and honest.
Finally, delighted with America, the two ships got under way,
took the westerly wind across the Atlantic and were back in
England by the middle of September in that same year. Thus
the round journey out and home had been done under five
months. Henceforth the name Virginia was given in an
unlimited, vague comprehensiveness to this general neighbour-

hood. It is quite likely that the sailors got the word " Wingina " mixed up with the " Virgin " Queen of England, and thus pronounced the Indian word anglicized. At any rate Elizabeth was flattered to have the new land called after her, and Virginia was the future appellation. Simon Ferdinando had accompanied this expedition, which included William Grenville who belonged to one of the numerous families to which Raleigh was related. The unqualified success of the prompt undertaking, and the optimism which it inspired for the future, soon led to Raleigh's receiving a knighthood. Throughout the winter of 1584–85 he was hard at work getting together a body of intending colonists, arranging for a squadron of ships, carefully selecting the leaders and specialists, so as to have everything up to time and ready by the beginning of spring.

Now before we consider this second voyage it is essential and fascinating to note how Amidas and Barlow found their way in 1584. They went by the route which a few years later was known by their contemporaries as the " Unneedfull Southerly course," which was the only one that was so far known, except that to the extreme north-east of the American coast. The navigational data to the New World were strictly limited so far as the English pilots were concerned. They knew whereabouts lay the West Indies, and they had been taught that Columbus reached that neighbourhood by the Canary Islands ; so this became the stereotyped route. Just why they did not always know ; but the Spanish and Portuguese before them had to learn by bitter experience, and summed up briefly the problem is as follows.

The best time for crossing the Atlantic, bound for the more southern half of the eastern coast of North America in a sailing ship was, and is, the spring or early summer, thus incidentally avoiding risk of hurricane. During the summer the favourable northerly winds will be picked up off Portugal, and blow with such regularity that they are known as the Portuguese " trades." These should continue right down to the Canaries, where the breezes become the north-east trades, so that on altering course to go west there will be favourable winds for the three thousand miles across to the West Indies. But the ship must go below the Tropic of Cancer to about Lat. 20° N., otherwise she will be gravely delayed by getting into the area of calms and variable airs which lies between Lat. 20° and 30° N. This region of squalls, strong head winds and flat calms, with trying, damp, muggy heat and sometimes a confused sea, will work havoc with the ship's gear as she rolls helpless and making no headway. These are known as the Horse Latitudes, because when ill-navigated sailing ships used to find themselves hereabouts the trying conditions killed off the horses and cattle mercilessly. So, too, hundreds and thousands of the passengers voyaging from England to Virginia became out of sorts, developed disease in those evil-smelling, filthy vessels, and died as if from an epidemic.

So long as the experienced pilots went sufficiently far south before turning west there were for the huddled-up passengers moderately endurable conditions, for they could keep on deck away from the odours of foul bilge water. Day after day, under an unvarying sky that followed the same grey dawn, the rough-built ships with everything set—spritsail, mainsail, lateen mizzen, topsails as well—went gaily along, while the blocks whined and the spars creaked and the ropes slatted. With a smother of soapy lather at her bows, creating rather more fuss than speed, each vessel would make good perhaps one hundred and twenty miles each twenty-four hours. The pilot would be busy with his cross-staff every noon, to the admiration and wonder of the travellers. After a gentle fall of warm, light rain at dawn, the sun had leaped right into the sky and flooded sails, sea and decks with a brilliant, fierce light. By midday these people who had never previously been outside England, or even their native parishes, were hunting round the bulwarks in an impossible effort to find some shadow.

Then at sunset this hard, white glare would give way as the crimson disk of sun vanished into the Atlantic, yielding place to a soft, caressing darkness. The roaring, rushing sound of tropical squalls, water-spouts, cataracts of rain would occasionally vary the routine, the cooper would be busy with his barrels to collect the heaven-sent drinking water, and in this way many a life was saved after the Plymouth or London supplies had gone bad under the heat.

As soon as the ship had left her English port the captain

had summoned the crew and divided them into starboard and larboard watches, the master choosing first and the master's mate second. Each man then chose his " comrade." About this time, in fact ever since the Portuguese coast, some enemy vessel might suddenly be sighted and a fight be imminent ; for by reason of that Papal Bull of Demarcation no Englishman had a right to use these waters. The look-out must therefore be strictly kept, especially during the dark hours. Consequently, if the watchman should be found asleep he was severely to be punished as follows : for the first offence he was to be " headed at the main mast with a bucket of water poured on his head," for the second offence his hands were to be hauled up by a rope and two buckets of water poured into his sleeves. At the third offence he was to be bound to the main-mast with gun-chambers tied to his arms and as much pain to his body " as the captain will." But if he committed this crime a fourth time, it was his very last. The sentence was that he be suspended at the bowsprit-end in a basket wherein were a can of beer, a loaf of bread and a sharp knife. He could then starve to death, be washed away by the seas, cut his throat, or cut himself adrift.

These ships were still much troubled with worm, so that, as Hawkins remarked, " I have seen many ships so eaten, that the most of their planks under water have been like honey-combs, and especially those betwixt wind and water." There were strange commands and wondrous words which the unhappy landsmen kept hearing aboard these ships. " Keepe your loufe," would bawl the master's mate at a careless steersman who had allowed the vessel to fall off the wind. " Keepe full ! Stidy ! [Steady !] Come no neere [*i.e.* not too close to the wind], be yare [*i.e.* dextrous, smart] ! Ugh ! A fresh man at the helme ! " Then on another occasion it would be the master calling to a boy, "Is the kettle boyled ? " " Yea, Master," comes the answer. Or, " Boy, fetch my celler of bottles. A health to you all, fore and afte ! " Or, " Boteswaine, call up the men to prayer and breakfast."

And so the long voyage would continue.

Having at last got into the Gulf Stream off Cape Florida, where the water was a deep purer, blue and they were heading north, there was the strange experience as through the pall of

Sir Richard Grenville

night the keel stirred up countless living marine jewels of light, leaving astern an emerald-green flame, a phosphorescent track. These crazy old hulls, surging on crests of great waves, at length came to the neighbourhood of Cape Hatteras, where the Gulf Stream flowing swiftly northward (as Gilbert and his pilots were aware), like a vast stream of hot water, hit the cold current from the American side and kicked up such heavy weather as the Virginia-bound ships were always encountering off here. Scared passengers, ignorant pilots without charts, inexperienced mariners, a savage "norther" springing up here out of a southerly wind and catching the sails all aback, leaving an ugly sea with tops torn off the waves into spindthrift—here came the last and greatest trial for all before reaching Virginia's fair and pleasant shores. Squadrons would become separated into units after having been in close company all the way from England. Some would be lost altogether off this Cape, others would heave-to for days ; some would work back to the West Indies and make themselves new masts or yards at one of the islands ; but others would up-helm and go right off to the Azores, and even England.

There were no clever gadgets in those days, no ingenious instruments, nothing aboard more mechanical than the capstan, no preserved foods, nothing but the very elementary essentials for existence afloat, and frequently not even those. From all these conditions it is hardly surprising that so many lives on board were lost through scurvy, dysentery and other diseases. Equally natural were the bitter feuds, the quarrels, assaults and mutinies, the general mutual hatred of one another owing to being cooped up in a small hull through weeks of the tropics and days of Gulf Stream gales. The environment was ripe for all kinds of discontent, and in this spirit the travellers came ashore to America.

It is impossible to compare the speed of these ships with that of modern Atlantic passenger carriers, but we can get a quite useful background if we just consider a few of the trips that have been done quite recently, and during the last century, under sail exclusively. For America has always been distant from England not so many miles but so many days ; and it is the decrease of the necessary sea-period which made all the

E

difference to the intending planter. Even Tudor and Stuart
pioneers could endure the ocean voyage for but a limited
number of days. Thus, when the pilots and the mariners had
proved by a succession of voyages that the journey ought not
to require more than a few weeks, investors could reckon up
roughly the cost of sending out so many people, and have some
assurance that the hoped-for treasure might not be delayed
indefinitely. To-day the steamship and the aircraft aim to
cross the Atlantic by the routes which are practically the
shortest geographically, but in the sailing-ship days the way
was determined not so much by numbers of miles as by the
regions of fair winds. So soon as it was established that by
taking advantage of the northerly and easterly winds outward
bound from Europe, and thus choosing a longer indirect way,
but contrariwise employing the westerly winds when running
home from America on a direct course, then there was begotten
a new confidence altogether. Humanity hates suspense, revels
in certainty, is made nervous and suspicious by the unknown,
but gains courage from factual knowledge.

Thus it was the ill-informed, experimental navigators whose
mistakes and strange adventures at last discovered where and
at what seasons the different regular winds of the Atlantic could
be relied on. The astrolabe and cross-staff made it possible to
interpret these data for the use of other ships, and so was
evolved an established routine, without which every trip
between the Old World and the New would have been
so uncertain as to discourage that flow of colonizers and
commodities requisite for any progress. As it is the hope of
reward that sweetens labour and attracts the capitalist to
release his purse strings, so there must first be conceded some
high probability that neither labour nor money will be risked
unnecessarily. Civilization, trade, the spread of ideas and
ideals, the production and exchange of wealth, have been
rendered possible for the most part just because man perfected
a ship ; but it needed a higher type of man to find out how
to employ her to the best advantage.

CHAPTER V

THE ATLANTIC PROBLEM

WHEN Columbus set out on his second voyage from Europe on 25th September, 1493, he was about to inaugurate another useful precedent for subsequent navigators. Instead of gaining contact with the New World as far north as the Bahamas, he was able to get hold of the trans-Atlantic land much nearer to the south, much less distant from the Canaries, and right in the very track of those favourable north-east trade winds. By this discovery the actual open sea-route was lessened, the chances of navigational errors and bad landfalls were minimized, the ships could be watered, and the crews exercised ; in a sentence, it was thus a strengthening of confidence.

On Sunday the third of November he discovered a volcanic island in that Leeward group of the West Indies which was an excellent landmark, since it contains the highest summits of the Caribbean chain. And because it was the Lord's Day he named it Dominica. Henceforth if, after many days, the European navigators could sight those mountains rising over five thousand feet from the sea, the continuance of the journey northward to the American mainland was rendered easy by a series of insular links till the scents of Florida smote the nostrils. So it became the practice of Tudor and Stuart ships to regard Dominica as a sign-post, where they must alter course if they would find Virginia.

By steering for either the Leeward or Windward Islands, a ship coming from the Canaries and keeping within the wind zone could hardly fail to find one of these very numerous detached West Indies stretched out fan-wise athwart her bows and extending over a wide area. If she missed Dominica and got too far south, there was Barbados (so named by the Portuguese from the bearded fig-trees there found) waiting

even farther seaward like a warning beacon to announce that
the New World had been reached and that the Spanish colonies
were to the westward, with Florida to the north-west. As a
kind of rocky ring, forming a series of natural buttresses,
these Windward and Leeward Islands seemed destined to guard
and shut out all comers from the Spaniards' Caribbean

When, as a result of much experimenting, the English
navigators learned that the best course after passing the
Canaries was to cross the parallel of about 20° north of the
equator somewhere between 20° and 30° of West Longitude,
then the rest was comparatively easy ; for the secret
entrance to America had been found, and the kindly north-
east winds did the rest. Captains Amidas and Barlow had
sailed from the Canaries to the West Indies in thirty - one
days, Columbus on his fourth voyage had done it in sixteen
days, and now in 1585 Sir Richard Grenville's squadron was to
accomplish it in fifteen days. " The 9. of Aprill he departed
from Plimouth with 7. sayle. . . . The 14. day we fell with the
Canaries, and the 7. of May with Dominico in the West Indies :
we landed at Portorico [Porto Rico], after with much a doe
at Izabella on the north of Hispaniola [Haiti], passing by
many Iles. Upon the 20. we fell with the mayne [land] of
Florida. . . ."

From this it is evident that Grenville's ships from Plymouth
to the Canaries were able to average about a hundred miles
daily, but that from the Canaries to Dominica, with every sail
set, they reeled off about seven miles each hour. Of course, a
square-rigged vessel is, for ocean work and running in the trade
winds, superior to the more modern fore-and-aft cutter and yawl,
both of the latter possessing superiority in handiness. But it
is an interesting comparison to note that in the year 1920 the
British yawl-rigged *Amaryllis* covered a similar voyage from
the Canaries to Barbados in twenty days, leaving Santa Cruz
(Teneriffe) on 19th October. During that period this thirty-six-
tonner always had an easterly wind which varied from N.E. to
S.E., but it was rather too light than too strong. As a further
comparison may be cited the British cutter yacht *Jolie Brise*,
which in 1926 sailed from Falmouth to Larchmont, Long Island
Sound, a distance of 5,525 miles, in forty-seven days. In this

voyage she put in nowhere, sighted the Canaries, and went as far south as about Lat. 19° N. before going on her western course toward the West Indies. I believe, however, that the fastest passage ever done by a sailing ship from the United Kingdom across to North America was that made by the British steel vessel *Howard D. Troop* (2,165 tons), which during the year 1892 got to New York in fourteen days by the more direct route of which even Gilbert was aware.

The problem of sailing from America to Europe, except in heavy weather, was more easily solved by our ancestors. The following instances will suffice. In 1602 Captain Bartholomew Gosnold sailed from New England to Exmouth in thirty-five days. Three years later Captain George Weymouth sailed from the same neighbourhood to Dartmouth in thirty-two days, and there are hundreds of later voyages concerning which no accounts exist. But, while the record for the fastest trans-Atlantic sailing trip belongs to the American-built *James Baines*, which in the year 1854 travelled from Boston to Liverpool in just over twelve days, we must not forget that she was of 2,275 tons. Much more akin to the smaller Tudor ships in size was the fifty-foot schooner *Primrose*, an American yacht, which in 1926 sailed from Boston to Falmouth after a passage of twenty-two days, the same summer in which the *Jolie Brise* sailed from the Bermudas to Plymouth in twenty-four days. In 1928 came a still further interesting episode, when the American schooner yacht *Elena* sailed from New York to Santander, Spain, in seventeen days.

While we keep before our eyes, then, the problem of the Atlantic as presented to brave enthusiasts who had nearly everything to learn, as we look into their minds and place ourselves in their positions, we cannot but admire the persistence of purpose which was manifested in spite of difficulties. But, within that general awakening to the call of the sea, there was the special urging of those two great Elizabethans, Sir Walter Raleigh and the Rev. Richard Hakluyt, without whose active inspiration much less would have been accomplished. The former was not merely carrying on Gilbert's work, but he was the first to get the colonization of the American continent on a practical basis. This was no small matter, coming at the end of so much theorizing and so many bad starts. Raleigh's strength was in his broad vision and his ability to transform dreams into realities ; his weakness was that he decentralized his keen influence by not accompanying these undertakings in person, and leaving the details to others less brilliant and energetic.

The admiration of Hakluyt for Raleigh, as the patron of colonization, was well-founded and fortunate. Hakluyt's was the voice crying to his countrymen, endeavouring to excite them to seize the big chances which the sea held out ; his was the scholar's appeal to men of action. Born about the year 1552, educated at Westminster and Christ Church, Oxford, where he took his B.A. in 1573, he had a passion for studying globes and for acquiring every bit of geographical knowledge. A true son of the Renaissance influence, he was filled with a burning desire to consume every record of voyaging, by land or sea, which could be employed for the good of his own country. He delivered public lectures on cosmography, introduced into schools the use of maps, globes and spheres, and with the true instinct of a modern journalist would make long journeys and suffer great inconveniences merely to get from some traveller his true rich story.

A few months before Sir Humphrey Gilbert had made the Newfoundland attempt, Hakluyt in 1582 had published his important *Divers Voyages touching the Discovery of America ;* and in the very year that Raleigh sent out the Amidas-Barlow expedition Hakluyt had written for Sir Walter a *Discourse on Western Planting*. More writings were to follow, as we shall presently note, and we must not fail to realize how invaluable was this highly - constructive propaganda when the average English citizen's mind was still dull, when the adventurous courtiers and captains of the time could scarcely be made to understand that piracy must not be associated with plantation, though both were subdivisions of maritime exploration. The debt of the United States nation to Hakluyt and Raleigh is that due to men of totally different natures ; the cleric was the intellectual patron of American colonization, the knight was the financial and business patron.

Amidas and Barlow had brought back to England not

merely glowing reports of the fertility and wholesomeness of the
Roanoke Island neighbourhood, but demonstrated that " a more
kinde loving people cannot be," by taking with them across the
Atlantic two of the natives.   Seeing, to simple minds, was the
surest way to believing.   Thus little time was lost this winter
in preparing a much bigger expedition, which required seven
ships to carry out intending planters, cattle, fruit and plants
which would make the beginnings of a colony in the New World.
The commander selected was Sir Richard Grenville, one of
Raleigh's cousins, who had been interested in the Amidas-
Barlow voyage as one of the " assistant " or financial partners
of that 1584 scheme, though he had remained at home.   It was
this same Grenville who was to achieve immortal fame a few
years later when aboard his ship *Revenge* he died fighting with
" a joyful and quiet mind, for that I have ended my life as a
true soldier ought to do, that have fought for his countrey."

Of the eight leading officers chosen to serve under Grenville
for the second voyage to Virginia, Ralph Lane is the principal.
The latter had as far back as 1571 received a commission from
the Queen to search for certain Breton ships reputed to be
laden with unlawful goods, and in 1584 he had got together at
his own expense seven vessels with the intention of making an
exploit on the coast of Spain.   He was a man of substance and
authority, who was chosen to act as the first Governor of this
projected Virginia colony, being then about forty-four years
of age.   With him went Thomas Cavendish, who was nearly
twenty years younger, and had been born at Trimley St. Mary,
Suffolk, where the fresh breezes from the North Sea mingle with
the clear country air of East Anglian meadows.   Cavendish was
one of those high-spirited, adventurous young men to whom
learning was a nuisance.   He had been for a time at Corpus
Christi College, Cambridge, but had failed to take his degree,
and in a few years had squandered most of his inheritance.   In
order to repair his finances he answered the sea's call, and it
was the sea which held him till the end.   He fitted out at his
own expense one of Grenville's ships, and on his return from
this voyage he sailed from Plymouth in July, 1586, and made
a predatory expedition against the Spaniards in the New World.
Proceeding by the Magellan Straits, and returning by the Cape

of Good Hope, he was back in Plymouth in September, 1588, as the third person and second Englishman who ever circumnavigated the globe. The value of the loot brought home amazed the Devonians, yet he soon was again in need of funds, and sailed in 1591 for a similar voyage, but he was compelled to turn back. He died at sea in the next year, and his body rests in the Atlantic.

Another of the eight was Mr. Stukely, who was a family connection of Raleigh, and had invested money in this American venture. He was father of Sir Lewis Stukely, Raleigh's cousin (otherwise known as " Judas ") who executed the order for Sir Walter's arrest in a later year. It is often that family quarrels are founded on disputes over money matters, and it has been claimed that the feud started as a result of this Grenville voyage. In contrast with the above colleagues for this Virginia voyage was Thomas Hariot, a young mathematical genius of twenty-five who had taken his B.A. degree at St. Mary's Hall, Oxford, when he was aged only twenty. Raleigh, who received mathematical instruction from him, had a high regard for his ability. Hariot corresponded to what we should nowadays call the scientist of the party, whose duties were to survey Virginia, observe the manners and customs of the natives and make his report in proper time. On his return he published in the same year as the Armada operations *A Briefe and True Report of the Newfound Land of Virginia*, which is now a book of extreme rarity. It was Raleigh who introduced him to Henry Percy, Earl of Northumberland, and this nobleman made Hariot an allowance of one hundred and twenty pounds a year. Hariot is also known to have drawn up observations on what is called to-day Halley's Comet. He was a man of many sciences that included philosophy and theology ; who understood all about "mathematicall instruments, sea-compasses, the vertue of the loadstone, perspective glasses," clocks and sun-dials. According to Aubrey he died in 1621 " of an ulcer in his lippe or tongue," but to the last Hariot retained his keen interest in Virginia.

That expert seaman Captain Philip Amidas was appointed admiral, or senior naval officer, while Simon Ferdinando again went as " pilot major " or fleet navigator. The squadron of

seven vessels sailed from Plymouth on 9th April, 1585, passed
by the Canaries, sighted Dominica on 7th May, landed at Porto
Rico on 12th May for a temporary rest, but took the precaution
of fortifying themselves from a possible Spanish attack. During
their sojourn they built themselves a pinnace. This was quite
an ordinary practice which continued for many generations,
the boat being usually taken from home in parts to save space,
and then assembled when near the ships' destination.

The squadron hoped to obtain fresh victuals from this island
after a month at sea, and the Spaniards promised to grant the
request. This contract was not kept, so Grenville captured two
Spanish frigates ; he was ever rather the fighting man than the
colonist. Now the expedition was bound for the Pamlico
Sound again, and finally they anchored off Wococon (Ocacock),
where Amidas' flagship got aground and was wrecked.
Ferdinando was blamed for his " unskilfulnesse," yet what
mariner would justifiably convict him for an error of judgment
in such tricky waters of which only a very rough chart could
have been made in the previous voyage ? Still, Ferdinando
never seems to have been very lucky off this coast, for they
" were put in great danger upon Cape Fear," the promontory
which is most of two hundred miles short of Cape Hatteras.
And on the next expedition we shall see that this pilot made
another mistake off that selfsame shore.

Grenville's party included Manteo, one of those two natives
whom the Amidas-Barlow expedition had taken to England ;
so, having sent a message to the native Chief Wingina, whose
acquaintance had been made on the previous visit, they landed
on Roanoke Island as well as the mainland, Manteo
accompanying one of the officers to the latter. Various native
villages were discovered on the continent by Grenville during
an eight-day march, but the Indians soon displayed their
proclivities for stealing. They were not quite the kindly, honest
people which had been supposed. It came as a surprise that
they should pilfer a silver cup, so the English explorers punished
them by burning the village and ruining their corn. Thus began
the first of those many unhappy experiences which continued
through generations of the white man's inhabitation.

But before the middle of August Grenville, having landed

one hundred and eight people, started for England ; yet instead
of returning straight across the Atlantic before the westerly
winds he could not resist going down to where he would be
likely to find a little loot. On his way he came across a richly-
laden Spanish ship of three hundred tons returning from Haiti
with ginger and sugar. He boarded her " with a boate made of
the boords of chests, which as soone as hee had boorded her
fell in sunder and sunke at the ships side." He arrived with
her at Plymouth on 18th September, 1585, thus well rewarded.

Now, over those colonists left behind, Ralph Lane became
Governor, and it was decided to settle on Roanoke Island at the
mouth of Albemarle Sound ; for it was always part of the early
English colonial strategy to choose an island where possible, so
as to be secure from attacks from the Indians. Here Lane's
party were to remain from August, 1585, till 18th June of
the following year. Their first impressions of the country
were decidedly pleasant, and that month Lane wrote a letter
addressed to Queen Elizabeth's Secretary of State, Walsingham,
announcing that Grenville had returned to England, that they
themselves had discovered in Virginia so many rare and
singular commodities in the Queen's new kingdom " as by the
universal opinion of all the apothecaries and merchants there,
no state in Christendom doth yield better or more plentiful."
Moreover, the climate was very healthy. They were resolved to
stay there so as not to " defer possession " of so noble a kingdom
to the Queen, their country and Sir Walter Raleigh. They felt
assured that they would there be free from Spain's tyranny, and
that God would not suffer the Papists to triumph at the overthrow of their venture, nor would He allow famine or other wants.

On this same summer day Lane wrote also to Sir Philip
Sidney, dating his letter from Port Ferdinando, thus named
after the pilot, and in this private missive we get another aspect
of colonial life. Already the history of the next two American
centuries was really foretold in Lane's lament that he has " the
charge of savages as well as wild men of his own nation," who
also are unruly. In these words we have colonial life as it
appeared from the standpoint of practically every Virginian
governor down to 1775 ; externally there was the ever-present
native threat, while internally there was that continuous unrest,

which might burst out into rebellion at any hour. It is part of my theme to show that by the nature of things this friction was bound to happen and inevitably destined to continue.

But why did this contentious unhappiness begin right from the very first ?

The answer is manifold. First, there was the discomfort of a long voyage. Next came the pangs of home-sickness, the strange shock of their new environment, the lack of housing, the necessity of working to keep alive, the anger of jail-birds being deported, coupled with the feeling that this was to be no earthly paradise after all. But even among the officers there was no lack of bad feeling also. It was an age of ignorance, and ignorance is the mother of mistrust. It was an epoch, too, when there was a good deal of underhand plotting, politically and privately ; the history of the Tudors and Stuarts is rich with examples of such activities in high places. Nor did this spirit suddenly vanish just because the characters transferred themselves across the Atlantic. Revolutionary changes in the realm of religion and politics always create counter-action and suspicion, and seem to impregnate the very atmosphere that is breathed. The sixteenth century with its Reformation and its strained relations with Spain, its back-biting and spying, its uncharitableness and deceit, created a mutual animosity that even the highest and noblest of souls had difficulty in evading. But there was something else as well. Civilization was not so deep as many have supposed ; in England, at least, I am convinced that in the true sense of the word it never even began till the nineteenth century was well under way. Did not the early nineteenth-century law of the land recognize two hundred and twenty-three capital offences ? Sir Samuel Romilly, the great English law reformer, asserted that there was no other country in the world where so many and so large a variety of actions were punishable with loss of life.

But it was worse in previous centuries. What can we think of the seventeenth century for having executed such a patriot, such a colonial genius as Raleigh ? Or what sea-picture in Spanish history is more ludicrous than that of Columbus returning home in irons, a prisoner, after the voyage in which he discovered the mainland of South America ?

So it was that Lane and Grenville, both men of more than ordinary distinction, fell out. The former writing to Walsingham from the Roanoke colony lamented the latter's intolerable pride and insatiable ambition ; and we can be sure that of the one hundred and eight serving under Virginia's first governor many said much harder things in accusation of Lane.

At the same time Lane's correspondence shows that he for himself was an optimist. He realized the value of minerals in the great scheme of colonization, and while his people had discovered a kind of wheat " that yields both corn and sugar," of which he was sending specimens to Raleigh, yet " the strength of Spain doth altogether grow from the mines of her treasure." By September Lane had erected a new fort, and wrote that if Virginia had kine as well as horses in reasonable proportion, no country could compare with it. The country was explored around Albemarle Sound and Chowan River, but also as far north as the land of the Chesapeake Indians, who lived on a small river at the south of Chesapeake Bay. Thus, in short, a general rough idea of the coast-line from the south-east tip of Florida up to Chesapeake Bay was already known to the English mind, though there remained that big gap thence to Newfoundland.

The net results of Lane's colonization were that rivers, bays, villages and other geographical details were ascertained, as well as some hydrographical, botanical, ethnological and mineralogical information ; but it became evident that this region was not that ideal area where English capitalists hoped to find (1) mines, such as had enriched the Spaniards, (2) a passage through to the South Sea (Pacific Ocean). " I conclude," reported Lane at last when optimism had been modified by hard facts, " a good mine, or the South sea will make this Country quickly inhabited, and so for pleasure and profit comparable with any in the world : otherwise there will be nothing worth the fetching. Provided," he emphasized, " there be found a better harbour then yet there is, which must be Northward if there be any." The last bit of advice was a valuable hint which was remembered twenty years later at the founding of Virginia, and made all the difference.

From the natives some useful intelligence was gathered, and

Hariot was able to collect many facts about the beasts, birds, fishes, fowls, fruits, roots, dyes, salts and so on. But especially important, historically, was the discovery that the Indians used tobacco. " Of their tobacco," reported Hariot, " we found plenty, which they esteeme their chiefe Physicke." And its introduction into Europe was entirely owing to this expedition. Elizabeth encouraged its use, Raleigh was wittily known as the first man who ever " turned smoke into gold," and during the seventeenth century it was the principal source of revenue which England was to derive from America. That good-natured gossip, John Aubrey, who was born in 1625 and possessed such a wide circle of acquaintances, has left it on record that Raleigh " was the first that brought tobacco into England and into fashion. . . . I have heard my grandfather Lyte say that one pipe was handed from man to man round about the table. They had first silver pipes ; the ordinary sort made use of a walnutshell and a straw." With remarkable rapidity this new habit was to spread to both sexes of European nations during the seventeenth century, and even as early as 1619 the London pipe-makers had become an incorporated body. But, if Raleigh got the credit for this social innovation, it was Lane who taught him how to use a pipe. And we know that just before he went to his execution Raleigh consoled himself with this weed.

But the Lane expedition was destined not to be the success that had been hoped. The party quarrelled with the Indians, found them treacherous, and this culminated in bloodshed. The provisions ran short, the Indians refused to supply them with any, and by June of 1586 matters began to look desperate. What was to be done ? Here was a company in a strange land, without friends and lacking means of support, or ships to carry them on. Obviously there was only one thing to do, and that was to keep a smart look-out for any ships that might pass the coast. It was the slenderest of hopes, for how many vessels had ever yet burst into that portion of the Atlantic ? And if a squadron should be seen, it would most likely belong to the Spanish.

However, Lane sent an officer named Captain Stafford with a party of twenty men to Croatan, which gave its name to the

sound separating Roanoke Island from the mainland ; and this
little band of watchers was to live as best it could, while seeing
if it " could espie any sayle passe the coast." Similarly, Master
Predeox was dispatched with ten men to the Cape Hatteras
vicinity for the same purpose, while other parties were sent to
the mainland, there to exist on roots and oysters. It was then
that one of the most dramatic incidents of American history
occurred, rivalled for its intense thrill only in the pages of
fiction. For Captain Stafford, looking out to sea, descried not
one ship, nor a squadron, but a whole fleet of twenty-three sail.
A marvellous and glorious sight to men marooned and starving !

These were no Spaniards but the great Sir Francis Drake's
force. In the previous year he had left England to make
reprisals on the Spaniards in the West Indies, with orders from
Elizabeth also to visit her new Virginian colony and supply its
wants. So here was the gallant admiral, after having taken
Carthagena. ready to furnish Lane with ships, boats, munitions,
victuals, clothes, ship-masters, men. Stafford brought Drake's
letter to Lane, and everything was all in readiness when the
notorious Hatteras weather piped up and nearly drove Drake's
fleet ashore, so Sir Francis with true seamanlike sense stood
out clear of the land. Finally, after the gale had subsided and
contact had again been made, Lane called the colonists together
to decide what was to be done. They unanimously urged Lane
to beg Drake to take them all away to England, for they had
suffered enough wretchedness, and there seemed no hope of
Sir Richard Grenville coming out to relieve them. Drake agreed
to this request, " so with prayses to God we set sayle in June
1586 and arrived in Portsmouth the 27. of July the same yeare."

When Raleigh heard the news that his planters were back
in England, he too was to have a great surprise, for he had no
thought of seeing them thus soon. On the contrary, he and his
associates had fitted out a one-hundred-ton ship and filled her
hold with supplies for the succour of Lane's men. Unfortunately
the ship was delayed in setting out. She did not leave England
until the beginning of April (1586) and arrived off Hatteras
just after the Lane colonials had deserted America. It puzzled
the mariners that no sign of their compatriots could be found,
and after spending some time ashore seeking them up-country,

the ship with her supplies came back across the Atlantic to England.

Now the relation of cause and effect is one of the most fascinating of all human studies, and when Fate seems to take charge of this procedure we sometimes get amazing results. It was so with this first Virginia plantation. For about a fortnight after the one-hundred-ton relief ship had left the American coast there arrived Sir Richard Grenville with three vessels and supplies. After searching everywhere in the neighbourhood and finding neither the above ship nor any of the one hundred and eight people he had landed nearly a year previously, but discovering only their abandoned habitation, he was perplexed. Fate had created a vicious circle and stopped all progress. But, being a man of resource, and appreciating that so goodly yet deserted a country might now become inhabited by other pioneers—of whom the Spaniards were quite the most likely—he decided after deliberation to land a nucleus party,[1] well furnished with provisions for two years, and so continue Virginia as a going concern. He placed them on Roanoke Island and then sailed off to England.

In the meanwhile Raleigh's undaunted faith in Virginia kept him planning and organizing, instead of repining. While Grenville, in accordance with his particular practice, fed his disappointment on the way home by calling at the Azores, and enriching himself at the Spaniards' expense, Sir Walter was getting together another emigration party. The leader was to be Master John White, who was to have twelve assistants, and they were incorporated under the title of " Governour and Assistants of the Citie of Raleigh in Virginia," and to take out with them one hundred and fifty people. The title of this undertaking is interesting, as it was in this manner that subsequent ventures were made. Here we have in effect a president and council selected to settle and rule in new territory as a community, and to export as a result of their labours such commodities as would reward the investors at home for the cost of the expedition.

Raleigh's instructions were that the party should first call

---

[1] Authorities differ as to its strength, but it consisted of either fifteen or fifty men.

at Roanoke, take off the nucleus colony left by Grenville, but then make a plantation farther north (as Lane had advised) on Chesapeake Bay, taking precautions to fortify themselves. Thus, profiting by sad experience, and in agreement with Hakluyt's views, Raleigh was aiming more accurately at the area which Fate had predestined as the birthplace of the American nation that was to begin two decades later. But effect was not allowed to follow cause directly and immediately ; circumstances were to delay and modify consequences.

Sir Walter Raleigh

CHAPTER VI

THE AMERICAN ATTAINMENT

IT was on 8th May, 1587, that this new enterprise started from England, and the navigation was again entrusted to Simon Ferdinando. The vigilant Captain Stafford also went ; his watchfulness was once more to prove invaluable. One of the twelve assistants was Ananias Dare, who had married Governor White's daughter Eleanor, and this lady also accompanied the party. Her courage in committing herself to such a trying voyage was all the more commendable since she was in a delicate state of health, but she was to become the mother of an historic child.

During this voyage we see the same suspicions, mistrust and plotting as before ; they had not yet learned, these officers and men, that the basis of success must be co-operation and disciplined obedience. From the very first there was an absence of the " pull-together " spirit ; the undertaking developed into so many separate forces each tugging against the other. The result was therefore doomed.

It was decided to sail by " the old course," that is via the Canaries and West Indies. Three vessels set forth, but they had not crossed the Bay of Biscay ere one of them deserted. The usual temporary rest in the West Indies was marred by the accident of eating poisoned apples, and when they had sailed north, leaving the Florida coast well astern, Ferdinando made another of his errors ; for he, " mistaking Virginia for Cape Fear, we fayled not much to have beene cast away, upon the conceit of our all-knowing Ferdinando, had it not beene prevented by the vigilancy of Captaine Stafford." Rightly or wrongly, this pilot was accused that he intentionally " did what he could to bring this voyage confusion." Whether he was in the pay of Spain, or whether he was merely the object

F

of unseafaring soldiers' jealous wrath, may be argued for ever.

At any rate, the ships escaped disaster and reached the Hatteras neighbourhood by 22nd July, after nearly eleven weeks' travelling. Forty men then landed at Roanoke Island, looked for Grenville's fifty men, yet found nothing but desolation — human bones, houses overgrown with weeds, and the fort destroyed. It was believed that these fifty had been suddenly attacked by three hundred Indians, that one Englishman had been slain but that the others had gone perhaps inland—no one knew. Presently the balance of the planters was landed to the number of a hundred and seventeen, and it is to be noted that instead of proceeding north to the Chesapeake country, as ordered by Raleigh, they disobeyed, with serious consequences. One can only further marvel at the Elizabethans' inconsistencies of character, which to the twentieth-century mind are so difficult to comprehend, so incapable of being pieced together into one uniform whole. Here were patriotic Englishmen, who as officers and gentlemen were genuinely keen on their high duties to their God, their Queen and their patron who had sent them out. They were zealous to bring Christianity to the Indian " savages," yet they did not hesitate to shoot any natives if danger threatened.

Hariot, being a man of religious instinct, had during his surveys and intercourse with these red men spoken " concerning our God. In all places where I came, I did my best to make his immortall glory knowne." The missionary spirit, which the colonizing Englishman had so frequently been accused of combining with the commercial impulse, was here at least a survival of pre-Reformation ideals. Thus at length on 13th August, 1587, there took place under White's brief Governorship the baptism of Manteo, who has been mentioned previously, and this faithful friend of the pioneers was the first of his race to receive Christianity. On 18th August Mistress Dare was delivered of a daughter ; this being the first child to be born of white parents in North America, the girl was christened Virginia.

But now came another of those foolish squabbles which show a curious lack of loyalty as between leader and colleagues.

Having resolved to settle at Roanoke Island, it became clear that supplies from England must be procured. Which of the party should be sent across the Atlantic ? All stoutly refused to go, except one man who was thought unsuitable. The Governor and his assistants argued and quarrelled, but finally White was persuaded to go himself, and on 27th August the two ships got under way. The smaller of this couple was just a fly-boat, but she was short-handed, and after sailing to the Azores in company with Ferdinando's vessel, fetched up not in the English Channel but at Smerwick on the west of Ireland. White and Ferdinando, however, reached England in due course, the former having got to Ireland on 16th October. From now there sets in a lull in colonial advancement, and over Virginia the curtain falls like a heavy pall, but when at length it was raised there was nothing visible. What had happened may be put briefly.

The crisis in Anglo-Spanish relationship was quickly approaching, and war was certain to break out before long. In 1583 Philip of Spain had been urged by his Admiral, the Marquis of Santa Cruz, to attempt a conquest of England, and three years later the suggestion was pressed forward again in consequence of the behaviour of Elizabeth's seamen in the West Indies and elsewhere. Santa Cruz died in February, 1588, but a vast Spanish fleet was being fitted out, the command of which was to be given to the Duke of Medina Sidonia, who loathed the sea and suffered greatly from *mal de mer*. The Armada set forth from the Tagus on 28th May, but the northerly wind that would have been so useful if they had been bound for the West Indies instead of the English Channel drifted the high-sided galleons a hundred miles to leeward. On 19th June, when the fleet was off Finisterre, it came on to blow hard, so many of them ran for Corunna, which was not left until 12th July, when the southerly wind wafted them across the Bay. Exactly one week later Medina Sidonia formed them in three divisions of an oblique crescent, and then they came sweeping up past the south coast of England.

The campaign was disastrous. As a result of English gunnery and fire-ships, together with gales and heavy seas, there returned to Spain only fifty-three of the hundred and thirty which had started from the Tagus. Thus, at the time of its zenith, Spanish naval power, which had been such a threat to English exploration and colonization, was now at last crippled though not destroyed. In England the reaction from this happy issue was to give her seafarers a greater confidence than ever in maritime endeavour, and to encourage many souls who had rather lost faith in the plantation notion. For years the anticipation and inevitable certainty of war with Spain had kept the English in suspense, and the clash had to come soon. Jealousy over prosperity by sea, embitterment through religious differences, and insults delivered from a singularly virile patriotism, could hardly fail to culminate in hostilities.

A tremendous climax had been reached in English history, which was to concern the whole future of America. Was Spain to people the future United States, or was the work to be done by England ? In February, 1587, Captain John Hawkins, writing to Walsingham, remarked : " I do see we are desirous to have peace, as it becometh good Christians, which is best for all men ; and I wish it might anyway be brought to that pass ; but in my poor judgment the right way is not taken. If we stand at this point in a mammering and at a stay we consume, and our Commonwealth doth utterly decay. I shall not need to speak of our estate, for that your Honour knoweth it far better than I do : neither need I rehearse how dead and uncertain our traffics be ; most men in poverty and discontented, and especially the poorer sort ; our navigation not set on work. . . . We have to choose either a dishonourable and uncertain peace, or to put on virtuous and valiant minds, to make a way through with such a settled war as may bring forth and command a quiet peace."

In that same 1587 Drake had destroyed Spanish shipping at Cadiz and upset the Spaniards' plan of invasion for a year. But during the following winter and spring it was well realized in England from merchants travelling abroad, and from spies, that the enemy would certainly have completed their arrangements which Drake had arrested. The English experts expected the Spanish Armada to arrive by the middle of May, and all this suspense kept English shipping at a standstill. But on 22nd April, 1588, Governor White, having obtained the supplies for the Roanoke colony, put to sea with a couple of small ships from that north Devon port of Bideford, but owing to meeting the enemy the two craft were back home within a few weeks.

Because of all the American set-backs and disappointments, which had cost the adventurer some forty thousand pounds without tangible rewards, Raleigh on 7th March, 1589, assigned to Thomas Smith[1] and other merchants the right to continue the Virginia plantation, and Sir Walter himself gave the syndicate one hundred pounds for establishing there the Christian religion. Nothing practical, however, was done till 20th March of the year following, when Governor White was sent from Plymouth by the new syndicate with three ships. They sailed by the north-west African coast and across to the West Indies, where they reached Dominica as usual, and arrived at the " low sandy Iles westward of Wokokon " on 3rd August. It had thus been a very long voyage. But bad weather off this coast once more hindered them, so that it was 11th August before they could anchor. On the next day they came to Croatan, and on the fifteenth anchored off Hatteras, nine miles from the shore, expecting to see the smoke rising from the Roanoke colony which White had left there in 1587. Ordnance was fired to attract the planters' attention, but, when two of the ships' boats came through the inlet and landed, there was no sign of these marooned men.

The next day the ships anchored two miles off the shore, and the boats made another trip. There was a hard north-east wind which caused ugly seas to leeward, and one boat in crossing the bar through broken water was half swamped. She got through, but the second boat was capsized with the loss of seven men, four only being saved. The effect of this mournful accident was to discourage the mariners from any further search for the lost planters ; but at last they were persuaded, and nineteen of them went ashore in two boats. A trumpet was sounded, but no response came from the missing colonists. Perhaps they had left Roanoke and gone inland up the continent ?

It had been their intention, White well knew, to go fifty miles " into the mayne," but it had been secretly agreed with him that they should before departing write on some tree, door

[1] *Vide infra.*

or post the name of their intended destination. If, however, they had been in distress this was to have been signified by making a cross. Now, after spending some time up and down Roanoke, White found no evidence of distress, but three Roman letters : " C. R. O." The houses had been taken down, the place strongly fortified by a high palisade, and on one of the posts in capital letters was carved the word " CROATAN," but again without any cross. The sailors next discovered some of the planters' chests which had obviously been hidden, dug up again and rifled. White was able to identify three of these boxes as his own, which had contained such things as books and pictures.

Much shocked, yet still hopeful, White returned with his men aboard. But that night it blew such a heavy gale that it was feared the ships would be driven ashore. On the next morning they were weighing anchor, intending to make for Croatan and meet their old companions, when there was an unfortunate accident which caused the loss of two anchors and part of their cable. Letting go their third and last anchor, they dragged badly before it could get a grip, and they narrowly escaped shipwreck. Finally they made sail, got into deep water and clear of that treacherous coast. Having only a single anchor, and realizing that their provisions after so lengthy a voyage were running short, they decided to give up the idea of visiting Croatan, but to run south to the West Indies, refresh themselves at one of the islands, remain there the winter, and next spring come back again to seek the lost settlers. Now again there was a sharp difference of opinion among the leaders, for the Vice-Admiral would have nothing to do with this plan, and promptly sailed away to England in a huff. The rest began to run before the north-easter in order to make the island of Trinidad, but within two days the wind flew round ahead, so they bore away and determined to get supplies at the Azores. Here they arrived on 23rd September, 1590, and found quite a number of English vessels. Truth to tell, these English captains knew that there was little enough money to be made out of planting America, but, their minds set on piracy, they had every chance of getting rich by attacking some Spanish ship in the neighbourhood of the Azores.

What, then, had happened to those settlers of 1587 ? There

had been landed ninety-one men, seventeen women and nine boys. Had they been all murdered, or had they moved elsewhere ? Although subsequent efforts were made to trace them, the people were never found. The tradition has persisted that they went inland, and it is claimed that a certain Indian tribe speaking Elizabethan English in the nineteenth century were the descendants of this party. The late Sir Clements Markham, President of the Royal Geographical Society and an authority on the history of exploration, wrote that " the colonists intermixed with the natives, and were finally massacred by order of King Powhatan, instigated by his priests. Four men, two boys, and one young maid were spared, and from them the Hatteras Indians were descended." [1]

Two centuries later there occurred on the coast of Africa an episode which in certain respects is similar to this strange, romantic mystery. In August, 1782, the East Indiaman *Grosvenor* while bound from Ceylon to England with a valuable cargo was wrecked on the Pondoland shore in the neighbourhood of where the modern maps mark Port Grosvenor. The passengers consisted of government officials and army officers with their families, the total number of persons, including the ship's officers and crew, numbering one hundred and thirty-five. After reaching the land, some of the survivors trekked along the coast, but some (including three English ladies, Mrs. Logie, Mrs. James and Mrs. Hosea) went inland. No further information has from that day ever been heard of them, though there was basis for the belief that the Kaffirs put the males to death while sparing the ladies and forcing them into marriage. Some few years later a Colonel Gordon trekking up the coast was informed by some natives that up country was a white lady with a black baby, over which she frequently wept, living with a chief. Gordon sent along a message offering her rescue, but no reply was returned. Recently a Danish ethnologist, Herr C. Redsted Pederson, has found in the native villages of Pondoland a number of sad-eyed, pale-skinned negroes, of a shy, aloof manner, with features more refined and regular than their fellows, and so pale that they

---

[1] *The Royal Navy*, by W. Laird Clowes, London, 1897, vol. i, p. 648.

might be taken for South Europeans. But this is another of those intriguing human mysteries that will never be solved in this existence.

For a moment, then, Virginia fades out of our picture. Raleigh and his associates had failed dismally, and all those thousands of pounds, which could so badly be afforded by a nation still poor, had apparently been thrown into the sea. But it were truer to say that this was only part of the result. There are noble ambitions growing in men's minds silently and unseen, which all of a sudden manifest themselves at the right moment as some great detailed scheme. Raleigh inspired in many an imagination the picture which he was never to paint. He presented thinking people of London and the West of England with a big idea which must still be weighed and pondered over. The final result was that the American nation really was founded by his unrewarded enthusiasm and self-sacrifice. The window which was placed in the Church of St. Margaret, Westminster, within a stone's-throw of the place where he was executed, was a gift of Americans who recognized what is due to Raleigh's memory.

All this seemingly unprofitable period of sixteen years which follows was really of great fruitfulness. It afforded an opportunity to think and mentally construct ; it enabled prudent merchants, ardent students, influential noblemen and bold navigators to clear their minds of piracy, and definitely to keep separate this activity from the business of planting. Hakluyt, for his part, was doing magnificent service in keeping before his countrymen the necessity to colonize. What had started him on his quest we know from his own words : how that when a boy at Westminster he chanced to visit his cousin of the Middle Temple, and found " lying open upon his board certain books of cosmography, with a universal map," and that after the cousin had instructed him and " pointed with his wand to all the known seas, gulfs, bays, straits, capes, rivers, empires, kingdoms, dukedoms and territories of each part," there was made in the youth " so deep an impression that I constantly resolved . . . I would by God's assistance prosecute that knowledge and kind of literature. . . . In continuance of time and by reason principally of my insight in

Portus Regalis, siue F.S. Helenx

Prom. Lingu.

The Coast of Florida

From the de Bry engraving made about 1595

this study I grew familiarly acquainted with the chiefest captains at sea, the greatest merchants, and the best mariners of our nation." And finally, " not seeing any man to have care to recommend to the world the industrious labours and painful travels of our countrymen," he undertook " the burden of that work wherein all others pretended either ignorance, or lack of leisure, or want of sufficient argument."

Thus in 1587 he published his *De Orbe Novo* and his translations of Laudonnière. Two years later appeared Hakluyt's monumental *Principall Navigations, Voiages, and Discoveries of the English Nation*, of which a revised edition was called for ere the century was ended ; and in 1601 he published *Galvano's Discoveries of the World*. But there now joins up with this new sea literature the new art of engraving, which was to give a still further stimulation to the imaginative appeal. In the year of the Armada there came on a visit to England Théodore de Bry, a most notable Continental engraver, then aged sixty. He signed the plates for the " Mariners' Mirror " of charts which Sir Anthony Ashley, Clerk of the Privy Council, was issuing to help English seamen ; but de Bry was particularly anxious to obtain permission to engrave the drawings made by Jacques Le Moyne, who had accompanied Laudonnière on his unsuccessful endeavour to found a Huguenot colony in Florida during the period 1563–65. Le Moyne had died ; the widow gave the necessary license, but de Bry met Hakluyt and was persuaded by the geographer to postpone the Florida engravings so as to commence the illustrating of a grand series of voyages and travels. And so it was that the engraver, with the aid of his two sons and two sons-in-law, issued to the world a vast number of prints and maps which gave life and actuality to marine incidents, explorations, ships, foreign lands in America, the East Indies and elsewhere. There were flying fish and sea-monsters for details ; naked natives with bows and arrows, but others with sacks full of pearls ; there were intriguing islands and mermaids, tall, well-gunned, well-manned European three-masters, boats, pinnaces and Indian canoes. Altogether these plates were calculated to have an immense influence even on those who could not read.

But Hakluyt introduced de Bry to an artist whom Raleigh had sent out, at the wish of Queen Elizabeth, with that Grenville-Lane expedition of 1585 to Virginia. The English artists had depicted the natives and their environment, and de Bry was now able to make copper plates of these illustrations. Hariot's book on Virginia, as already stated, came out in London during Armada year, so de Bry's engravings were used for the new edition of this little tract. The publication, therefore, appeared in a new and beautiful form during 1590, three years before Ralph Lane received a knighthood. The name of the English draughtman was John White, and his original water-colours are still preserved to us in the British Museum.

The closing years of Elizabeth's reign are marked by a concentration of effort to use the sea for the expansion of trade, now that the might of Spain's naval strength had been fully tested. The establishment of trading factories in the Levant by English merchants was to whet their ambition to reach the Far East. Five years before the Armada year there had reached India three Englishmen by the overland route, though it was not till later that the seaway thither was used by Tudor ships. But in April, 1591, three tall ships under that adventurous Captain James Lancaster sailed from Plymouth, called at the Canaries, and got to Table Bay. Here one vessel was sent home with the sick. The voyage was resumed, but a second ship went down in a heavy gale. Lancaster, however, carried on, called at Zanzibar, crossed the ocean to the Nicobar Islands, visited Penang, and cruised off the Malacca coast, returning via St. Helena, West Indies, Newfoundland and so back to the West Indies again. Here off the island of Mona the carpenter cut the ship's cable while only five men and a boy were aboard, and the vessel drifted out to sea, thus leaving Lancaster with his party on the island. They were landed at Dieppe in 1594 by a French vessel.

The Indian route having thus been discovered, it remained only to find the capital for establishing trade with the Orient. Five years later the sum of seventy-two thousand pounds was subscribed by the London merchants and adventurers. It was necessarily considerable because a squadron of ships had to be obtained, fitted out on the Thames, and their holds filled with valuable merchandise. But a Dutch squadron had already made its first voyage to India, and there was every likelihood that the investors would make a handsome profit when the holds returned with Oriental goods. On the last day of 1599 Elizabeth granted to this association, numbering one earl, two hundred and fifteen knights, aldermen and merchants, the charter of incorporation of the East India Company, of which the first Governor was to be Alderman Sir Thomas Smith. With this man's career the history of the Virginia colony is most intimately connected, and we shall see much of his determined business policy later.

Hakluyt assisted this important Indian voyage by supplying both information and maps. On 13th February, 1601, the ships left Woolwich, were delayed in the Downs till 2nd April, but, proceeding by the Canaries, Table Bay and the Nicobars, reached Sumatra not till June of 1602. By September of the year following the East India Company's first voyage was completed in the Downs. Cinnamon, pepper and cloves of great value had been brought home ; a great commerce had been initiated which was to raise England from a poor to a wealthy nation, and eventually establish the British Empire.

The importance of the East India Company to the future of America was this : at a period when it seemed unlikely any longer to persuade sane individuals to squander more money on overseas ventures, there came just the right proof that such undertakings could become most remunerative. Plantation schemes could not be launched without capital ; the only people in England that possessed liquid capital were the nobility, the gentry and such prominent citizens as Sir Thomas Smith. Therefore if they could be so encouraged as to lend their wealth and general support to developing Virginia, in the firm hope of being plenteously rewarded, would it not be possible to try once more where Raleigh's project had failed ?

But even a few months before Sir Thomas Smith's East India ships had returned there was a venture which was undertaken by Captain Bartholomew Gosnold, Captain Bartholomew Gilbert and other gentlemen in a small ship. The party consisted of thirty-two, of whom eight represented the

crew. The intention of this voyage was to reach America, find
a suitable spot, land every person with the exception of a dozen
who were to bring the little vessel back to England ; those
remaining being about to try their luck as settlers. Now the
voyage itself, and localities visited on this occasion, were
entirely different from any of those which we have been
recently considering.

CHAPTER VII

EXPLORING THE AMERICAN COAST

BEFORE 1584 the American continent was known by the name of Florida. Next came that undefined area called Virginia, which embraced just as much of the land to the northward as the imagination cared to include. Now the Gosnold enterprise was dominated by an effort to find a short, quick way across the Atlantic and get hold of this vaguely-conceived territory without going by the "unneedful" southerly Canaries-West Indies route.

From Gosnold's point of view this was therefore rightly called a Virginian voyage, though it belongs geographically speaking to that region which was to be peopled later and is to us known as New England. He had hoped to go straight across the Atlantic, and he knew from accumulated experience that if he started in the spring he might get fair winds. He left Falmouth on 26th March, 1602, with the two ships *Concord* and *Dartmouth*, but for the first part of the journey he could not lay his course and was compelled to go as far south as the Azores, St. Mary's Island of that group being sighted on 14th April. From there Gosnold ran, as he believed, "directly west"; a week later he reckoned he was two hundred leagues west of that isle and in Lat. 37° N. On 8th May he got soundings with his lead in seventy fathoms. On the next day he found twenty-two fathoms, and "we held our selves by computation well neere the latitude of 43. degrees." On 14th May, about 6.0 a.m. land was sighted, and there came toward them a small boat with sail and oars containing Indians whose shoulders were covered with deerskins.

These natives must have already had dealings with the various unrecorded mariners who had been off this coast previously, fishing or bartering; for the visitors came aboard

with a few articles that had been made by Christians. They
" with a piece of chalke described the coast thereabouts, and
could name Placentia of the New-found-land. They spake
divers Christian words, and seemed to understand much more
than we. . . . These people are in colour swart, their haire
long up tyed with a knot in the part of behind the head. They
paint their bodies, which are strong and well proportioned."

So wrote Gabriel Archer, a " gentleman " who accompanied
Gosnold. And on 15th May the expedition came to anchor at
a cape where they caught such a lot of codfish that they
named this promontory Cape Cod, by which it is known to this
day. The voyage from England had tuhs taken about seven
weeks, which was a great improvement on some of the former
achievements, and it was a further advantage that by this
route they had been able to keep in a temperate zone of climate.
It followed that there was no injury to their health. Gosnold
was very proud of this, and in a letter to his father written in
the following September he remarked, " . . . for our selves
(thankes be to God) we had not a man sicke two dayes together
in all our voyage ; whereas others that went out with us, or
about that time on other Voyages (especially such as went upon
reprisall) were most of them infected with sicknesse, whereof
they lost some of their men, and brought home a many sicke,
returning notwithstanding long before us."

Having made a mental note of the fact that the Cape Cod
neighbourhood would yield a " good fishing in March, April,
and May," they came to that island which they found most
lovely with springtime blossoms and affording such promise
of " strawberries, respises, gousberries, and divers other fruits :
besides, deere and other beasts we saw, and cranes, hernes, with
divers other sorts of fowle, which made us call it ' Martha's
Vineyard ' "—the name which it retains to this day. Another
island, about " two leagues from the Maine," they visited with
further pleasure, sowed therein wheat, barley, oats which in a
fortnight had sprung up nine inches, the soil being " fat and
lusty." Fine oaks, cedar, cherry and other trees were noticed,
and it was decided to call this Elizabeth's Isle, though we now
are more familiar with the title Cuttyhunk Island.

After viewing the mainland of America, it was finally

concluded that the most suitable place for " our abode and plantation " was certainly that island of Elizabeth which they had named after their Queen. They began to busy themselves on 28th May making a fort and building a house. A new keel was put on the shallop ; they collected sassafras (the medicinal value of whose bark they found valuable for curing one of the party " that had taken a great surfet by eating the bellies of dog-fish), and on 31st May Gosnold sailed over to the American mainland, where he went ashore. The Indians entertained him well, presented him with skins, tobacco, turtle, but no pearls could be found along the beach. Still, Gosnold's people thought " this Maine is the goodliest Continent that ever we saw, promising more by farre then we any way did expect : for it is replenished with faire fields, and in them fragrant Flowers, also Medowes, and hedged in with stately groves, being furnished also with pleasant Brookes, and beautiful with two maine Rivers that (as wee judge) may haply become good Harbours, and conduct us to the hopes men so greedily thirst after."

These are weighty words written under the influence cf American springtime beauty, but foreshadowing that spiritual springtime which eighteen years later came to the sad-visaged people of the *Mayflower*. Gabriel Archer's language, just quoted, with its poetical enthusiasm, suggests the kind of phrases that Shakespeare might have used had he been of the party. Everything in this new sphere was idyllic to their simple and uncritical minds ; it was so satisfying after those monotonous days, rolling and pitching to the heavy Atlantic swell. It was so good to see budding, blossoming Nature in her bridal garments, and to smell the sweet odours of virgin land after the stench of filthy ship-holds.

On the eighth of June the expedition's victuals were divided in two parts : those for the planters on Cuttyhunk Island, and the rest for the returning mariners. But, when it was realized that there would be only six weeks' supply available for the former, trouble began. Again, there was also that old bugbear of suspicion and mistrust. They might possibly sustain themselves even for six months, bnt there was a secret rumour that they would never be sent any more supplies. The outcome was that after a few days of wrangling and bad-tempered consultations this first English settlement in New England came to a sudden end. The house and little fort that had been built by ten men in nineteen days and could have protected at least twenty persons was left, and on 17th June the expedition anchored at Martha's Vineyard, where the crew loaded up with fat geese and other birds. Next day the explorers set sail for England ; on 20th July they sighted the red cliffs of Devonshire and anchored off Exmouth. The trans-Atlantic trip had thus taken thirty-two days, but had it lasted much longer they would all have been starved ; there was practically neither food nor drink aboard except a little vinegar. What they did bring was considerable information of this new continent, its natives and products, its exceeding beauty, its healthy climate.

Apart from the trees, fowls, fruits, plants, herbs and fish, the reports contained data as to the dyes available, as well as copper in great abundance, and emery stones suitable for England's glaziers and cutlers. All this information reached Raleigh, and in this year he had sent a small vessel, which left the Dorset port of Weymouth in the same month as Gosnold had started forth. Raleigh was still mindful of the Roanoke settlers, and had selected Samuel Mace, " a very sufficient mariner " and " an honest sober man," who had been to Virginia twice before. But nothing came of this voyage, although Sir Walter took the precaution to buy the ship and hire the crew by the month with definite wages. The ship sighted America forty leagues to the S.W. of Hatteras. But the foul weather and the loss of their ground-tackle off that treacherous coast were the excuses they brought home for not having sought out the missing planters.

That was a busy year for American enterprise, for on the 2nd May, 1602, Captain George Weymouth left the Thames with a couple of fly-boats of seventy and sixty tons respectively, financed by the London merchants of the Muscovy and Turkey Companies, in yet another attempt to find a North-West Passage to China. He sighted Greenland, and picked up the western shore near that opening we know as Hudson Straits. Mutiny broke out aboard, but the culprits were punished, and on the way back the coast of Labrador was partially examined.

Weymouth got back to Dartmouth with the great riddle still unsolved.

At the beginning of 1603 came the death of Queen Elizabeth and the end of that brilliant Tudor period. Men's eyes were still blinking at its dazzling brightness, unable quite to understand all that shone around them. Everything in life seemed in a state of flux; the old safe but unprogressive settlement had gone. Prices had become high in proportion to wages. In every parish were many poor, but now that the monasteries had been swept away there was no Christian charity to afford poor relief. The mariners wounded in the Armada operations were given not pensions but licences to beg. It is true that in 1601 the maintenance of the impotent poor, and the setting of able-bodied men to labour in workhouses, became a duty of regular guardians. But that by no means ended the difficulty.

In the country and towns were great swarms of idle men who developed by the easiest stages into criminals. Landlords raised the rents of tenants, who in turn became bankrupt, or (to quote the current expression) "bankerout." The centre aisle of St. Paul's Cathedral was now the recognized rendezvous for business men, servants looking for jobs, rogues awaiting the opportunity to carry on their existence as cut-purses, while others were hoping for the chance of a free meal. A " Paul's man," in fact, was a recognized type of sponger or hanger-on. Professional perjurers could be bought for a few shillings as false witnesses in lawsuits. In this aisle was focused an amazing but accurate picture of that curious life which the Renaissance had produced in England by the beginning of the seventeenth century. The house of prayer had become the city of London's centre of restlessness. Brokers and usurers were bargaining, jostling and shouldering each other; while others were begetting drunken quarrels. Then along came the wealthier swaggering sort, brave with feathers, distinguished with beard and moustache, their cloaks thrust open to display their new clothes and the gilt rapier by the side. Knight and gallant, gentleman and captain, lawyer, scholar, puritan, cut-throat, mariner, merchant, traveller, ruffian, professional rascal were all here at work about 11.0 a.m. during divine service when (says a contemporary writer) " men, devoutly given,

G

do up to hear either a sermon or else the harmony of the choir and the organs."

What was a gentleman at this time ? Ben Jonson makes Carlo say in *Every Man out of His Humour* : " First, to be an accomplished gentleman, that is, a gentleman of the time, you must give over house-keeping in the country, and live altogether in the City amongst gallants ; where, at your first appearance, 'twere good you turned four or five hundred acres of your best land into two or three trunks of apparel . . . and be sure you mix yourself still with such as flourish in the spring of the fashion, and are least popular." There was a biting truth in this sarcasm. English life was undergoing a violent change, and during that process it was causing discontent. " The causes and motives of seditions," wrote Francis Bacon in 1597, " are : innovation in religion ; taxes ; alteration of laws and customs ; breaking of privileges ; general oppression ; advancement of unworthy persons ; strangers, dearths ; disbanded soldiers ; factions grown desperate ; and whatsoever in offending people joineth and knitteth them in a common cause. For the remedies . . . the first remedy or prevention is to remove by all means possible that material cause of sedition whereof we spake ; which is want and poverty in the estate."

" Traffic," wrote Barnabe Riche in 1581, " is so dead by means of these foreign broils that unless a man would be a thief to his country, to steal out prohibited wares, there were small gains to be gotten " ; while, for the farmer, " lands be so racked at such a rate that a man should but toil all the days of his life to pay his landlord's rent. But what occupation . . . might a man then follow to make himself rich, when every science depends on new-fangled fashions ? For he that to-day is accompted for the finest workman, within one month some new found fellow comes out with some new found fashion, and then he bears the prize, and the first accompted but a bungler. . . . Such is the miserable condition of this our present time. This is the course of the world, but especially here in England, where there is no man thought to be wise but he that is wealthy. . . . What little care of the poor and such as be in want ! What feastings of the rich and such as be wealthy ! "

London in those days, with its utter lack of hygiene, was a breeding-place for epidemics, especially when the summer was hot and rainless. Plague came as too regular a visitor, and there was a particularly bad outbreak of this torment in 1603, shortly after the Queen had died. Thomas Dekker, writing of that year in London, drew a terrible picture of its " still and melancholy streets . . . the loud groans of raving, sick men, the struggling pangs of souls departing ; in every house grief striking up an alarum ; servants crying out for masters, wives for husbands, parents for children, children for their mothers ; here he should have met with some frantically running to knock up sextons ; there, others fearfully sweating with coffins to steal forth dead bodies lest the fatal handwriting of death should seal up their doors."

To people thus unsettled in mind and estate the bright prospects of the New World inevitably brought great temptations to quit. Gosnold's related facts and infectious enthusiasm gave to the title Virginia a fresh vitality, and Hakluyt (now Prebendary of Bristol Cathedral) was keener than ever that the land should be explored. Bristol, since the days of the Cabots, had not forgotten its interest in North America ; it needed only the persuasion of this ardent cleric to get busy once more. Hakluyt's influence over the leading merchants of that western city was such that, after various meetings and consultations, a resolution was made to send an expedition for the further discovery of northern Virginia. As Raleigh still had to be consulted, the Bristol merchants sent Hakluyt, together with Master John Angel and Master Robert Saltern (who in the previous year had accompanied Gosnold), to obtain the requisite permission from Sir Walter. This having been granted, two ships were fitted out, the first being the *Speedwell* of fifty tons burden, manned by thirty mariners and boys under the command of Captain Martin Pring, with the above Robert Saltern as pilot. The second ship was the *Discovery* of twenty-six tons, with thirteen men and boys under Master William Browne. Victualled for eight months, and furnished with a cargo of hats, stockings, shoes, tools, knives, looking-glasses, scissors, fish-hooks, beads and other articles for barter with the Indians, the vessels sailed on 20th March, 1603, bnt were held up for a fortnight in Milford Haven (where they heard of Elizabeth's death), and then sailed via the Azores on a route similar to that of Gosnold's voyage. Thus June saw them arrive among those islands of New England south of Cape Cod Bay, which (says Pring) " we found very pleasant to behold," with " an excellent fishing for cods, which are better than those of New-found-land." They then sailed to the south-west, and visited the mainland in the neighbourhood of what we now call New Bedford, investigating the inlets. Afterward they went south " into that great Gulfe which Captaine Gosnold over-shot the yeere before, coasting and finding people on the North side thereof. Not yet satisfied in our expectation, we left them and sailed over, and came to an Anchor on the South side in the latitude of 41. degrees and odde minutes."

With their rude navigational instruments these old mariners were not always strictly accurate in getting the latitude, b' t it would seem that Pring reached Long Island Sound, and here they bartered with the Indians, who were much afraid of two mastiff dogs which had been brought from Bristol. Wheat, barley and oats, as well as garden seeds, were planted by Pring's people, and came up so quickly that there was ample proof of America's rich soil. It was all very encouraging for the future. " And," remarked Pring, " as the Land is full of Gods good blessings, so is the Sea replenished with great abundance of excellent fish." By the end of July the little *Discovery* was loaded with sassafras and sent back to Bristol, where she safely arrived after being away from England five and a half months. About 8th August the *Speedwell* left her " excellent Haven," which they found to be as winding as " the shell of a Snaile, and it is in latitude of one and forty degrees and five and twentie minutes." Crossing the Atlantic, she went north of the Azores and reached soundings off the English coast, but had the bad luck to be delayed there by easterly winds. On the 2nd October she arrived, however, in Bristol.

The net result of Pring's expedition was to confirm and slightly increase the knowledge obtained by Gosnold concerning this northern part of America and the direct way thereto. But in that self-same year was made another voyage, which, for the relation it bears to a most historic undertaking begun less than four years later, is worthy of especial attention. We have already mentioned Captain Bartholomew Gilbert, who in 1602 had been across with Gosnold. In the spring of 1603 Gilbert, together with Master Thomas Canner of London, Richard Harrison as mate, Henry Kenton the surgeon, a Dutchman named Derricke, and others provisioned a fifty-ton vessel at Southampton, sailed down-Channel, left Plymouth on 10th May, and went by the southern route.

The navigation during this voyage was not good. They failed to sight Madeira, and then on 1st June, altered course when in Latitude 27° N. to reach the West Indies. On 15th June they had made quite a good passage and sighted land, which Gilbert and others took to be the Bermudas. Had that conjecture been correct, they would have been most considerably to the north of their intended position. Next day some natives were seen, and made signs for the visitors to show their colours. Gilbert's people then hoisted their flag at the maintop and called back " *Ingleses ! Amigos !* " (" English ! Friends ! ") A rope was thrown to a canoe, some bartering went on, and it was learned that this was the island of the West Indies named Santa Lucia. On 17th June Dominica was sighted, and two days later they brought up off the island of Nevis, which is one of the Leeward group, and was not colonized by Gilbert's countrymen till a quarter of a century later.

The object of this voyage was to fetch lignum-vitæ. Now the day of their first landing here was a Sunday, and Canner (who was a Puritan in attitude) believed their ill-fortune " a just plague unto us for prophaning the Sabbath in traveling about our worldly business, when there was no necessitie," since trees seemed to be scarce. After a fortnight Gilbert decided to sail farther north and seek for more plentiful wood in Virginia ; so on 3rd July (another Sunday) he weighed anchor, called at St. Christopher, where they obtained fish and tortoises with their nets. Steering on N.W. and N. by W. courses, they carried the same north-east wind which had blown constantly ever since the Canaries, but on 10th July it began to veer through south to west. They began to feel, also, the effect of the Gulf Stream setting out from the Gulf of Mexico. On the eleventh they steered north, and then suffered

from calms as well as extremely hot weather, during which
their fish went bad. It was on the twentieth they expected to
sight Chesapeake (or, as they called it, Chesepian) Bay, whither
they were bound. But a cast of the lead gave them no bottom
until they got thirty fathoms about 6.0 p.m. on the twenty-first.
Gilbert had feared that the current had set them too far to
leeward, and in fact he went a long way to the north, thus
missing his objective.

It was not till 23rd July about 8.0 a.m. that the American
continent was picked up—" very fine low land, appearing farre
off to bee full of tall Trees, and a fine sandie shore." But this
was in " 40 degrees and odde minutes " and no harbour could be
found   Next day the wind went round from W. to N.E., so
they presently put about and ran before it in the hope that
" then we should fetch the Bay of Chesepian, which Master
Gilbert so much thirsted after, to seeke out the people for Sir
Walter Raleigh left neere those parts in the yeere 1587 : if not,
perhaps we might find some Road or Harbour in the way to
take in some fresh water : for now wee had none aboord."

They were off Chesapeake Bay on the night of the twenty-
fifth, but again bad luck dogged them. Owing to the fresh
wind and heavy sea it was thought inadvisable to run in toward
the land. Next day and the following the conditions were
again unfavourable. Water, beer, food and wood (for the
galley) having practically ended, matters began to look critical ;
but on 29th July the ship lay-to about a mile from the mouth of
Chesapeake Bay, where the shore " appeared unto us exceeding
pleasant and full of goodly Trees." So in the ship's boat
went Captain Gilbert, Thomas Canner, Harrison, Kenton
and Derricke with their arms, and landed, leaving a couple
of youths to mind the boat. Thus, at last, was a temporary
acquaintance made of that territory which was destined in a
few years to become the birthplace of the United States nation.

But the exploring party had not gone far when the two lads
saw their shipmates attacked by Indians, who slew the whole
lot except Canner. The boys with great difficulty saved the
boat, and returned to the ship with heavy hearts. This first
landing, in what we may rightly refer to as " New " Virginia
in contradistinction to that " Old " Virginia (extending from

Cape Fear to the entrance of Chesapeake Bay), had thus been another of those inconclusive affairs that seemed ever to keep America inviolate from all permanent intruders. One disaster after another ; the accumulated toll of missing men and wasted voyages ; the struggles against bad weather, hunger, thirst, disease and wretched discomfort ; the quarrels and mutinies, the failure to give merchants a tangible reward for the capital risked ; the continuous series of disappointments—all these were the preliminaries and conditions before England was to come in active possession of northern America, and to hold her colonies for only little more than a hundred and sixty years.

With eleven men and boys all told, in great distress of thirst, the ship delayed no longer but made for the Azores. Thence she entered the English Channel, picked up the first land at Portland, and came up the Thames to Ratcliffe about the end of September, 1603, there to receive still further bad news from the inhabitants of London ; for they found " the Citie most grievously infected with a terrible plague." No home-coming could have been less encouraging.

Still, failure is to be computed only in its ultimate consideration. Success that has no history behind it, no fruitless efforts and no difficulties, is hardly likely to endure, and is not worthy of retention. Pioneering is rarely a paying proposition in the sense of direct profit-making. It is not the man who discovers the best place for a plantation that becomes rich, nor is it the first generation of planters. But these, with all their sad stories of mistakes and misfortunes, alone make it possible for the reaper and the trader to turn nature's products into gold and bring prosperity to a virgin region. The business of colonization, like any other avocation, requires and demands a previous apprenticeship. The grandparents of America had entirely failed to appreciate this obvious fact. They embarked bravely, though imprudently, on a task that needed more complete preparations and a greater knowledge. The merchants were so eager to get an immediate return for their money, and the mariners were too optimistic while possessing such limited information. Thus it was all a succession of gambles. The shipowner naturally wanted to hire out his vessel, but the merchant was very much at his mercy, and had to believe so many things just because the hardened old sea-dogs and a few geographically-minded enthusiastic idealists made certain unproved statements.

And yet without these ventures and lost fortunes, these risks and disappointments, progress and development would have been delayed indefinitely. The time had now arrived when there was just sufficient information available as to where the first permanent colony in northern America might be settled, and there were plenty of warnings from the past indicating the dangers to be avoided in the future. But one generation, or one family, is jealous of another not infrequently, so many of the old mistakes continued to be made for a long time to come.

Queen Elizabeth

From a contemporary print

CHAPTER VIII

THE PLANTATION PLAN

THE sixteenth-century Englishmen were very emphatic in the claim that Sir Sebastian Cabot on behalf of England's king had been the first that ever set foot on the American shore as representative of any Christian prince. This gave to them a confidence and a buoyant courage when otherwise the task might scarcely have seemed worthy of the labour. Whatever Spain or France might pretend, the men of England felt that this North-American coast belonged by right to England. But the latter had the sagacity to leave Florida strictly alone.

Laudonnière had discovered rivers in Florida, and relations had been established with the Indians, but the first attempt at colonization had been frustrated by a mutiny among the French. A second attempt by the French was again marred by mutinous outbreaks. The third effort was rendered impossible by the arrival of a Spanish squadron, but a fourth French voyage to Florida reuslted in extermination of the Spaniards. While these events were given every consideration by Raleigh's colleagues in the Virginian venture, Hakluyt was careful that his own countrymen should not forget that Jacques Cartier had in 1534 sailed from St. Malo, crossed the Atlantic, called at Newfoundland on his next voyage, landed on the Gaspé side of Quebec, of which he took possession in the name of France's King. Still, no effort at permanent occupation was made until 1608. In 1541 Cartier had made his third voyage to Canada, but there followed yearly voyages from France by others who profited from the fish and beaver skins.

It was not till March, 1603, that Samuel de Champlain, then aged thirty-six, sailed from Honfleur and went up the River St. Lawrence, otherwise known as the River of Canada. It did not take the French long to find (as the English had discovered) that the Indians were treacherous liars and thieves. The River Saguenay was partially explored, and Champlain for a time anchored off Quebec during June, being favourably impressed with the country, its trees and wild vines. Nor did he fail to notice sites suitable for settlers. Several natives were brought back to France, where Champlain arrived before the end of September. As a result of this voyage, a patent was granted by the King of France in the following November, and by this authorization the area from Lat. 40° to 46° was to become French for possession and habitation, with a view to profit and also to incite the savages to the knowledge of God and the Christian religion. So another voyage began in the next March. It was while on the other side of the Atlantic that the acquaintance was made of Captain Savalet, a most experienced old mariner, who came from the Biscayan port of St. Jean de Luz. This was the forty-second voyage that he had made to the north-east American waters, and this is proof enough that by the opening of the seventeenth century more unrecorded trips from Europe to that region had been prosperuosly accomplished than has been generally conceded. Savalet went to the Newfoundland seas for the fishing, and managed to earn one thousand pounds each voyage, and it was such inducements which were building up a small but increasing fleet of European ships that before long would be required in carrying the people to dwell permanently in America. French families came across in 1608, and Quebec was founded as a town by Champlain, who in 1609 discovered that celebrated lake which still bears his name.

French colonial enterprise was thus working in a manner similar to English activity that was confined to more southerly latitudes. Champlain was a man of great geographical attainments, and skilled in the sea arts, but he was also a brave, bold pioneer, content to suffer untold hardship. The old Cathay fascination was alive in him, and he was resolved to go on exploring till he had found a northern or western passage toward China. The River Saguenay seemed to suggest a possible northern route. That he failed was no fault of his own. A flourishing fur trade was established by him, the first baptism of instructed Canadians included a hundred and twenty, and a great beginning had been made in a vast territory. But in these French settlements were laid the seeds of future international trouble, which was unavoidable since England claimed priority through Cabotian cruises. Especially did this apply to Acadia, the name by which the early French settlers knew Nova Scotia. In 1629 Quebec fell to the British and Champlain was carried to England, though in 1632 the Treaty of St. Germain restored Canada to the French and Champlain again became Governor. It was in 1621 that Sir W. Alexander, afterward Earl of Stirling, obtained a charter and tried to colonize Nova Scotia, but it was not till the Treaty of Utrecht, 1713, that this Gallicized island became definitely British, and even then the French settlers continued to give trouble until their deportation occurred forty odd years later. For the dominion of Canada a long struggle was bound to be waged between Britain and France, which went on till only a dozen years before British-American colonists insisted on their own independence.

But our story centres round the origin of the United States, and we have only one more voyage to consider before we witness the inauguration of the first of those states. In the early spring of 1605 Captain George Weymouth was sent from the Thames on another of those endeavours such as Gosnold had made. We are now well into the reign of James I., and the conditions for overseas energy have been altered. Only two years before her death Elizabeth had by royal proclamation prohibited all trade whatsoever with Spain and Portugal. James, however, was anxious to be on good terms, and in 1604 had made peace with Spain, thus putting an end to those marauding privateering expeditions which had found employment for so many of England's mariners. Incidentally this new policy threw the latter into the awkward predicament of either becoming pirates (which not a few preferred) or getting odd jobs when crews were wanted for the Atlantic.

Being a lover of peace, James was anxious to assist rather than obstruct merchants. He enlarged the privileges of the East India, the Muscovy, the Turkey, and the Merchant Adventurers' Companies as early as 1604. No monarch has ever been so closely connected with the trend of young America. Whatever his virtues and defects, he loved the English nation and was desirous to encourage its commerce. A very human man, who swore like a soldier, hated war and enjoyed hunting, delighted in literature and art, appreciated the possibilities of colonization, it was he who laid the basis of the English-speaking influence throughout the world. Even the somewhat unsympathetic Alexander Brown in his well-known *Genesis of the United States* has remarked of this Stuart sovereign : " It may be that he has found but few friends among the historians of America, yet I am sure that America has more cause to bless him than to blame him."

Elizabeth's legacy to her mariners was the supremacy of the seas ; therefore the time was ripe now for such as would pass over the ocean for commerce, exploration or the settling of a colony. Peers, knights, aldermen and others quite early in James's reign were already planning overseas schemes now that the horrors of the Plague had been swept aside. It was the Earl of Southampton in partnership with Lord Arundell of Wardour who sent Captain Weymouth forth. The crew consisted of twenty - nine first - class sailors, who had been waiting aboard the vessel at anchor in the Downs weather-bound, but at 5.0 p.m. on Easter Day, the last of March this 1605, the wind came N.N.E. and enabled them to get under way.

She was furnished with such sea-charts as recent voyages along the American coast had provided ; a magnetic piece of loadstone ; dogs ; a pinnace ; munitions ; victuals, and the following five articles for navigation and observation : an astrolabe, a semisphere, a " ring-instrument," a cross-staff " and an excellent Compas, made for the variation." The proximity of the invisible American shore was ascertained on 13th May, when a cast of the lead gave one hundred and sixty fathoms, and five hours later one hundred fathoms. Weymouth, not wishing to close the land till daylight, therefore lowered sail, and next morning a hand was sent aloft who descried a whitish sandy cliff.   In accordance with contemporary marine practice a boat was now lowered and went ahead in charge of the mate to take soundings. Shoal water was discovered, and they were compelled to keep away seaward, for they had narrowly avoided getting ashore somewhere within a small radius of Martha's Vineyard.

The wind was between south and west, they were uncertain of their position and unable to see the land again. " Wee found our Sea Charts very false laying out Land where none was, for though we bare in directly with it according to them, yet in almost fifty leagues running we found none." They were further anxious, as they lacked wood and drinking water. But on 17th May land showed up to the N.N.E., and on the following day (being the eve of Whitsun) they let go anchor in forty fathoms to the north of an island where there was everything that they desired in streams, fruit, fish and fowl. Hence were visible the Elizabeth Islands, and the mainland stretching away from WSW. to ENE. On Whit-Sunday they weighed and found a less deep anchorage under one of these islands, the mate as before going ahead and sounding cautiously from the boat. This excellent haven "whereof here before we reade none to have made either description or relation," they named Pentecost Harbour.

The crew, who were soon at work constructing the shallop, digging wells, finding clay suitable for making bricks, obtaining lobsters, felling wood, digging the ground, planting garden seeds and barley, noted that the fir trees yielded turpentine " so sweet as our Chirurgeon and others affirmed they never saw so good in England," and of course even the small pearls in the mussels excited them. On 30th May Weymouth went in the shallop to the mainland and explored what was apparently Narragansett Bay. Some trade in skins was done from the ship with the Indians, and Weymouth having previously magnetized his sword with a loadstone mystified these natives by attracting their knives. " This we did to cause them to imagine some great power in us, and for that to love and feare us."

The Indians presented them with tobacco, but these natives soon proved treacherous to the English adventurers. Five natives were kept on board, who were to be taken with their two canoes, their bows and arrows, to England. In the meantime Weymouth was very busy exploring the coast and especially safe anchorages with a view to future settlements contemplated by his noble employers. This was absolutely essential. " The first and chiefest thing required for a Plantation is a bold coast, and faire land to fall with. The next, a safe Harbour for Ships to ride in." That was how Weymouth rightly reasoned, and when he brought the ship up to Narragansett Bay with a gentle wind " wee all consented in joy." In that mixed ship's company were men who had seen the principal rivers of France, others were familiar with the Rio Grande that flowed into the Mexican Gulf, while some had been with Raleigh in the 1595 expedition to Guiana and had beheld the mighty Orinoco ; yet in their enthusiastic admiration not one of these rivers seemed comparable with Narragansett.

Weymouth could not resist the thought that by this noble inlet a way might be found to the South Sea, *i.e.* the Pacific. But he was prudent enough to keep that notion to himself, and remember that he had been sent out for the purpose of finding suitable places for settlement. Finally, having completed his survey and found (as he thought) the correct latitude, he started on 16th June for England, sighted the Scillies a month later, but did not reach Dartmouth for another two days owing to calms and light winds.

Now the resultant value of Weymouth's trip was this : it added to the slender existing knowledge that this part of America was most suitable and tempting for any who cared there to settle. Detailed information was brought back concerning all the natural products, and a beginning was made of an Indian dictionary. All these data were a few years after to be of considerable assistance when English thoughts turned to consider New England's possibilities as a home from home. Bnt even immediately important results were to upspring, and fresh patents were to be obtained. As yet the title New England had not been bestowed or even considered, though New France in Canada suggested it. For the present the whole vast American territory known to Englishmen only partially, but extending roughly toward Newfoundland, was just simply Virginia, and all the Indian tribes were Virginians. This was definitely and officially set down in the patent which will now be examined.

The year 1606 is one of the most important dates in the whole of America's story ; it is from this point that all the previous failures fade away and become forgotten. Sir Humphrey Gilbert and Sir Walter Raleigh had kept alive an idea, but now the right men gathered together and seized that idea as their own. Under the conditions of this new reign, and young seventeenth century, there was a little more opportunity for contemplation and quiet working out of problems. Even men of action, who had travelled and fought on the European continent, were now exercising their intellect and reasoning powers in a less warlike and more constructive manner. Some even regretted that the Reformation had robbed them of cloistered opportunities for withdrawing from the world and meditating in quietness. " I wished monastrys had not been putt downe," expressed the genial Aubrey later on in this century ; " that the reformers would have been more moderate as to that point. Nay, the Turkes have monasteries. Why should our reformers be so severe ? . . . there should be receptacles and provision for contemplative men. . . . What a pleasure 'twould have been to have travelled from monastery to monastery."

That great thinker Francis Bacon, who used to have " musique " played in the next room while he meditated, once remarked to his servant Hunt : " The world was made for man, Hunt ; and not man for the world." And wise men were beginning just to realize that there was something other than warring, privateering and piracy worth while. Of these individuals there stands out conspicuously Captain John Smith, who had spent a most adventurous life soldiering in the Low Countries, then wandering through France to the Mediterranean, where he narrowly escaped death by drowning, and took part in piracy. After visiting Italy, as so many English gentlemen at this period were accustomed, Smith fought for the Christians against the Turks, distinguished himself in single combat, was eventually taken prisoner to the Black Sea neighbourhood, whence he escaped from slavery. Finally, after passing through Russia, France and Spain, he went afloat again, served in an English man-of-war against some Spanish warships in a hot engagement but with victory. And then in 1604, full of experience, he was back in England. At once he threw himself whole-heartedly into the colonial enthusiasm which was now so well established, being ready to give his own personal fortune and his very self.

The first thing was to get together a company of able men with money, and next to obtain the requisite royal patent, or authorization, to colonize. To quote his own words, " I haue spared neither paines nor money according to my abilitie, first to procure his Maiesties Letters pattents, and a Company here to be the means to raise a company to go with me to Virginia ; " and this cost him " more than 500 pounds of my owne estate." It was that great leader Captain Bartholomew Gosnold who was really the prime mover of this scheme, and he had been spending many monotonous months soliciting his friends' interest, but without avail, until Master Edward Maria Wingfield and Captain John Smith got certain of the nobility, gentry and merchants to help. At last James I granted this company its patent on 10th April, 1606, and this was destined to become of such historical importance that we must briefly examine it.

The grantees included the following : Sir Thomas Gates, Sir George Somers, Prebendary Hakluyt, Edward Maria Wingfield, George Popham and another of the Gilbert family whose Christian name was Raleigh. Gates was a Devonshire man, an expert on fortifications and military matters. He had distinguished himself in the taking of Cadiz in 1596 (when Howard, Essex and Raleigh were fellow-campaigners), and received a knighthood. Later on he served abroad under the States-General, and was soldiering in South Holland during the autumn of 1606. He petitioned the States for leave to go to Virginia, and this was granted in April, 1608. Somers was a Dorset man, born at Lyme Regis and now aged fifty-two. Of a good family, he was at heart the real roaming adventurer whom life in a quiet little seaside town could never restrain for long. He had first gone roving when quite young, and at forty sailed on a buccaneering voyage to the Spanish Main, where he displayed considerable heroism. Other warlike expeditions followed, especially in the neighbourhood of the Azores, and he led a charmed life, narrowly escaping death both afloat and ashore. A friend of Raleigh, he was knighted in 1603, and after spending a few years in England as Member of Parliament and Mayor of his native town, he became one of the principal supporters of the Virginia Company. He was wealthy,

accustomed to command men, had considerable knowledge of
ship life, was full of recources, and continued always the kind of
gallant fellow who was not afraid of suffering for the good of so
noble a cause as planting a colony. Neither of these two,
however, went out to Virginia in the first voyage. Wingfield,
who became one of John Smith's enemies, was in religion a
liberal Roman Catholic, but a somewhat difficult person with
whom to work, rather too self-reliant and a little too unpractical.
His obstinacy became even dangerous at times.

The wording of this 1606 patent makes clear that it was
a "license to make habitation, plantation, and to deduce a
colonie . . . into that part of America commonly called
Virginia, and other parts and territories in America, either
appertayning unto us, or which now are not actually possessed
by any Christian Prince or people, situate lying and being all
along the sea coast betweene thirtie foure degrees of Northerly
latitude from the Equinoctiall Line, and fortie five degrees of
the same latitude, and in the mayne land betweene the same
thirtie foure and fortie five degrees, and the ilands thereunto
adjacent within one hundred miles of the coast thereof." The
area was thus roughly that from Cape Fear to the present north-
easternmost boundary between Canada and the United States.

Further, " for the more speedie accomplishment of the said
intended plantation and habitation " the project was to be
divided into two colonies and companies. The first was to be
the undertaking of " certaine Knights, Gentlemen, Merchants,
and other Adventurers of our Citie of London," whose sphere
was restricted between 34° and 41°; that is to say as far
north as about Long Island Sound. The second was that
of adventurers belonging to the cities of Bristol, Exeter and
Plymouth, whose area was to be in some suitable place between
38° and 45°.

Just as the French King hoped that plantation in Canada
might lead to the spread of Christianity among the Indians, so
James I commended this plantation for Virginia " which may
by the providence of Almightie God hereafter tend to the glorie
of his Divine Majestie, in propagating of Christian religion to
such people as yet live in darknesse." The licensees were to
have the land, havens, rivers, mines, fisheries ; they could erect

H

forts, and no other British subjects should be allowed to plant
on the landward side without permission of the Council in
England.

Thus, there were two Virginian plantations contemplated :
the southern one under the London Company, and the northern
under the West of England Company. " Neither Colonie shall
plant within one hundred miles of each other," and each colony
was to be ruled by a Council of thirteen. Of any gold and
silver discovered one - fifth was to be paid to the King of
England, and of any copper one-fifteenth was demanded. On
the twentieth of November this same year James established
the " King's Council for Virginia," in which were to serve such
distinguished citizens as Sir Thomas Smith, Sir Francis Popham
and Sir Ferdinando Gorges ; but in the following March his
Majesty added Sir Edwin Sandys and a number of other
prominent names.

The London Council was to have full authority in the King's
name to direct the Council resident in America for the good
government of the people ; at the same time power was
reserved to the Crown to alter the London Council. This
proviso was likely to have far-reaching effects, and thus from
the very first we can see potentialities of plantation trouble.
According to whether this controlling power was exercised
arbitrarily, or with human prudence, would depend the whole
American colonial future. There must come a year when the
mother-country's child would grow to manhood and the age of
discretion. Would the grown-up offspring disown the parent,
and sever all relationship, with a view to complete independence
and full self-expression ? Obviously that must be decided more
by the parent than by the descendant. Autonomy, in other
words, must be the whole basis of happiness ; excessive
interference must inevitably rouse the most loyal colonists
to rebellion. But the ruling minds in seventeenth-century
England could not see what a dangerous policy was being
inaugurated.

It was to be lawful for the American Council to choose its
own President for a year or longer, and to remove him. It was
further ordered " That the said President, Councils, and the
Ministers should provide that the true Word and Service of God

be preached, planted, and used, not only in the said colonies, but also, as much as might be, among the savages bordering upon them, according to the rites and doctrine of the Church of England." But the whole legislative power was placed exclusively in the hands of the Presidents and Councils, without any representation of the people. And, as we have just seen, the King could "increase, alter, or change the said Council" at his will and pleasure. Liberty was thus circumscribed in a vicious circle. How long would such a condition be tolerated?

The death penalty was to be the punishment of "tumults, rebellion, conspiracy, mutiny, and sedition, together with murder, manslaughter, incest, rapes, and adultery." This comprehensive regulation well indicates the barbaric character of those days, and a degeneracy in English moral standards had already set in. It had become notorious, for instance, that the wealthier men who left England to travel in Italy came back home only after a surfeit of wickedness. "Vanity and vice," wrote Roger Ascham, "and any license to ill living in England was counted stale and rude unto them." Even the Italians had a saying that "an Englishman Italianate is a devil incarnate." But there was no mutual happiness in family life, or trustful friendship between father and son. "In those days," recorded Aubrey, "fathers were not acquainted with their children."

The same authority refers to a peer of that age as "damnably proud and arrogant." A man might be a popular knight, famous at Court for his repartee and sparkling wit, a great gallant, but an incorrigible gamester both at bowls and cards, so that shopmen would not trust him for sixpence. Gentlemen would quarrel outrageously over their mistresses as well as their gaming, and end their disputes in a duel with swords. Few of them could write a letter, but most of the nobility were proud and insolent in their manner. With the exception of churches, and some of the best rooms in a few gentlemen's houses, glass windows were still very rarely found, and never in the poor people's dwellings. Until Queen Elizabeth's spacious days caps were worn but not hats, and trunk hose were in fashion till the latter end of James I's time. It was not yet a very civilized country below the surface.

But among the regulations for Virginia were two that

stressed the communal character which the colony was to assume : " That for five years, next after their landing on the coast of Virginia, the said several colonies and every person thereof should trade altogether in one stock, or in two or three stocks at most, and should bring all the fruits of their labours there, with all their goods and commodities from England or elsewhere, into several magazines or storehouses, for that purpose to be erected. . . . And lastly, that every person of the said colonies should be furnished with necessaries out of the said magazines for the space of five years." Nor could a colonist be allowed to embark for Virginia until he had taken oaths of obedience.

The London Virginia Company being duly formed, who should be appointed " Treasurer " (that is, the chief director in its management and its chairman at the Council meetings) ? The choice fell easily on that conspicuous citizen Alderman Sir Thomas Smith, whom we have seen in a previous chapter already selected as first Governor of the East India Company. This wealthy merchant was born in 1558, and the son of a father with the same Christian name. The latter had amassed a fortune as farmer of the Customs, a method that made more than one such speculator rich, as, for instance, Sir Thomas Wolstenholme, to be mentioned in a later chapter. Sir Thomas Smith's father was able to lend Queen Elizabeth one thousand pounds when she required it.

Sir Thomas's mother was daughter of a Lord Mayor of London, so the boy was brought up in an atmosphere of prosperity and finance derived from both sides of the family, and in his early manhood he began straightway to be a person of some commercial importance. After being educated at Oxford, he became at the age of twenty-three an incorporator of the Turkey Company previously mentioned, six years later he was one of the chief men of the Russia Company, and two years later still he gains further attention as one of those to whom Raleigh assigned his Virginia interest. We see Smith helping to send ships to the East Indies even in that 1591 expedition. In 1603 he received his knighthood, and from 1604 to 1605 was Ambassador to Russia. He was one of those appointed to the London Virginia Company's Council in

November, 1606, and his influence in keeping the colony going through storm and stress, disputes and disheartenment, was a very able piece of administration. That he was liable to fierce criticism will in due time become apparent too. At present we can think of him as to-day we think of some consummate shipping magnate whose money and judgment reap high rewards.

Sir Thomas Smith was financially adventurous without being rash ; far-sighted and big-minded while still preserving the sanity of a business man. He believed that Virginia would be as productive as the newly-established trade with India promised ; he had in mind the probability of there being found in America gold, silver and pearls, though previous voyages had never brought home any definite facts. It was, however, well established by those adventurers whom we have already been considering that America yielded hemp, masts, tar, pitch, resin —all of which were much required for the increasing English navy—together with such useful commodities as sassafras. That was why he and his colleagues were willing to raise the necessary funds. Virginia was to be planted primarily for the enrichment of English investors, not for the development of America. Most of those emigrating were in effect slaves, though in name servants. Thus, those who tilled the ground, raised crops and made a new country productive, were not to enjoy the full fruits of their labours, but to work for others living three thousand miles away—several weeks.

Thomas Smith and his friends were merely following the precedent of Spain, who had exploited the New World with the most satisfactory results financially. But the Anglo-Saxon mind was of a peculiar sort. Centuries of history had given to the insular-bred English character a keen sensitiveness regarding freedom. England, from her geographical position and the paucity of shipping, had been aloof from European influences to a surprising degree. But she had worked out during the Middle Ages an extension of liberty to her people. The suppression of the Barons, the legal reforms, the summoning of the first representative Parliament under Edward I, the forbidding of taxation without Parliament's consent, the sixteenth-century assertion of national freedom from Rome, the strenuous resistance of Spain's maritime exclusiveness, all these and many smaller movements had made Thomas Smith's fellow-countrymen almost fanatical in their attitude toward unfettered right to live as they pleased. The psychology of the English crowd is such that it will endure every kind of misery and physical suffering in behalf of freedom ; but in the absence of liberty it will magnify every small inconvenience, lose all interest, become rebellious and fight to the last ditch against tyranny and injustice. In those days the intellect was less quick to reason and resolve than modern education and experience have enabled. It took one hundred and sixty-nine years, or several generations, before the American colonists broke out in revolt against the very principles which had been laid down by a London company of hard-headed, keen, astute, but unsympathetic men in 1606. Lack of imagination, neglect to consider the possible reaction of a tight policy on struggling human beings, are faults quite as serious as slackness or rashness ; and the last years of Thomas Smith's life were made full of worry by these two defects.

St. John's, Newfoundland

From an early nineteenth-century print

CHAPTER IX

TO THE PROMISED LAND

BY the late autumn of 1606 three ships had been chartered for the London Virginia Company, viz. the *Susan Constant* (one hundred tons), *God Speed* (forty tons), and *Discovery* (twenty tons), which was one of the smaller ocean-going types classed as a pinnace. The promoters entrusted the entire transportation details to Captain Christopher Newport, because of his previous experience in sailing to the American coast. He was a genuine mariner, aged about forty-one, who was destined to make another four voyages to Virginia and back before he entered the service of the East India Company in 1612. Newport sailed as Admiral (or senior officer) of the squadron for Virginia, with his flag on the *Susan Constant*. That well-tried Atlantic navigator, Captain Bartholomew Gosnold, was chosen Vice-Admiral, with his flag on the *God Speed*. The Rear-Admiral was Captain John Ratcliffe (alias Sicklemore) with his flag on the *Discovery*.

Until the landing was effected at Virginia Captain Newport was to be in supreme command. According to Purchas the colonists numbered one hundred and forty-four, of whom seventy-one travelled in the Admiral's flagship, fifty-two in Gosnold's vessel, and twenty-one in the pinnace. According to the Hon. George Percy's account the party on arrival at the Virgin Islands, West Indies, 4th April, numbered " eight score persons." But we must remember that shipping documents show how weak was the arithmetic of this time. Meticulous accuracy in figures was not characteristic of the period. From the Virginia Company's " Instructions given by way of advice," we know that the number of emigrants originally contemplated was one hundred and twenty, and if we think of this historic band as roughly one hundred and fifty we shall not be far from the truth.

They included Master Edward Maria Wingfield, Captain

John Smith, Captain John Martin, Captain George Kendal, the Hon. George Percy (brother to the Earl of Northumberland), the mild and patient chaplain Master Robert Hunt, and Captain Gabriel Archer, a somewhat officious intolerant person who had accompanied Gosnold on his New England voyage in 1602. Anthony Gosnold (a brother of Captain Bartholomew Gosnold) and another Anthony Gosnold (nephew of the Captain) also set out on this Virginia voyage ; the rest of the party consisting of gentlemen, soldiers, a drummer, carpenter, labourers, bricklayers, a blacksmith, a barber, a tailor, a mason, a surgeon and a few boys. At least one of the colonists was a Dutchman.

The London Virginia Company issued instructions to be observed by officers and men ; these being additional to those ordinances already set forth by the King. Thus, before sailing from England, a clear idea was manifested as to what were the intended lines on which the American plantation was to be conducted. It was directed that, after the coast of Virginia had been sighted, " you shall do your best endeavour to find out a safe port in the entrance of some navigable river, making choice of such a one as runneth farthest into the land, and . . . bendeth most toward the North-west for that way you shall soonest find the other sea." (An entrance into the Pacific Ocean was hoped for.) Next " let Captain Newport discover how far that river may be found navigable," so that they might choose " the strongest, most wholesome and fertile place " for a plantation. They were advised, if possible, to select a site well up the river. " For if you sit down near the entrance, except it be in some island that is strong by nature, an enemy that may approach you on even ground may easily pull you out. . . . And to the end that you be not surprised as the French were in Florida by Melindus [i.e. Don Pedro Melendez], and the Spaniard in the same place by the French, you shall . . . first, erect a little stoure at the mouth of the river that may lodge some ten men, with whom you shall leave a light boat, that when any fleet shall be in sight, they may come with speed to give you warning. Secondly, you must in no case suffer any of the native people of the country to inhabit between you and the sea coast."

After discovering the locality up the river for settlement, victuals and munitions were to be landed. One third of the colonists were then to build a store-house for the victuals and fortify the place. The second third was to be employed preparing the ground and planting corn as well as roots, but ten men were to be on sentinel duty at the haven's mouth. The remaining third, numbering forty-odd, were to spend a couple of months under Captains Gosnold and Newport exploring the river above. They were to try to find minerals, avoid offending the "naturals" (*i.e.* natives), but trade with them for corn and other victuals at once so as to get food into the store. The soldiers must " never trust the country people with the carriage of their weapons. . . . You must take especial care that you choose a seat for habitation that shall not be burthened with woods near your town. . . . Neither must you plant in a low or moist place."

The mariners of these ships were paid by wages, but care was to be taken that these sailors did not carry on a little trade privately with the natives and so lower the rate of exchange. The carpenters and other workmen were not to build houses for individuals until first the public buildings had been set up ; " let them all work together first for the company and then for private men." Nor was the town to be laid out without plan, but " set your houses even and by a line, that your streets may have a good breadth, and be carried square about your market place, and every street's end opening into it." Captain Newport, after landing the colonists, was to return to the Thames bringing for the London Company " a perfect relation . . . of all that is done," where they were seated, and what commodities had been found. No man was allowed to come back to England except by passport from the President and Council, nor to write any letter " that may discourage others. Lastly and chiefly the way to prosper and achieve good success is to make yourselves all of one mind for the good of your country and your own, and to serve and fear God the Giver of all Goodness, for every plantation which our Heavenly Father hath not planted shall be rooted out."

These sensible and practical instructions were derived from the accumulated experience of men who had served in a military capacity afloat, or ashore in Holland, and had studied the mistakes of other colonial attempts. " The land - service," wrote William Powell in his *Tom of all Trades* twenty-five years later, "where a man may learn most experience of war discipline, is in the Low Countries, by reason of the long exercise of wars and variety of strategems there," and we shall see presently how also Dutch discipline was to be enforced upon these new Virginians.

A box containing sealed orders with the seven names of Virginia's Council, selected by the London Council, was to be opened within twenty-four hours of the ships' arrival at their destination, and these seven were to choose one of themselves as President. He was to have a casting vote and govern the colony with the advice of the Council's majority, but immediately on election he was to take the oath of allegiance to the King. The two bigger ships were to return home, but the *Discovery* was to remain in Virginia. Working to a time schedule, *Susan Constant* and *God Speed* were to leave Virginia by the end of May, 1607, loaded with local produce.

Well may we sumpathize with the band of people who braved a raw English winter and went aboard the ships lying in the Thames below London off the village of Blackwall, without waiting the few days till Christmas. It was farewell to those cosy English homes with their panelled rooms, their moulded ceilings, their shining refectory tables that had once been in pre-Reformation monasteries, the large open fire-places with the crackling yule-logs, and the candle-lit portraits of grave-faced aristocrats looking down out of starched ruff. It was good-bye to the swearing, swaggering jostle of St. Paul's aisle, to the sound of the pottle-pots[1] in the city taverns, and the wild carousings ; to the wrestling at Bartholomew Fair, and the shoving, itching crowds that flocked to philander at the theatre before the plays began. " Welcome, gentlemen ! What wine will you drink ? Claret or canary ? Cider, or perry, to make you merry ? " They would never hear that greeting again at some inn, famous for its comfort and good cheer. Even the well-fed gentlemen would have to adapt themselves to new conditions. No more six-course meals of delicate meats ; no more coloured jellies, or crystallized plums, or confectionery, or marvellous creations in sugar-work. It was going to be a

---

[1] Each holding a couple of quarts.

hard life, with starvation following famine, and death coming as a merciful release. But, luckily, at present optimism and want of imagination kept these pilgrims blindfolded.

On Saturday, 20th December, the squadron dropped down on the ebb-tide, and we can picture the planters standing in the waists of these three-masted ships listening to the strange sea language of the mariners " flatting " the sheets, " hauling home a cluling," or, getting awkwardly in the way of some sailors busy at the capstan, waving their Monmouth caps at the retreating shore. England's fair and pleasant land looked sad and gloomy under that dull, leaden sky, but the day would quickly come when they would consider it as a paradise. Their outfit for an all-weather Atlantic voyage, and American habitation, was slender enough : three shirts each, a waistcoat, three suits, three pairs of Irish stockings, four pairs of shoes and one pair of garters. As bedding, seven ells of canvas were given to make a bolster for two men in Virginia with one pair of canvas sheets. Aboard ship two men had to manage with five ells of coarse canvas and one coarse rug. In addition to these items there were kettles, frying-pans, dishes and wooden spoons, tools, muskets, swords, powder, shot and some light armour.

That setting-forth will always be one of the most momentous events in Anglo-American history ; though it was not till June, 1928, that a bronze tablet was erected (by the Association for the Preservation of Virginia Antiquities) at Brunswick Wharf, Blackwall, to commemorate the sailing of those who were to found the first permanent English colony in America. But the cardinal mistake was made by the London Company of supposing that shiploads of lazy labourers, fugitives from justice, inexperienced and spoilt younger sons of good families who never had done a day's work, could succeed, even under the guidance of a few hardened, well-travelled leaders, in quickly transforming a virgin land into a self-supporting plantation, yielding everything from unlimited corn to mines of precious gold.

This voyage was unfortunate from the first. Instead of taking a couple of days to pass the Kentish coast, round the North Foreland, and come to anchor in the Downs, they were a fortnight. Here they remained for several more weeks riding out those gales of wind for which the English Channel in January is notorious. Rolling and pitching, creaking and groaning, jerking at their hempen cables, the ships made life intolerable. Sea-sickness was the least of the troubles that broke out ; the ships were in danger of destruction, illness seized the passengers, and the Rev. Robert Hunt became so weak that his recovery was despaired of. Only twenty miles away over the Kentish flats lay his home, but he stuck to his duty and never once expressed a wish to go ashore. He was determined to set a good example to the others ; he would fulfil his mission of taking Christianity, as requested, to the savages of America. For, as the saintly poet George Herbert (1593–1633) some years later expressed the situation :—

> " Religion now on tip-toe stands
> Ready to goe to the American strands."

But many of the ill-assorted rabble—" little better than Atheists " Captain John Smith dubbed them — became mutinous at the monotony of ship-life and were already anxious to give up the whole undertaking. And this was a beginning of all those discontented activities which characterized Virginian endeavours as long as England held that plantation.

Still, among the party were long-tried pioneers, or resolute-minded principals, such as Newport, John Smith, George Percy and others, who could never look back having once set their gaze toward the New World. Michael Drayton a few years later interpreted in one of his *Odes* the attitude of his countrymen at home toward such men who made America :—

> " You brave heroic minds,
>   Worthy your country's name,
>   That honour still pursue
>   Go, and subdue,
>   Whilst loitering hinds
> Lurk here at home, with shame.

> " And cheerfully at sea
>   Success you still entice
>   To get the pearl and gold
>   And ours to hold,
>   VIRGINIA,
>   Earth's only paradise."

This squadron ought never to have started before March, but there was the eternal dread lest Frenchman or Spaniard or Dutchman might forestall them. As it was, the three ships did not proceed by Gosnold's short way but by the " unneedful " route. They sailed south to the Canaries, where they took in fresh water, whence they used the trade winds across to the West Indies, reaching that customary island of Dominica on 24th March. Three days later they called at Guadeloupe, and on 28th March they reached Nevis Island (also in accordance with previous ship practice), and here Newport for most of a week encamped his men to give them a chance of recuperating from the scurvy and dysentery, which were the ills of these long voyages, as contrasted with the healthiness which Gosnold had found on his short route to New England.

After bathing their travel-stained bodies in the island's mineral springs, shooting birds and rabbits, and obtaining plenty of fish, they weighed anchor, called at the Virgin Isles, Lesser Antilles, where they obtained more fish and fowl and turtle also. Having sailed by Porto Rico, they next came to the island of Mona lying to the S.E. of Haiti. Drinking water was necessarily here shipped, as the Nevis supply had gone bad in the heat, and so stank that no one could touch it. The men were clearly still in bad health, for, while some of the sailors were filling the casks with water, the gentlemen and soldiers marched six miles inland to find food, whereupon many of them fainted by the wayside, and a gentleman named Edward Brookes died of heat and thirst.

On 10th April they said good-bye to the West Indies, steered to the north, and four days later passed the Tropic of Cancer. On the twenty-first in the evening there burst such a Gulf Stream gale that they had to heave-to while it blew, rained and thundered alarmingly. The ensuing few days were anxious even when the storm passed ; for they could see no land, they could find no bottom at a hundred fathoms, and they were three days out of their reckoning. Such " sea-cardes " as they possessed were of scant use, no one of the party had ever in his life seen this part of America, and Captain Ratcliffe in the *Discovery* was in the mood to " beare up the helme to returne for England."

But at 4.0 a.m. on 26th April they sighted a promontory,

which was later on named by them Cape Henry, as to-day it is still known, and without any further difficulty entered Chesapeake Bay. Here they anchored after four long months from Blackwall, weary, care-worn and not too healthy. But at last the beginning of the American nation was to be made, the dawn of a new era in the world's story had burst its effulgence. The three ships rode gently in the sheltered water where, three hundred years later the *Deutschland*, the first submarine from Europe bound for America, was to enter, and in 1928 the airship *Graf Zeppelin* was to make the American coast after being as many days on the way from Germany as Newport's vessels had been months coming from the Thames. Surely Cape Henry is one of the landmarks that deserves to be noted with a very special regard in the evolution of travel !

Newport, Gosnold, Wingfield and thirty others went ashore soon after anchoring and advanced a short way. What were the Englishmen's first impressions of this new country ? How did they react ? Let George Percy answer the question. He was delighted and charmed with the " faire meddowes and goodly tall trees, with such fresh-waters running through the woods, as I was almost ravished at the first sight thereof." But that night, when they were about to repair on board, there came the Indians " creeping upon all foure, from the hills, like beares, with their bows in their mouthes." Their arrows wounded Captain Gabriel Archer in both hands, while a mariner named Matthew Morton was dangerously hurt in two places. Both men recovered, but it was an unpleasant welcome to Herbert's " American strands."

After having repelled this attack and driven the Indians into the woods, Newport's men got safely back to the ships. In accordance with their instructions from London, that same night the box was opened and the orders read. It was now learned that the Council for Virginia was to consist of Bartholomew Gosnold, Wingfield, Newport, John Smith, John Ratcliffe, John Martin and George Kendal. They were to choose from among themselves their President for a year. " Matters of moment were to be examined by a Jurie, but determined by the major part of the Councell in which the Precedent had 2 voices."

Now, here again within the first few hours of reaching America began the long list of troubles in the administration of England's colonial expansion. John Smith was not allowed to become a councillor ; he was outside the pale, a man who had been condemned to death, a criminal. It is perfectly true that with all his strength and independence of character Smith had the defects of his own qualities. Force will always create opposition and misunderstanding, and Smith was an exceedingly forceful personality who was frequently misunderstood. Like many another, who has been through all sorts of narrow escapes and won through by his own self-assertiveness, his own bold initiative, he had developed through life a direct method of going for his objective and thrusting all impediments ruthlessly aside. A man of action before all things, he was not the diplomatist. Nor was he good at team-work. He was a strong individualist, who, left to his own resources, triumphed, but by his very technique created jealousy, suspicion and hatred among his colleagues.

Friction was manifested in the squadron while still in the Downs, as we have seen. By the time the ships had come to the Canaries Smith was considered a dangerous fellow, suspected of the intention to murder the principals and take charge of the whole outfit. It was believed that he was plotting with certain others to this end, and for this reason it was decided to keep them separate by distributing them in the different vessels. Apparently the voyage across to the West Indies did not improve people's tempers, and during the sojourn at Nevis a pair of gallows had been made where Smith was to have been hanged. Luckily for Virginia his life was spared, but he entered on his great work in that country as one not to be trusted or promoted. From such a situation there is one infallible way out ; that way is to make oneself, by certain proof, absolutely indispensable. The opportunity must be awaited patiently, but in Smith's case it was not long coming.

CHAPTER X

THE VIRGINIA SETTLEMENT

HAVING at length reached the intended territory, the next thing was to explore the immediate neighbourhood with a view to choosing a suitable site for the plantation. This kept them busy till 13th May. In accordance with the marine practice of this seventeenth century and later, a shallop had been brought out from England in parts. On 27th April the ships' carpenters and their mates began assembling the frames and fastening the planking, so that by the next day here was a small craft capable of carrying twenty-five men and suitable for making discovery of adjacent rivers, bays and creeks. Such little craft were clinker-built and could be rigged either (a) with a fore-staysail, one mast, and sprit mainsail that was laced to the mast, the mainsail being readily lowered by withdrawing the sprit ; or (b) with two small masts on each of which was set one squaresail.

Every item of procedure during these initial days demands our interest, as we watch the first steps in the founding of a great nation. Here were three shiploads of colonists waiting in a state of suspense and curiosity as to their future, while Newport with one party of gentlemen explored the lower end of Chesapeake Bay, landed, gathered oysters (and of course promptly opened them for pearls). Another party of gentlemen and soldiers marched eight miles inland, at whose approach the Indians fled. Illumined by the vernal sunshine, America seemed to these pioneers a goodly place. " We past through excellent ground full of flowers of divers kinds and colours, and as goodly trees as I have seene, as cedar, cipresse, and other kindes," related the Hon. George Percy. " Going a little further, we came into a little plat of ground full of fine and beautiful strawberries, foure times bigger and better than ours in England."

Such environment was most soothing and encouraging after all those weeks of weary monotony gazing at the restless Atlantic. Before night came down to close the 28th of April soundings were taken for a suitable ship anchorage at the mouth of what was to be named James River. On rowing over to the northern shore they found a channel by " a point of land " containing six to twelve fathoms of water, " which put us in good comfort. Therefore wee named that point of land, Cape Comfort." Such was the first title of that seaside resort, which continues to be known as Old Point Comfort. On 29th April the custom of the Spanish explorers was followed when a cross was erected near the entrance to Chesapeake Bay, and that headland which marks the southern extremity of the bay was named Cape Henry in honour of Prince Henry, elder son of King James I, who was to die five years later. The white sandy dunes with pines and firs that greeted these first settlers of America are still the scenery which belongs to the Cape Henry of to-day. On the opposite side was a promontory which they later designated Cape Charles, after the Duke of York, second son of James I, and destined in 1625 to become England's king.

Thus history must ever regard that channel between Capes Henry and Charles as the gateway through which civilization poured into America during the ensuing years. Physically this approach was excellent, since shipping from Europe would not merely have good landmarks, but a wide easy entrance into the big Chesapeake Bay, with rivers extending from inland at the western side. In many respects Virginia was therefore ideal, and some years later Captain John Smith was still able to say of it that " heaven and earth never agreed better to frame a place for man's habitation being of our constitutions, were it fully manured and inhabited by industrious people. Here are mountaines, hills, plaines, valleyes, rivers and brookes all running most pleasantly into a faire Bay compassed but for the mouth with fruitfull and delightsome land."

On 30th April the three ships changed their anchorage to that of Point Comfort, and Captain Newport went ashore to Kecoughtan—where Hampton now stands—and established friendly relations with the Indians. Thus began that

I

association between the white colonist and the red native of the
American continent ; here commenced the first chapter of a
story that was to be punctuated by treachery, opposition,
bloodshed. Now these English people named the river in
honour of King James, but its Indian appellation was
Powhatan. It was clearly Newport's duty to explore it, firstly,
to select a site well up the waterway, but secondly because this
river " bendeth most toward the North-west," and might reach
to the Pacific. So the shallop, leaving the ships swinging to
their cables in the somewhat open roadstead of Point Comfort,
proceeded up James River and on 4th May reached the
Paspahegh country, being hospitably entertained by the local
Indian chiefs. The scenery was favourably impressive. " Wee
passed through the woods in fine paths," related Percy, and
there were " most pleasant springs which issued from the
mountaines. Wee also went through the goodliest corne fieldes
that ever was seene in any countrey."

Still proceeding up river, they were at first opposed by
Indians, but afterward allowed to come ashore. Now on
12th May they started down-stream and sighted a point of land
which they named Archer's Hope (after Captain Gabriel
Archer). Here the soil was good, with excellent timber, vines
" in bignesse of a mans thigh," and with a little labour this
location could have been fortified, but there was not deep
water close up to the bank. " If it had not been disliked
because the ship could not ride neere the shoare, we had setled
there to all the Collonies contentment." But on 13th May they
came to a peninsula, which was joined to the mainland by a
narrow neck and reached out into deep water. Because this
site could also be defended easily from the Indians, it was now
selected as the settlement's headquarters. The explorers,
however, in their concentration on convenience and strategy
had omitted to obey the London instructions as to wholesomeness. This low ground, with its malaria-breeding swamps and
brackish drinking water, was an unfortunate choice for which
many lives would be paid ere long. It was a pity that the
higher ground of Archer's Hope had not been possible, for it
was only eight miles away.

On 14th May the three ships that had come from Blackwall

were secured so close to the shore that the warps were made fast to trees. There were six fathoms of water right alongside, and now all the colonists, numbering over a hundred, came ashore. At once they were employed in fortifying the peninsula, keeping watch against the Indians, felling trees so as to clear sites for their tents, providing clapboard for reloading the ships bound for England. Others began making nets for fishing, or digging gardens. The spot was dedicated to the glory of God by the chaplain, the Rev. Robert Hunt.

The Council was sworn, Wingfield was chosen the first President, and a speech was made as to why Captain John Smith was not admitted to the Council. The Chief of Paspahegh came with a hundred of his Indians to call on them on 18th May, though an unfortunate incident caused by a redskin pilfering a hatchet, and an Englishman striking the thief, resulted in the visit being quickly terminated. But, at any rate, there had now been founded that little colony which in letters sent to England was referred to as James Fort, or more frequently Jamestown, in honour of the Stuart King. It was not long before President Wingfield was at variance with his colleagues. Here nearly forty miles from the sea, on the north side of Powhatan River, thousands of miles away from their beloved English homes, this community of men, always in danger of some Indian treachery, could not avoid quarrelling among themselves. Team work, communal spirit, the necessity of every man pulling his full weight and of all pulling together for the good of the town, these were not yet appreciated. That personal mistrust, suspicion, underhand scheming and jealousy which had been so familiar in London now became planted in America. They had yet to learn that one may change one's environment a thousand times without modifying one's character.

So we find Wingfield at enmity with Archer because the latter's choice of Jamestown's site had not been acceptable ; because Archer preferred to live aboard the pinnace instead of in the town ; and because Wingfield would not elect him to the Council. Then a report got about that Wingfield was an atheist, because he never seemed to have a Bible. But when about to leave England Wingfield had packed a Bible among his other

books, together with " divers fruite, conserves, and preserves,"
which were sent in a trunk to London and deposited in the
house of Master Crofte at Ratcliffe ready to be put aboard.
But Crofte had evidently opened this trunk, eaten " my
sweetmeates " and kept some of Wingfield's books, including
the Bible. Still Wingfield could not help making himself
unpopular with Smith, Martin, Wotton the surgeon, as well as
others. And a further cause of friction was Wingfield's refusal
to allow either " exercise at armes " or any fortification other
than the branches of trees put together crescent-shaped by
Captain Kendal's skill; for the President was nervous of
causing offence to the Indians.

These pioneers were a strangely-assorted company of hardy
adventurers, " soft-handed sons of small squires," stern soldiers,
double-faced intriguers, sane practical men, unimaginative but
respectable, who had never been at pains to realize what a hard
life must needs await them. Wingfield, although one of the
promoters of the Virginia scheme and liberal in his religion as
a Catholic, was in these post-Reformation days suspect ; yet,
in his own defence he pleaded that his first act had been
to appeal to the Archbishop of Canterbury " to make a right
choise of a spirituall Pastor," with the result that Robert
Hunt had accompanied the expedition. The latter was the
son of the Rev. Robert Hunt, M.A., Vicar of Reculver, Kent,
whose cliff remained a noted sea-mark for mariners. The
future Jamestown chaplain had been educated at Trinity Hall,
Cambridge, where he took his LL.B., and received ordination
in the year 1606; that is to say, not long before sailing for
America. Hakluyt was largely instrumental, with the approval
of Archbishop Bancroft, in Hunt's appointment, so there was
no question about this cleric, to whom Wingfield referred as
" truly, in my opinion, a man not any waie to be touched with
the rebellious humors of a popish spirit, nor blemished with ye
least suspition of a factious scismatick, whereof I had a speciall
care."

At the same time there was a basis for mistrust in the camp.
Kendal was suspected of being a Spanish spy, and was
eventually executed for plotting against the settlement's
welfare. Others showed themselves before long only too ready

to spoil the Jamestown effort by running away. George Percy, loyal as he was to the colony, a man of honour and industry, though not a strong character, and coming of a famous family, was none the less brother of that Earl of Northumberland who had been suspected of being concerned in the Gunpowder Plot of 1605 and imprisoned in the Tower. There is ample historical evidence to show that during 1607 the Spanish ambassador to England was, at his sovereign's request, transmitting every particle of news concerning the Virginia colonization and how to wreck it. Just how many men of English nationality were working on behalf of Spain to this end it is impossible to state, though the probability is that at least one spy set forth in every ship that sailed to Virginia from England during the first few years. And no less an authority than Dudley Carleton, writing on 18th August, 1607, from London, says : " One Captaine Waiman a speciall favorit of Sir Walter Copes was taken last weeke in a port in Kent shipping himself for Spaine with intent as is thought to have betraied his friends and shewed the Spaniards a means how to defeat this Virginian attempt," for Captain Newport had recently arrived back in England with the first account of Jamestown.

Little enough information had been available in England concerning the Indian's character, and much had to be learned. That he was to be regarded with suspicion the settlers well understood beforehand, but it took time to size him up. A man of physical strength, but cunning and treacherous and cruel, yet hospitable ; one who lived by the soil rather than hunting ; childishly simple in many desires, yet no fool; who, with his own self-contained and self-supporting territory, was unable to understand pioneers or traders coming across the seas to disturb the land ; he was not easily understood by the people who had never previously been outside the city of London. Only the more travelled leaders, such as John Smith, were quick to adapt themselves to the Indian mentality and make of him a friend instead of an enemy.

On 22nd May, in accordance with the instructions brought from London, a party of twenty-three went up the James River to continue the exploration. The trip was under Captain Newport and included Captain John Smith. The fact that the latter was no longer under arrest but was already regarded as a man likely to be of valuable use is a proof that Newport was sufficiently discerning not to be swayed by idle suspicions, and it is a further proof that Smith's outstanding personality was beginning to make itself felt. The shallop was again provisioned, so off they started up-river, while the rest of the settlers were kept busy till the middle of June making the Jamestown peninsula into a camp triangular in shape, with no chapel as yet but a reading-desk nailed between two trees, where Hunt preached to his congregation twice every Sunday, except on those occasions when an alarm was raised that the Indians were approaching. On several Sunday mornings the service was thus brought to a stop, and the sermon dispensed with. It never seemed to have occurred to the colonists that the redskins themselves could hardly help being suspicious of the white men who were so anxious to strengthen their position. No wonder that armed with bows and arrows the natives of America watched with uneasy suspense all these proceedings.

The shallop's expedition after six days reached Powhatan village, consisting of a dozen houses on a hill at the north side of the river, where resided Little Powhatan, a chief subordinate to the Great Powhatan ; and on this site in 1737 was to be founded that capital of Virginia which to-day we know by the name of Richmond. Above the falls Newport's party found the river no longer navigable ; so on Whit-Sunday, 24th May, a cross was erected on one of the islets at the mouth of the falls with the inscription " Jacobus Rex, 1607," and Newport's name below. The land was thus taken over in the name of the English King. Now on the way up the party had made friends with the Indians, but on the way down Newport became suspicious that the natives had been causing trouble at Jamestown. The wind veering fair, the shallop got under way and reached the settlement on 27th May, only to learn that on the previous day several h ndreds of the Indians had assaulted and very nearly overthrown the young colony, causing the deaths of one man and a boy besides wounding others. Wingfield was untouched, but an arrow flew through his beard with marvellous danger to his life. This alarming assault had occurred at a time when the colonists were busy sowing their corn and were unarmed, but the artillery and muskets from the three ships moored in the river saved the situation. However, it had the good result that Wingfield now allowed the place to be fortified as strongly as possible with ordnance mounted, while the men were well armed and exercised. One can well understand Wingfield's previous, though unpopular, reluctance to give this permission ; he was clearly obeying the London Company's order " not to offend the naturals." Still, a large-minded president would from the first have remembered also the instruction for the settlement to be fortified.

There was certainly no monotony in this early Jamestown life. From 28th May all hands were rapidly palisading the plantation, and several more attacks occurred before 5th June which brought about more deaths—the thickets and long grass affording the enemy excellent cover. But by 6th June there was a good deal of dissatisfaction both among the gentlemen and the others as to the administration of the settlement. Archer, still hostile to Wingfield, was the prime mover, and a petition was made to the Council for " reformatyon." But, thanks to the broadmindedness and tactfulness of Newport, hot tempers were cooled down and peace restored for a while. More interesting still was the fact that Captain John Smith was this 10th June sworn a member of the Council, and thus after thirteen weeks of being under a cloud he became one of the Jamestown government as had been originally intended by the Council in England. It was the good influence of Robert Hunt which finally restored peace between this singularly able man and his detractors.

There was now over Jamestown an air of peace, save for the sniping which the Indians still continued, and so we come to 21st June, the third Sunday after Trinity, when the colonists received Holy Communion, and later on Captain Newport came ashore to dine with these pilgrims whom he had brought to the New World. That evening he invited many of them, in return, to a farewell supper with him aboard the *Susan Constant*. Hearts were touched, quarrels were forgotten, there was a sense of sadness permeating his " great " cabin, but there was no little joy among the crew ; for on the following morning, loaded with a cargo of timber and sassafras, but with no gold or pearls, the *Susan Constant* sailed off down the river, leaving behind one hundred and five people whose dimmed eyes saw the topsails disappear out of sight as the long voyage began. About forty of those that came out from England had either died or been sent home, and who could say what would be the fate of the others ? For there remained provisions that could last not more than fourteen weeks.

With the ship, which arrived in the Thames before the middle of August, was sent by the Virginia Council to the London Council a report of the colony, and it mentioned *inter alia* that they had already built some of their houses, sown wheat, and that the soil was most fruitful ; at the same time they entreated " your succours with all expedition." " This note doth make known where our necessities do most strike us, we beseech your present relief accordingly." It was for this reason that the London Council decided to dispatch to the Virginians a double supply of provisions. " The great counsell of that State," wrote Dudley Carleton to John Chamberlain from London on 18th August, 1607, " hath resolved of a dubble supplie to be sent thether with all diligence."

Newport brought back to the expectant London Company, some nine months after having left England, a description of the newly-discovered James River and country of Virginia, how that the fort—" triangle wise "—had a bulwark at each of the three corners " like a halfe moone," with four or five pieces of artillery mounted therein, that most of the corn had been sown on two hills and by the middle of June had already sprung up to " a mans height from the ground." He informed Sir Thomas Smith and the other distinguished founders all about the Indians and Powhatan, how that there was not a grey eye among all these " naturals," that the women did all the work, while the men went about at their pleasure, how that forty or fifty redskins dwelled together in one small village, that they were all well practised in the art of stealing, and were naturally treacherous yet not unkind. They were both witty and polygamous.

The weakest characteristic of these early efforts to plant Virginia lay in the commissariat department. The London Company cannot be accused of having been over-generous in the supplies sent out with these three ships, and it was expected of the colonists that they would become practically self-supporting within a few weeks of arrival. The quickly-growing corn, the fish in the rivers, the fowl of the air, and the animals of the land should prevent all possibility of starvation. On the other hand, the Company was really gambling with men's lives if for any reason food was not readily discovered and stored ; and in those days, when such few articles of sustenance could be carried undamaged through the tropics, it was difficult to send much variety other than grain, wine, oil, peas, salt pork and a little aqua vitæ. Nor must it be forgotten that most of these settlers were totally inexperienced when it came to providing for themselves. Accustomed to life in London, with its plentiful food and taverns, the men could not quickly adapt themselves to primitive existence in a virgin country. The general organization, though it contained a common store, was weak, inefficient, inadequate and short-sighted. This defect was not appreciated during the first few weeks, for Newport's flagship became an unofficial supply vessel plus tavern, whither many a man resorted for a bit of food or refreshing drink, but when once the *Susan Constant* had sailed, and a floating store vanished, it was then that the hearty-living roysterers with empty bellies began to blaspheme and protest violently.

As to the West of England Virginia Company mentioned in a previous chapter, it may here be added that on 9th March, 1607, an ordinance was made enlarging the number and augmenting the authority both of that Council and of the London Council. The latter was to consist of thirty members, while the Plymouth was to have ten members. It was on 31st May, 1607, that two ships commanded respectively by Captain George Popham and Captain Raleigh Gilbert were sent out by the Plymouth Company to that northern part of the all-inclusive area of "Virginia," which was a few years later to be known as New England. This expedition was organized by Sir John Popham, who got together both the money and the men. North America was reached on 11th August, a site being chosen in what to-day is called Maine. Here a settlement by a hundred people, with a fort, store-house and church, was made for a time ; but that winter of

1607–8 was so severe and the provisions were so scanty that all the people with the exception of forty-five were sent back. In 1608 their President, Captain Popham, died, and some supply ships arrived with the news of Sir John Popham's death, so this northern (or Plymouth) scheme was abandoned, and the party all returned to England from a region which they described as " a cold, barren, mountainous, rocky desart." A dozen years must pass before New England was destined to be settled permanently.

Sir John Popham, Lord Chief Justice of England, was one of those curious characters of Elizabethan-Jacobean civilization which was so typical of that inexplicable period and so puzzling to us moderns. Born in Somerset about the year 1531, he lived a profligate youth, was educated at Balliol College, Oxford, entered the Middle Temple, and was elected to the Privy Council in 1571, by which time he was already a famous lawyer. Still, here was one who had actually incurred criminality as a highwayman, and finally accumulated the largest fortune which had ever been made by a member of the English bar. As a judge it would not be uncharitable to say that his decisions were sometimes influenced by fraud. Shortly after James I came to the throne it fell to the lot of Popham to preside at the trial of Sir Walter Raleigh, when Popham very feebly interposed to mitigate the Attorney - General's violence. Now, as a Member of Parliament, Popham had sat on several committees to devise some means for effectually punishing rogues and vagabonds by setting them to work.

It is here that we get the connecting-link, already alluded to, between colonization and banishment. As Lord Chief Justice, Popham assisted in drafting an Act during Elizabeth's reign whereby banishment beyond the seas was for the first time employed as punishment for vagrancy. Thus we shall hardly overstate the case if we insist that ex-highwayman Popham during his exertions of 1606 to procure patents for the London and Plymouth colonization of America was actuated partly by the problem of dealing with England's wastrels and partly by his greed for wealth. While he was known as an able lawyer, he was exceedingly severe on thieves, just as naval history shows us how austere were the reformed pirates of James I's day against those who still continued in piracy. (Of this we have a perfect example in Sir Henry Mainwaring.) That Popham was able to leave an enormous estate behind him on his death in 1607 with ten thousand pounds a year to his son was the result of a grasping nature. Of this big, heavy, bovine personality, whose influence on the selection of the first settlers sent to Virginia cannot be disregarded, Aubrey wrote that it was Sir John who " first sett-afotte the plantations, *e.g.* Virginia, which he stockt or planted out of all the gaoles of England." And while the same authority credits him with having first revived brick building in England, we shall easily perceive why besides bricklayers there were sent out in the *Susan Constant* expedition some of the most undesirable of England's citizens, and ever prone to break forth into mutiny.

In the creation of a new tradition, such as a colony over-seas, or a university or a great school at home, much depends on the first administrators and the first members who form that body of learners. A high tone inspired by lofty ideals, and supported by generous-minded administrators, after meticulous care that only hand - picked candidates are accepted, will continue through generations to maintain happiness in times of trial, and a determination to let nothing spoil the venture. But when the policy was actuated by such self-seeking men as Popham and such tight-fisted, money-worshipping magnates as Sir Thomas Smith, who were inhumanly mean as to allowance of stores and provisions, but expecting an immediate dividend in the shape of gold, silver and pearls, can we really wonder Virginia was condemned to go through such intolerable suffering that the colony almost failed ? Notwithstanding the daring, the imagination and financial ability of these early company promoters, it cannot be denied that on them rests the grave responsibility of inaugurating a tradition of dissatisfaction, which was to be handed on down the years till the crisis came in an inevitable outburst of independence.

CHAPTER XI

DISCOVERY AND DEVELOPMENT

WHEN Captain Newport sailed from Jamestown, he left
behind Captain Ratcliffe and the twenty-ton pinnace
Discovery, and also Captain Bartholomew Gosnold. The latter,
no more than Archer, was one of Wingfield's enemies and had a
popular following.   Discord quickly broke out again between
the President and the Council, and then within ten days of
Newport's departure the community was afflicted with sickness,
so that there were not more than ten of them able to move or
stand. Says Studley in explanation, " Whilest the ships staied,
our allowance was somewhat bettered by a daily proportion of
bisket which the sailors would pilfer to sell, give, or exchange
with us, for money, saxefras, furres or love. But when they
departed, there remained neither taverne, beere-house, nor
place of releife but the common kettell. Had we beene as free
from all sinnes as gluttony and drunkeness, we might have bin
canonized for Saints."

The President allowed each man for daily sustenance half
a pint of wheat and as much barley boiled in water, but this
grain was full of worms through having been so many weeks
in the ships' holds. As a result of bad and inadequate food, the
heavy work of erecting palisades in the hot July weather, and
the continuous vigil that was nightly maintained by four or
five men at each of the three bulwarks, the living had scarce
strength to bury the dead. Thus there was now at Jamestown
the two-fold drama of discord and death. Kendal was dismissed
from the Council and imprisoned ; on 22nd August died that
tough seafarer Captain Gosnold, and now only half a dozen men
remained fit. Captains Ratcliffe and John Smith fell ill, but
recovered, though there remained the perpetual fear that the
Indians might learn of the opportunity to wipe out the settlement in one attack.

Wingfield's position was acute. Certain of the Council demanded larger allowances of food for themselves and their sick friends, but this had to be resisted, since the date of Newport's return was uncertain (owing to winds and weather) ; it would be a long while before the Jamestown harvest was ripe ; and there was no telling how long the Indians would continue friendly. Fortunately the latter daily assisted the town with corn and meat, so that twenty men were now able to work. Finally, on 10th September the Council deposed Wingfield and sent him aboard the pinnace under arrest as King's prisoner, Ratcliffe being made President in his stead, Archer being chosen as Recorder, afterward joining the Council.

Men whose chief drink had been from the river, which was salty on the flood but full of slime and filth at low tide, died of " the bloudie flixe," of swellings, malaria and of mere famine. From August to the following January " wee watched every three nights," related George Percy, " lying on the bare cold ground, what weather soever came," and " warded all the next day. There were never Englishmen left in a forreigne country in such miserie as wee were in this new discovered Virginia." Chaos had reigned through all this hunger and hardship, nor did it stop yet awhile. While some of the Councillors occasionally did themselves well on swans. geese and roast duck, many eyes beheld with starving pain.

Wingfield was tried for having said that a man named Jehu Robinson was about to steal the shallop and run away with others to Newfoundland ; for this statement the late President was sentenced by the jury to pay Robinson one hundred pounds. For having accused Captain John Smith of an intended mutiny Wingfield was ordered to pay the latter two hundred pounds " damages for slaunder." All that the ex-President possessed was therefore seized in part payment, which Smith presently handed over to the common store for the colony's good.

Kendal having been arrested on the charge of mutiny, Wingfield having been deposed, Gosnold having died, and Newport having sailed, the governing power at Jamestown rested in the triumvirate of Ratcliffe, Smith and Martin. This policy was contrary to the London Council's orders, though the circumstances were unusual, seeing that there was a dearth of strong, independent, sane men. Neither Ratcliffe nor Martin was highly regarded, so that the enterprising and determined John Smith by sheer force of character and courage became in fact, though not in title, the President. Impatient of all this mismanagement, of the lack of houses, and the want of food, Smith, who was a born organizer (while he never suffered fools and loiterers gladly), set about a new order of things. While some of those who had recovered, thanks in part to the attentions of the colony's surgeon, Thomas Wotton, were made to mow, others were employed binding thatch for roofs, while others began building houses in place of tents.

On 9th November, 1607, Smith set forth in the useful shallop with a few men to Kecoughtan, the Indian village at the mouth of James River, and, partly by force but also by tactfulness, he was able to bring back to starving Jamestown fish, oysters, bread, deer, turkeys, fowls and nearly thirty bushels of corn. Several more journeys were made by him, and thus besides establishing a very essential corn trade he succeeded in exploring the Chickahominy country, whose river flows into the James River to the north of Jamestown. Now in the meanwhile Smith had given orders for the refitting of the pinnace *Discovery*, which he intended to use in the new year for furtherance of this work. But the imprisoned Wingfield and Kendal saw here an excellent opportunity for themselves. Taking advantage of Smith's absence, of Ratcliffe's unpopularity, and of Martin's illness, it was no difficult matter to get together the pinnace's sailors and other disgruntled confederates with a view to sailing off for England. It was a disgraceful plot, seeing that Smith was trying to get food for a crowd of unsatisfactory settlers, but this experienced traveller's unexpected return, and his use of " sakre and musket shot " which " forced them to stay or sinke in the river," put an end to that subtle attempt. Kendal was tried by jury and shot. Wingfield was still kept in the pinnace, but troubles did not subside, and we find him with Archer planning to forsake the country, though once more the project was prevented by Smith.

Further plots to seek England were for the present halted by the fact that with winter's approach the rivers became covered with swans, geese, ducks, cranes, which were eaten with bread, Virginia pease, fish, fowl and other local products. And this cessation in grumbling enabled Smith to start out on 10th December for the purpose of finding the source of the Chickahominy River, which is ninety miles long. Having turned out of the James River to starboard, he reached the Indian village of Apocant. After another ten miles he sent his boat back to Apocant with seven men. Then, proceeding up the narrowed stream in a hired canoe accompanied by Jehu Robinson (whom Wingfield had maligned), a carpenter named Thomas Emry, and two Indians for another twenty miles, Smith and one Indian landed, but a loud shouting soon convinced him that the redskins had betrayed him.

Quick to think and act, Smith bound the Indian guide's arm with a garter " to my hand " and got ready a pistol. Then an arrow struck Smith on the thigh, but without injury to him. More arrows followed, so Smith used the guide as a shield until two hundred Indians surrounded the explorer. He was taken prisoner by Opechancanough, brother of Powhatan, but amused the chief by presenting him with an ivory compass which led to an interesting diversion on the subject of the earth, sun, moon, stars and planets. For Smith was too old a wanderer over the world, too cunning a student of primitive humanity, and had too often been at the point of death, not to employ any ready means to side-track execution. Robinson and Emry had been slain, and one of the boat's crew left at Apocant. But Smith they tied to a tree, though Opechan-canough prevented the Indians from shooting their arrows. Situated between the upper portions of the Chickahominy and James Rivers lay Orapaks, where the modern maps indicate New Kent County. Hither triumphantly the white man prisoner was taken and exhibited, while the inhabitants of thirty wigwams with strange yells danced around him. He was fed well, but a few days later they tried to bribe him with the offer of life, liberty, land and women, if only he would advise them how best they could attack Jamestown. Smith employed the opportunity to the best advantage. For he wrote down " in part of a table booke " a message to the effect that the Indians contemplated attacking the fort, and requested that certain specified articles be sent him. This December was exceedingly cold in Virginia (as we have seen it was also in Maine), while in Europe it was of unusual severity. But through the snow and frost went three Indian messengers with this note that meant to them nothing, and to their surprise they came back with the promised gifts.

Smith's treatment next consisted in being carried about the country from one tribe to another, visiting the Rappahannock and Potomac Rivers, witnessing weird native ceremonies, till at last on 5th January, 1608, they brought him to Werowocomoco, situated on the Pamunkey River, where the Great Powhatan was seated. This tall, well-proportioned, strong and hardy but sour personage was by heredity and conquest in possession of all the territory bounded on the south by the James River from its mouth up to the falls, and extending northward to where Maryland now touches. Here in a royal wigwam Smith was received by the grave and majestic semi-naked savage, seated on a matted platform surrounded by two hundred of the Indian men and women. Never before had the Great Powhatan beheld a white man.

Having entertained Smith kindly, a long consultation ensued, two great stones were brought before the big Chief to form the executioners' block, the Englishman was seized by violent hands, his head laid on the stones, and just when the executioners were about to beat out the white man's brains with clubs, there rushed forward Pocahontas, the young daughter of Powhatan, who laid her head upon the Englishman's. By this dramatic appeal of a child so dear to the Chief was the white man's life most marvellously saved. Smith should not die, but live to make hatchets for the Chief, bells, beads and copper for Pocahontas.

At the time of this incident Smith was aged twenty-eight, and Pocahontas was about thirteen. Although the former was by no means unattractive to the opposite sex, there is no reason for assuming any sexual romance in this incident. Natural feminine pity, and the exercise of that right (common to all Indian women) which claimed a life as a woman's property and for adoption into the tribe, are the logical explanation, together with a desire to preserve as something unusual the first pale-faced human that this girl had ever beheld. Smith never married ; he regarded his colonial work as " my wife, my hawks, my hounds." He considered the young girl's act as divine intervention, and was most grateful, but, for his own good reason, he did not allow the adventure to be mentioned in his writings until he wrote his *The Generall Historie of Virginia*, which appeared some sixteen years later. The people at home in England were quite sufficiently disposed to put a wrong construction on a man's conduct, without affording him a free opportunity.

Not till Charles Deane in 1860 published at Boston his suggestion that the Pocahontas affair was a mere embellishment did the world question the reason for Powhatan's change of mind. But, indeed, he who denies that the girl was the saviour of John Smith creates a whole catena of difficulties for himself. In my own biography of Captain Smith I have endeavoured to argue the case in full, and after full examination of the pros and cons beg leave to associate myself with William Wirt Henry, J. Poindexter, Professor Arber, Mr. A. G. Bradley, and other critics, both American and European, who stoutly defend the authenticity of the time-honoured Pocahontas legend. It was "La Belle Sauvage," who was to give her name to many a seventeenth-century English hostelry, nor can we readily believe that Smith would of deliberation tell a lie to Queen Anne, James I's consort, when in 1616 the Captain, writing to her Majesty, stated of Pocahontas that "at the minute of my execution, she hazarded the beating out of her owne braines to save mine." Those were hardly the days when a subject would go out of his way to fake facts for royal consumption. While the claim that truth is stranger than fiction can be insisted upon till it becomes wearisome, anyone who has spent his life in the channels of history is almost daily amazed at the dramatic surprises, the coincidences and curious twists which spring naturally out of human happenings. In few spheres are these unexpected occurrences as numerous as in the narrative of the American nation.

Those who view the world's evolution unphilosophically may find it hard to believe that no event is irrelative ; but others, like John Smith, hold the view that there is a connected

K

meaning at the back of apparently isolated actions. Pocahontas
from this January, 1608, till the following year was the very
salvation of the perishing Jamestown settlement. Every few
days she and her attendants used to bring food into the town,
so that (in John Smith's words) " she next under God, was still
the instrument to preserve this Colonie from death, famine and
utter confusion." No novelist would dare to arrange such a
succession of " accidents " as the following. On 7th January,
that is a couple of days after the interrupted execution, Smith
was allowed by the Great Powhatan to proceed to Jamestown,
but must send a present of two guns and a grindstone.
Travelling through the night with a dozen of the Chief's men,
Jamestown was reached next morning, where a couple of
demi-culverins were exhibited to the Indians. Inasmuch as
these weighed each forty-five hundred pounds, the visitors
found them too heavy to be carried ; and when Smith had them
fired, the men were so terrified that with difficulty they were
pacified and given such presents as toys for Powhatan's family.

But when the redskins had gone and Smith was apparently
safe once more, he was actually within range of death. For
during his absence Ratcliffe had sworn Archer into the Council
without Martin's consent, and Archer now had Smith indicted
in accordance with the Levitical law for the unfortunate deaths
of Robinson and Emry. He was tried and would have been
hanged forthwith, had it not been for another divine
intervention. " Hee had had his tryall," wrote Wingfield in a
diary, " the same daie of his retorne, and, I believe, his hanging
the same, or the next daie, so speedie is our laws thear : but it
pleased God to send Captain Newport unto us the same
eevening, to our unspeakable comfortes : whose arryvall saved
Master Smyths leif and mine, because hee took me out of the
pynnasse and gave me leave to lye in the Towne. Also by
his comyng was prevented a Parliament, which ye newe
Counsailour, Master Recorder, intended thear to summon."

The sight of a vessel, with her weather-stained sails and
spars, coming up the James River at the end of a wintry day
was miraculous in its many effects. Smith had found the
colony in confusion, Ratcliffe with others was about to run
away in the pinnace, and the famine was still serious, when all

of a sudden came the long-overdue first supply ship. This was not the *Susan Constant* (as has been erroneously stated by some historians) but the *John and Francis*, a vessel that hereafter was to visit America more than once, and became a fairly regular passenger-cargo carrier from England. Newport had been a disappointingly long time coming. He had left Jamestown, be it remembered, on 22nd June, reached England by August, and had been dispatched by the London Company "with all diligence." This would mean that he probably set sail in October, and was therefore about three months on the voyage. With him had started Captain Nelson's ship, *Phœnix*, but the pilot of the latter ship was not so experienced an Atlantic navigator as Newport, so the *Phœnix* never reached the colony till 20th April, having worked her winds badly.

Between them the two ships brought " a dubble supplie " of food and one hundred and twenty more settlers. The latter were vital to the whole future of America ; for such were the ravages of disease, famine and other enemies of humanity, that Captain Newport found of the one hundred and five whom he had left behind in Jamestown only thirty-eight now alive. And there would have been fewer still, had not frost and heavy wintry weather delayed the desertion by the pinnace. Still, we must in our criticisms of these brave and terribly tried first settlers not forget that Englishmen as yet knew nothing about the art of colonization except settlement in Ireland. They lacked the experience which teaches what to avoid and what to emphasize. Spain, in her plantations and discoveries, had passed through just those same dissensions, mutinies and general unhappiness, and England could learn only by making mistakes. The London Company had to realize that Virginia was not just one big gold mine requiring only to be quarried ; but it would need a few more shocks before these gentlemen appreciated their true and unsatisfactory position.

It requires no imagination to appreciate the bitter disillusionment of the *John and Francis* passengers, freshly come through the tropics to a frozen wilderness of starving men, representing less than one quarter of the people who had first sailed away from Blackwall. But Newport's influence always was uplifting, and Smith was able to enliven pessimists with

the information, gained during seven weeks of captivity, that
Powhatan's country contained plenty of corn. And there were
good souls, such as Anthony Gosnold, Thomas Wotton and
Parson Hunt, who could be relied on to work for Jamestown
without thinking of themselves. With sailor - like method,
Newport, having landed, lodged and refreshed his passengers,
set them to work building a store-house and a communal stove,
while the mariners he employed in erecting a rude church. And
what was more, he saw that these items were done speedily.

But then came another of those disasters which seemed
to indicate that Virginia was eternally doomed, that North
America was never intended to be inhabited by the white man.
For about the middle of January, just when things were
settling down, but while the frost still continued, the town,
accidentally got on fire, " which being but thatched with reeds
the fire was so fierce as it burnt their pallizadoes (though 10 to
12 yardes distant), with their armes, bedding, apparell, and
much private provision. Good Maister Hunt our preacher,
lost all his library, and al that he had but the cloathes on his
backe, yet none ever see him repine at his losse." A new
church was made in the spring, but Hunt, who had been
seriously ill on the way out from England, now soon died.

The *John and Francis* remained at Jamestown three months.
Four acres of ground were cleared for the colony, and much
useful work was accomplished. But there were disadvantages
to be reckoned. Contrary to the London Council's instructions,
Newport's mariners engaged in trade with the Indians, and
thus lowered the rate of barter, so that where an Indian had
been content with an ounce of copper he now demanded a
pound. Also, while it was natural enough that a stay of a week
or two after a long voyage should be desired, yet it meant that
so much beef, pork, oil, aqua vitæ, fish, butter, cheese and beer,
intended exclusively for the colonists, now was being shared by
hungry mariners. Someone would have to go on short rations
for certain. And, inevitably, the ship brought rats which came
ashore while she lay alongside the bank ; thus the colony's store
would suffer still further. Unfortunately, too, the London
Company had sent out this time (in spite of the fact that no
precious metals had been brought back to England in the *Susan*

Constant) expert gold refiners, who wasted valuable days and effort that should have been expended in other and more useful ways. " The worst," wrote Anas Todkill, " was our guilded refiners with their golden promises," which " made all men their slaves in hope of recompences ; there was no talke, no hope, no worke, but dig gold, wash gold, refine gold, loade gold, such a bruit of gold, that one mad fellow desired to be buried in the sands least they should by theire art make gold of his bones." Thus was valueless, glittering dirt loaded aboard for home.

In February the refitted pinnace *Discovery*, with Newport, Smith and about fifty others, sailed to what is nowadays York River, whence the party landed and visited Powhatan. Smith, already a *persona grata* with the big Chief, acted as interpreter ; and after several days were spent in feasting, trading and enjoyment, the party was able at the expenditure of a few coloured beads to return to Jamestown with two hundred and fifty bushels of corn as well as other commodities of food. Newport then got to work with the Council, effecting some improvements in the personnel, and set sail for England on 10th April, taking with him (to the colony's great relief) both Wingfield and Archer. The *John and Francis* had a passage of six weeks, and reached Blackwall on Sunday, 21st May.

While the little colony once more settled down with the returning spring to rebuild the burned town, and they were all busy hewing trees, making a fresh roof for the store-house, or sowing corn in the fields, a ship came up the river on 20th April to the surprise and alarm of the workers. It was no Spanish invader, but Captain Nelson's *Phœnix*, which had thus missed seeing Newport by only ten days. By good management Nelson (whose vessel had long since been given up for lost) had been able to obtain plenty of supplies at the West Indies for feeding his people ; so that she arrived at Jamestown with several months' provisions for the colonists, which did " so ravish us with exceeding joy, that now we thought our selves as well fitted as our harts could wish."

It illustrates the mind of the London Company when we observe that of the one hundred and twenty people brought out by the *John and Francis* and the *Phœnix* there were (besides twenty-nine gentlemen) twenty-one labourers, six tailors, a blacksmith, a surgeon, a cooper, a couple of apothecaries, but also a jeweller, a perfumer, two refiners and two goldsmiths. As there survived only thirty-eight of the original settlers who left Blackwall in 1606, the white population of Virginia on 20th April, 1608, numbered one hundred and fifty-eight. The rate of mortality, the immense period of time separating the colony from supplies of food and men necessary to be dispatched from England, the impossibility as yet for Jamestown to be self-supporting : these were already problems which must inevitably cause the settlement grave danger. Moreover, Newport had been too friendly and trusting toward Powhatan, even bartering twenty swords for twenty turkeys, in defiance of the London instructions forbidding the natives to have arms. Captain John Smith, with a sterner discrimination of the primitives' mind, refused afterward to continue trade on such terms, and there was a growing truculence on the part of the Indians which suggested yet another problem. For the story of Spanish conquest had been that of destruction and annihilation, but the London Company desired to be at peace with the " noble savage." How, then, could Smith and his fellow - settlers still defend the young colony from insidious attacks while obeying the Company's policy ?

On 2nd June, 1608, Captain Nelson started his return voyage in the *Phœnix*. Martin, who was one of the keenest enthusiasts for gold discovery, wanted to load her with the so-called gold-dirt, whereas Smith insisted on filling her up with cedar. It was with the latter cargo that she reached England before 7th July, and on that day Dudley Carleton wrote to John Chamberlain that " I heare not of any novelties or other commodities she hath brought more then sweet woode." But she also brought back to England Martin himself, who had been awkward, useless and an invalid.

In a small craft Smith took a party to explore Chesapeake Bay, who discovered and named Smith Isles (not after himself but in honour of Sir Thomas Smith), established relations with the Accomack Indians on the Cape Charles peninsula, sighted a group of islands which he named after Russell (a Doctor of Physic, who had come out to Virginia by the *Phœnix*), got badly caught in one of the powerful squalls for which the Chesapeake has ever been notorious, and finally, having discovered the Potomac River, arrived back at Jamestown on 21st July. Once more he was to find that community not a happy, prospering little town, but full of sick men ; for the *Phœnix* people had already got infected with the local fever, and the planters generally were up in mutiny against President Ratcliffe for his harshness, prodigality of provisions, and his having built himself a fine house. Smith concurred in the popular demand that Ratcliffe should be deposed, that Smith himself should succeed him, though the latter's personal enemy Scrivener—another of the *Phœnix* passengers—should carry on as acting-President for a while.

The weather was hot ; the Jamestown swamps were anything but conducive to health ; Scrivener was really very ill with fever, and delirious. Still, exploration must not be halted, so on 24th July Smith again set forth in a little voyage of discovery past Kecoughtan. The result of this excursion was that he went up the River Tockwogh (identified with the modern Sassafras in Maryland), became acquainted with the local tribes, penetrated to the northern end of Chesapeake Bay, bestowed names on rivers, falls, bays, islands, examined the Patuxent and Rappahannock Rivers, called in at Gosnold's Bay (to the north of Point Comfort), again endured heavy squalls, proceeded several miles up the Nansemond River, and finally reached Jamestown on 7th September.

This trip had been accomplished not without dangers, hardship and encounters with the Indians, but he had brought back as much corn as his small craft could carry, and he had amassed as a result of sailing many hundreds of miles an invaluable amount of geographical information. From these two expeditions he was able to make the first map of Virginia, which was eventually published in 1612, being engraved by William Hole. It is not to be stated that Smith created this bit of cartography unassisted, but when the claim is made by some of Smith's modern inimical critics that the President merely copied from the previous " plots " of Gosnold and others, such a suggestion goes too far. Captain Gosnold had been dead since 22nd August, 1607, and Smith was the first white man to

penetrate bays, rivers, creeks and many of the Chesapeake
Indian villages.

On board Captain Nelson's *Phœnix* Smith sent to a
distinguished friend in England—not for publication but as a
private communication—*A True Relation of . . . Virginia,*
which was presently printed and entered at Stationers' Hall on
13th August, 1608. It was issued as having been written " by
a Gentleman of the said Collony," and was the earliest printed
account of Jamestown ever to appear. And now in the autumn
of 1608 Smith was able to send to the London Company his
" Mappe of the Bay and Rivers, with an annexed Relation of
the Countries and Nations that inhabit them." This was just
the very information which the Company needed to obtain
concerning their colony. It afforded the nearest visual
representation that was practicable concerning Virginia's
potentialities, and was invaluable to those directors who
stayed at home in London, enjoying good cheer, hunting
and falconry.

News from Virginia came to England with much the same
interest as if to-day explorers sent to Europe letters from Mars.
English intellectual and religious life was still in a revolving
and unsettled condition. The growth of Puritanism which
had risen during the period of 1559–1604, with its Calvinism,
its attack on episcopacy and heated animosities, had been
stemmed. The historical claims of the English Church to be
part of the Church Catholic were now asserted unequivocally.
Both England and the Church of England were in a curious
state of isolation, and, since isolation always tends to develop
independence, there was an extraordinary vigour now alive.
Richard Bancroft, who had succeeded Whitgift as Archbishop
of Canterbury in the year 1604, was one of those highly-placed
clerics whose difficult double duty now lay in justifying alike
the clerical attitude toward Puritanism and toward the political
side of Roman Catholicism. It was Bancroft who as far back
as 1589 had preached in St. Paul's Cathedral his famous
sermon proving the claim of episcopacy to be a divine and
Scriptural order.

Much of the success which attended the Authorized Version
of the Bible is traceable to Bancroft, and he was the very

expression of the anti-Puritan but anti-Popish attitude. It was, however, an age not of mutual tolerance but of force and compulsion. His own personal disposition was arbitrary and bad-tempered, partly arising out of those abnormal troublous times, but partly because he had long suffered physically as a result of an internal stone. Now one sequel of Bancroft's inflexible attitude toward the suppression of schism, and the enforcement of conformity, was that in this year 1608 many of the Puritans resolved to settle in Virginia, and thus incidentally antedate by twelve years the *Mayflower* enterprise. But it was Bancroft himself who prevented this departure, for he sought a proclamation from the King, who, fearing that the unhappy Puritan element would be a source of danger to the young colony, readily complied with the Archbishop, who was to die two years later.

Smith, on his return to Jamestown in September, immediately took over the duties of the Presidency and began reforms, which included rethatching the store-house, erecting new buildings, altering the shape of the fort, exercising the men at arms every Saturday. And then, by Michaelmas, arrived at Jamestown Captain Newport from England with what was known as the " Second Supply " in the ship *Mary Margaret*. There had died in Virginia between that time and the " First Supply " (brought by the *John and Francis* and *Phœnix*) twenty-eight persons. But the *Mary Margaret* had brought from England some sixty to seventy people, so that Virginia's population was now about two hundred all told. Newport's passengers included Captains Peter Wynne and Richard Waldo, who were to be Councillors ; Master Francis West (Lord de la Warr's brother) ; Mistress Forest (wife of either George or Thomas Forest), together with her maid Anne Burrowes ; gentlemen, artizans, labourers, a couple of boys, as well as some Dutchmen and Poles for the purpose of making pitch, tar, glass, soap ashes, and of erecting mills. Thus the Company in London were still working on the wrong assumption—that Virginia was sufficiently developed to start manufacturing— whereas it had not yet emerged from the hunger zone. Smith's opportunity to inaugurate sound management ; firm, fearless, but fair governance ; energetic system and careful hoarding of food supplies, had only just been created. But his hopes and schemes were to receive a shock.

Newport had been sent with definite instructions (*a*) to find gold, (*b*) discover the South Sea, (*c*) search for those missing Raleigh colonists referred to previously, (*d*) crown Powhatan, and (*e*) start manufacturing. Smith was angered at such futility when the first and undivided duty should be the obtaining of corn from the Indians now that the harvest was gathered in and the anxieties of winter approached. But orders were orders, and the Virginian Councillors were inclined to agree with Newport. First of all Smith, Newport and others went to the modern - named York River, where they with difficulty persuaded Powhatan to kneel while Newport thrust a crown on the Chief's head. This ridiculous and useless ceremony was accompanied by such presents as a scarlet cloak and bedroom furniture. But a few bushels of corn were brought back to Jamestown, where the *Mary Margaret* was now unloaded and her hold filled with pitch, soap ashes, as well as cochineal, clapboard and wainscot, for England. While Smith and eighty men were seeing to this, Newport took a hundred and twenty up the James River to seek for gold and the South Sea. They came back from the site of modern Richmond disillusioned, disgruntled and starving.

Of the five instructions sent from London four had thus been carried out, and the fifth would be attempted later. But the corn problem was now again pressing, so Smith went with a couple of small craft to the Chickahominy country and with difficulty obtained what he wanted ; only to discover on his return that Newport and Ratcliffe were planning to depose him from the Presidency. Were there ever such underhand schemers as these men of the sixteenth and seventeenth centuries ? As to Newport's crew, they behaved as illegal traders, turning the *Mary Margaret* into a tavern where the Indians brought furs and blankets in exchange for butter, cheese, beef, pork, aqua vitæ, beer, biscuit and oatmeal. Thus was the red man introduced to the white man's strong waters. The Stuart mariner was a notoriously unruly fellow, but it was too cruel of him to steal the poor Jamestownian settlers' axes, chisels, pickaxes, powder and shot as additional implements of Indian trade.

Evidently Newport had been ordered not to waste time in Virginia this trip, for he sailed away about November and was back in England by January, 1609. The negative news which he brought was displeasing to Sir Thomas Smith and the London Council, who had expected those quick returns of gold and silver such as the Spaniards had fetched from the New World. It was the *Mary Margaret* which carried home from Smith that " Mappe of the Bay and Rivers," a duplicate of the same, and a blunt letter from him in reply to one sent by the London Council. The duplicate map was for Henry Hudson, who set forth on the following 25th March in the *Half Moon*, thus fortified with data suggestive of a north passage to the Orient being likely to be found somewhere north of Virginia. At any rate, on 26th August Hudson in this small vessel was actually off Cape Charles, but did not enter Chesapeake Bay. Being temporarily in the employ of the Dutch East India Company, he had more sense than to complicate matters, so two days later he reached Delaware Bay, and the early days of September saw him exploring what we now call the Hudson River, which had been discovered actually by Verazzano eighty-five years previously. But the interesting link is between Smith and Hudson, and thus between Virginia and the later Dutch settlement of the future New York. The chain of history was being forged more rapidly than was quite visible to individual beholders, whose gaze was concentrated on their own particular section.

CHAPTER XII

ADMINISTRATIVE DIFFICULTIES.

THE state of friction now existing between the unproductive
Virginia and the dissatisfied London Company was well
illustrated in the correspondence between Captain John Smith,
on the one hand, with the Treasurer and Council on the other.
The latter, because the ships had not been sent to England
heavily laden with valuable commodities, wrote that " if we
failed the next returne, they would leave us there as banished
men." The Company was tired of being fed " with ifs and
ands, hopes and some few proofes." Every time Captain
Newport came out meant a cost of two thousand pounds, which
was so far not defrayed by return cargoes. The end of patience
had been now reached, but Jamestown seemed to be wasting
time in factions.

Smith in reply wrote that he disbelieved in the probability
of finding the South Sea, gold mines, or any of the lost Raleigh
colony ; that he had " begun workes of pitch and tarre, glasse,
sope-ashes, and clapboard ; whereof some small quantities we
have sent you," yet " you must not expect from us " much
result since the personnel consisted of " ignorant miserable
soules, that are scarce able to get wherewith to live, and defend
our selves against the inconstant salvages." Frankly he told
Sir Thomas Smith and Company that the coronation of
Powhatan and presentation of gifts " will be the confusion of
us all ere we heare from you againe ; " that from Newport's
ship " we had not provision in victuals worth twenty pound,
and we are more than two hundred to live upon this : the one
halfe sicke, the other little better," while the sailors " daily
make good cheare."

" Captaine Ratcliffe is now called Sicklemore, a poore
counterfeited Imposture," continued Smith. " I have sent you

him home, least the company should cut his throat. What he is, now every one can tell you : if he and Archer returne againe, they are sufficient to keepe us alwayes in factions. When you send againe I intreat you rather send but thirty carpenters, husbandmen, gardiners, fisher men, blacksmiths, masons, and diggers up of trees, roots, well provided ; then a thousand of such as we have," since the present colonists consumed food without producing anything in return. It were better to buy commodities cheaper up the Baltic than expect glass, pitch and tar in any quantities till the Virginians had been able to get the more essential articles of food from the colony. " As yet," concluded Smith, " you must not looke for any profitable returnes."

To the London merchants hoping to have got rich rapidly this heart - to - heart talk was calculated neither to give satisfaction nor to increase Smith's popularity. But while Newport was on the high seas, winter was again approaching with cold, clammy hand ; the anxieties of the corn supply now had to be faced with fearlessness and enterprise. The situation was of this delicacy : while it was in the power of the Indians to exterminate the English by mere inaction, it was Smith's aim to compel the redskins—by force, daring, tact, applied at the right moment and in the right gesture—to keep on supplying Jamestown with the minimum of food, till a race of settlers should become so physically strong as to coax from the ground the essential articles. If, however, the unimaginative London merchants still kept pressing for manufactures and tangible dividends, then the fate of Virginia was sealed. A man must be fed before he can work, and be able to defend himself against the natives before he can enrich Sir Thomas Smith's friends. The fact that Jamestown survived these critical months was due to Captain John Smith's knowledge of the Indians' psychology : when to cajole them, and when to bully them.

So this winter, besides extending his own pleasure in discovery, he obtained corn from the Nansemonds, but he also dispatched Michael Sicklemore (not to be confused with Captain Ratcliffe, already sent home) and two native guides toward the Chowanock country, whither Sir Ralph Lane had penetrated in the 1585–86 expedition. But, while this was carrying out both the letter and spirit of the London Company's instruction, Smith knew that it was a hopeless quest. Sicklemore indeed failed, and came back with the report that he " found little hope and less certainte of them [that] were left by Sir Walter Raleigh." The expedition had proceeded as far as the upper reaches of the River Chowan, and thus finally the ill-fated Raleigh colony fades away into dim history.[1]

From a trip to the Great Powhatan Smith during January (1609) realized still more the increasing truculence and treachery of Indians. As Smith had prophesied to the London Company, all these presents had spoiled the big Chief ; all this bartering by sailors had ruined the market, and the price of corn had inconveniently gone up. Powhatan no longer fancied bits of copper ; he preferred swords and guns, although Smith had lent Dutch workmen who were building Powhatan a house. The Indians surrounded Smith and were about to kill him, but the President in a characteristic counter-attack by sword and pistol extricated himself and was able to sail back to Jamestown with further bushels of corn. It was the Pocahontas maid, that loyal friend of Virginia, who in the darkness braved her way through the woods to warn Smith that her father Powhatan was still planning to kill the expedition. Two Dutchmen were presently sent overland by this Chief to obtain, deceitfully, arms and ammunition. A visit to Opechancanough up the Pamunkey River certainly rewarded Smith with more corn, but it was yielded reluctantly, and again the party was trapped by seven hundred, surrounding, well-armed Indians. But once more Smith's boldness, swift and determined, his scathing denunciation of Indian treachery, and the Englishman's employment of bluff at a critical moment, together with the display of sword plus pistol, turned likely disaster into victory, which included those large quantities of corn that were the most vital of all matters.

Smith's forceful character, his determination to obtain that which he believed to be necessary and proper, not merely ensured the enmity of Powhatan and Opechancanough but the jealousy of such men as Scrivener, who was one of the

[1] Nathaniel Powell and Anas Todkill also investigated inland of Roanoke Island unsuccessfully.

Jamestown Council, and had been brought out from England in the First Supply. Scrivener, during Smith's absence, had been left in charge of Jamestown, but employed the time basely working for the interests of Powhatan. In order to forestall Smith, a party of eleven that included Captain Waldo, Anthony Gosnold and Scrivener himself had set out by water. The boat was overloaded, and a winter's gale caused her to sink, the bodies being afterward found by Indians.

Smith got back to Jamestown by about 8th February, 1609, after cruising up and down icy rivers, and there was now enough food in the store till the next harvest. That was entirely owing to his energies. The first Christian wedding had taken place between Anne Burrowes (who had come out as Mistress Forest's maid) and John Laydon (who had arrived with the very first settlers as labourer). A well had been sunk at the fort giving excellent water, about a score of houses had been erected, the church newly covered, with a blockhouse in the neck of the island to receive the Indian trade but allow neither Indian nor colonist to pass without the President's order. Some thirty or forty acres of ground had been planted, and the live stock was increasing. Three sows had produced sixty pigs in eighteen months, and there were five hundred chickens. The hogs were sent to Hog Island down the river, where a blockhouse was placed with a garrison to give warning of any approaching ships.

In spite of all Smith's efforts at organization, such as dividing the working parties into tens or even larger units, and making them toil six hours a day, even erecting a notice-board which showed a man's deserts at a glance—whether he were a slacker or an industrious worker—it was impossible to make the community a satisfactory hive. The Dutchmen about the month of March, at the instigation of Powhatan, plotted to murder Smith, and the latter even had a hand-to-hand encounter with the Chief of Paspahegh, nearly killing the Indian. But during this spring Powhatan realized that it would be better to tolerate than fight the English, and an improved condition of affairs followed as a result of the President's resolute firmness. Turkeys, deer, squirrels and other food thus came in as presents from the natives.

While Smith had since November pulled the colony through with only seven deaths (other than those drowned in the Scrivener party) out of two hundred inhabitants, notwithstanding the threats of cold, famine and savages (in spite, also, of the ravages by rats), it was not a happy family, but one that was always planning among themselves to run away in the pinnace to Newfoundland. Smith tried the experiment of splitting this family into several sections, so as to fend for themselves in groups down the James River, or above the Falls, and even to be billeted with the Indians (whereby, incidentally, the white man and the red got to respect each other more thoroughly), but this decentralization weakened the presidential authority, and rather encouraged those who schemed to escape in the pinnace.

Always in the supreme crises of Virginia's history the influence of the sea entered to save landsmen from their own misdemeanours. There seemed at this juncture a kind of insoluble difficulty in respect of disunity and food deficiency. The Hog Island blockhouse was an outpost lest some Spanish ship should (as certain of the malcontents hoped) come and sweep the colony away. And now early in July a ship did arrive. But she had been sent from England, though not by the London Company. Her commander was Captain Samuel Argall, an experienced mariner, her Master being Robert Tindal, who had first been to Jamestown in that original voyage of 1606-7, and explored up-river in company with Newport and Nelson. Argall had been sent out by a Master Cornelius, not for relief of the colony but for the purposes of trade and fishing in the James River for sturgeon.

Now strictly speaking it was illegal for Argall to attempt either of these undertakings, but, being a kinsman of Sir Thomas Smith, this adventurer by sea, now about thirty years old, was allowed to defy regulations. A man of good family and education, he was one of that steadily increasing number of Englishmen who took to the sea as a career. Leaving England on 5th May, he avoided calling at any of the Atlantic islands, but (after the example of Captain Gosnold in 1602) struck a more direct way across, avoiding the torrid zone. Thus, either he had been to America before, or was relying on the knowledge

Captain John Smith

obtained through Bartholomew Gosnold, or Martin Pring, or George Weymouth, or even Robert Tindal.

Argall's ship was well supplied with wine and provisions, and if these were not intended for Virginia, he was glad to let this semi-starving crowd receive them. Indeed, it was a matter for keen surprise when Argall saw with his own eyes the true but sad state of affairs. Argall's unofficial arrival caused the President increased worry ; for there came in the ship letters from London in the usual complaint against Smith (a) for his " hard dealing with the salvages," (b) for not having sent back " the shippes fraughted." Nor was that all ; there was information heralding great changes in the London government, the preparation of a large " Third Supply " that was coming out in a squadron of nine ships, and the foreshadowing of Smith's end as President, since Lord de la Warr had been appointed as Captain - General and Governor - in - Chief of Virginia.

All this was unsettling, and Smith decided to detain Argall's ship till the rumours should take definite shape in the James River. None the less there was born a new hope that Virginia was not to suffer the fate of the unfortunate Raleigh colonists ; food—lots of it—that was all which concerned the average Jamestown settler. The sooner those nine ships arrived the better would be the plantation's condition.

There had been made a great change in the minds of the responsible men in London. They had been made to realize that Virginia was neither a ready-made gold mine nor a close-confined investment for a few speculators. The news brought back by Newport and others, the slowness of the colony's development, the need for many more settlers, together with increased provisions, indicated that the scheme and outlook of 1606 must now be considerably widened. Therefore the Company petitioned for a new charter, and this was granted on the 23rd May, 1609, to " The Treasurer and Company of Adventurers and Planters of the City of London for the First Colony in Virginia." The grantees include Robert Earl of Salisbury, Thomas Earl of Suffolk, Henry Earl of Southampton, William Earl of Pembroke, Henry Earl of Lincoln and numerous other rich, influential men whose names occupy as many

L

as twenty-eight pages. But the powerful City Companies, such as the Grocers', the Haberdashers,', the Carpenters' and the Stationers', and even yeomen, all joined in this larger undertaking in response to the efforts to obtain more capital.

On the Council was again that busy Sir Thomas Smith, who subscribed seventy-five pounds to the enterprise, and his services were to be of immense importance, if not always well inspired. Only a few weeks later—on 4th July—Sir Thomas was again elected to the high duty of Governor of the English East India Company. And on the last day but one in that same year, when the King and Queen went down majestically with Prince Henry to launch that wonderful new East Indiaman, *Trade's Increase* (eleven hundred tons), which was unfortunately to be lost at the end of her first voyage by an accident when being careened, Sir Thomas was ceremoniously invested by his sovereign with a gold chain.

But besides this popular person as Treasurer, the Council included such well-known names as Sir Oliver Cromwell,[1] Sir Francis Bacon, Sir Robert Killigrew, Sir Thomas Gates, and John Wolstenholme, all true Englishmen of standing and intellect. The anxieties of the time, the nervousness in regard to England's religious and political differences, are well exemplified by the final clause of the new patent which stipulated : " . . . we should be loath that any person should be permitted to pass that we suspected to effect the superstition of the Church of Rome ; we do hereby declare that it is our will and pleasure that none be permitted to pass in any voyage . . . but such as first shall have taken the Oath of Supremacy." Thus, while England did not hesitate to send away from her shores the very scum of the streets, jail-birds and candidates for the gallows, she was determined that Virginia should not be made a dumping ground for disloyalists. As for Captain John Smith and his colleagues, this new charter had the force of " straightly charging and commanding the President and Council now resident in the said colony, upon their allegiance, after knowledge given to them of our will and pleasure, by these presents signified and declared, that they forthwith be

---

[1] Uncle of the future Protector.

obedient to such Governor or Governors as by our said Council here resident, shall be named and appointed."

Armed with this authority, the London Council appointed Lord de la Warr as Captain-General of Virginia, Sir Thomas Gates as his Lieutenant-General, Sir George Somers as Admiral, Captain Newport as Vice-Admiral, Sir Thomas Dale as High Marshal, Sir Ferdinando Wainman as General of the Horse. This new project created such great enthusiasm in London that not only were large sums of money subscribed but five hundred intended emigrants offered themselves and were accepted. And it is expressive of the secrecy maintained at home concerning the true and sad state of Virginia that so large a party was able to be hoodwinked. Had their eyes been open, many if not all would never have quitted the Thames' side. On the other hand, it was good that England should rid herself of a crowd largely composed of "unruly sparks, packed off by their friends to escape worse destinies at home," poor gentlemen, rakes and libertines, broken tradesmen and ne'er-do-wells. Thus, in the hurry to develop Virginia, was the fatal policy again short-sightedly imposed. A selection of the most demoralized riff-raff, whose fathers had lost much of their spiritual piety by the Reformation shock, and had handed down a weakened religious grip on personal conduct, now was to sail by the shipload toward a colony already surfeited with mutinous laggards.

Included in this, the largest party that had ever permanently forsaken the shores of England (exceeded only by those who in medieval days used to sail as pilgrims for the shrine of St. James of Compostela), were women and children. Henry Spelman (third son of that wealthy Norfolk historian and antiquary Sir Henry Spelman), who was one of the five hundred, has left behind in manuscript the statement that he himself went to Virginia for those two simple reasons of "beinge in displeasuer of my friendes, and desirous to see other cuntryes." On 15th May, 1609, seven vessels sailed from Woolwich, down the Thames and English Channel, reaching Plymouth on 20th May, where they were joined by two additional small ships.

It is expressive of the London Company's disregard for

Captain John Smith that not only was Ratcliffe again now sent out to Virginia, but so also were even Martin and Archer. On 2nd June the nine ships set forth from Plymouth Sound, an excellent time of the year, normally, for ensuring fair winds till clear of the English coast. This squadron consisted of the *Sea Venture* (flagship of Sir George Somers), the *Diamond* (originally intended as flagship of Captain Newport), the *Falcon* (flagship of Captain Martin, with whom was that experienced Atlantic mariner Nelson), the *Blessing* (in which Captain Gabriel Archer travelled), the *Unity* (which carried one of the famous English shipbuilding family Pett), the *Lion*, the *Swallow*, together with the ketch *Virginia* which had been built in North America by the short-lived Popham colony, and a pinnace. But the normal June winds did not blow, the squadron had to beat against a south-wester, so put into the easy harbour of Falmouth, which only a century later was to run its famous packet ships to the West Indies and Virginia.

On 8th June the squadron once more made sail and began their southerly course, the instructions being not to go by the long route of calling at the Atlantic islands or anywhere in the West Indies, but to leave the Canaries a hundred leagues to the eastward " and to steere away directly for Virginia . . . except the Fleet should chance to be separated, then they were to repair to the Bermuda, there to stay seven dayes in expectation of the Admiral ; and if they found him not, then to take their course to Virginia." The fact that so large a squadron carrying women, children and horses would have to endure heat and difficult conditions, and would be an easy target for sea-rovers, doubtless accounted for the Company's anxiety to avoid all delays on passage.

The voyage, however, was typical of the mismanagement and misfortune which dogged these early Virginian events. Before setting forth there was a jealous quarrel between Gates, Somers and Newport as to who should be in supreme command, for de la Warr was not to start out just yet. A compromise was effected by berthing all three in the *Sea Venture*. In this ship went one hundred and fifty passengers, most of the provisions intended for Jamestown, bills of lading and other important documents. Six days out from Falmouth the small vessel *Virginia* bore away for England, evidently not liking Atlantic weather. The squadron seems to have sailed well south of the Tropic of Cancer before bringing the trade winds on their starboard quarter. " We ran a southerly course from the Tropicke of Cancer," related Captain Archer, " where having the sun within sixe or seven degrees right over our head in July, we bore away West ; so that by the fervent heat and loomes breezes, many of our men fell sicke " of fever, " and out of two ships was throwne over-board thirtie two persons." In Newport's ship there was said even to be the plague.

These Stuart seamen had still to learn that from about the end of July to October was the West Indian hurricane season, and unfortunately the squadron when off the Bahamas on 25th July became caught and scattered by the tail of a hurricane which raged for some forty hours. Seven ships now proceeded independently amid the greatest danger, to the unspeakable terror of the passengers, of whom many were still in a bad state of health resulting from tropical travel. But on 11th August, three months out from the London river, the *Blessing*, *Lion*, *Falcon* and *Unity* came up the James River, and four days later arrived the *Diamond*, in which Newport was originally intended to travel but actually was commanded by Ratcliffe, alias Sicklemore. The *Diamond* had been compelled to cut away her mainsail and many of her people arrived ill, while in the *Unity* two poor women had each given birth to a boy. Both infants died, however. On 18th August, leaking badly, and with the loss of her mainmast, the *Swallow* arrived. Thus six of the eight were now accounted for. One little ketch became a total loss, but the fate of the *Sea Venture* will be related presently. Those who remember that not long ago the small warship H.M.S. *Valerian* foundered in the same waters during a hurricane, and recollect the injury done to Florida with its shipping, may well wonder that small seventeenth-century sailing vessels could weather such winds and seas. But, while these Jacobean mariners were indifferent navigators, they were very able seamen who knew how to handle unhandy craft. A modern steamer is unable to slow down sufficiently while still under command, but the ships of the Tudors and Stuarts were content to lower sail, " lye at hull," and never contend with

Nature's tyranny. For a little ship left to herself will often come through a gale unhurt, whereas a thirty-thousand-ton steamer suffers many hundred pounds' worth of damage.

The arrival of half a dozen storm-battered, spar-spent, sail-torn, weary vessels, with less than three hundred survivors caused a great sensation at Jamestown, where the look-outs took the first arrivals for some dreaded Spanish squadron. Argall was of course still there, and it was gratifying to note that, for the most part, the latter's provisions had for the time restored the Jamestownians' health. But to John Smith Fate had dealt a nasty blow. De la Warr not having yet arrived, Somers and Gates being presumably drowned, here were at hand, ready for mischief, the President's old enemies, Ratcliffe, Martin and Archer. As a result of this dangerous triumvirate on the one hand and Smith's fierce determination on the other, there quickly broke out factions and quarrelling that were further intensified by the " lewd company " of " many unruly gallants," who were now very active since they could stretch their legs ashore. They had come out with foolish " guilded hopes of the South Sea Mines," of which the few well-informed people at home had never dared to enlighten them.

Smith's reaction was to oppose this interregnum of anarchy by casting Ratcliffe, Archer and others into prison, while he sent West (de la Warr's brother) with one hundred and twenty men to start a plantation at the Falls, and Martin with a similar number to Nansemond. West made a failure of the settlement and returned to Jamestown. As to Martin, he and Smith at this date were the only legal members of the Council, seeing that the new Governor with a fresh authority had not yet arrived. Inasmuch as Smith was within a few days of the completion in office as President for twelve months, someone had to be chosen to succeed him. Martin at first accepted, but resigned three hours later. He also failed in his mission to Nansemond, with the loss of several men.

Early in September, while returning from one of his up-river trips, Smith was sleeping in an open boat. A clumsy companion accidentally fired Smith's powder bag and set him on fire, so that the President had to leap overboard. The flames were quenched, but Smith was nearly drowned and his thighs severely burned ; he reached Jamestown in severest pain. This state of helplessness tempted his enemies to murder him in his bed, but at the last moment the intended assassins, named respectively Coe and Dyer, lacked courage. Unable through physical weakness any longer to contend with unruly schemers, Smith was taken aboard ship in the second week of September, and on 4th October sailed for England, the intervening delay having been caused by his enemies for the purpose of framing a whole catena of charges against him. In this way some half-dozen or so of the settlers were able to reach England as witnesses.

Captain John Smith was nominally sent home " to answere some misdeameanors," as Ratcliffe dictated in a letter to the Earl of Salisbury on 4th October. But stalwart pioneer Smith, who had saved Jamestown from starvation and annihilation, left behind a population of about four hundred and fifty, with ships and boats, ten weeks' provisions in the store, three hundred muskets and twenty-four pieces of ordnance, six mares and a horse, five hundred pigs, besides chickens, hens, goats and sheep, nets, tools and a strongly palisaded town with fifty or sixty houses. It was thus a going concern needing only prudent administration. He was not responsible for the unhealthy site of Jamestown, but one of his last acts was to purchase from the Lesser Powhatan the Powhatan village with two hundred acres of ground where Richmond was some day to be built in an atmosphere more suitable for Europeans. And nothing is more eloquent of Smith's rule, his ability as organizer and provider, than the fact that after his departure Virginia was compelled to encounter failure. Within six months of this strong man's farewell the population dropped to sixty poor miserable creatures, who were scarce able to keep alive on roots, herbs and fish.

It was only by such contrasts, harsh and terrible, that Virginia was to appreciate a good administrator late in time.

CHAPTER XIII

VIRGINIA'S CRITICAL DAYS

ON the very day before Smith started off for England there
came up Jamestown's river that little vessel *Virginia*, which
in the previous June had been seen to turn back for the English
Channel. But now, many weeks overdue, she had fetched up
with sixteen men, thus reducing the missing ships to the
number of only two.

Captain the Hon. George Percy became the new President,
but he was a sick man, and was unable to uphold authority.
Ratcliffe was sent to the Great Powhatan for corn, but was
murdered with most of his party.   Indeed, now that Smith's
powerful personality was removed, the Indians despoiled and
massacred whenever there was a chance. Jamestown during
this winter of 1609–10 became a state of anarchy, chaos, waste,
bitterness, famine, so that it is known to this day as " The
Starving Time." When the last food was gone the settlers ate
the skins of horses ; when those were finished they became
cannibals, eating the corpses of Indians. One man even killed
his wife, pickled her, and had devoured part of her before he
was discovered and executed.

And then occurred one more of those surprises from the sea.

On 23rd May, 1610, who should come to anchor off Cape
Henry but those long-mourned knights, Gates and Somers.
For, while one little craft had foundered with all hands in the
hurricane, the flagship *Sea Venture* was miraculously saved.
There still exists among the State Papers in London Sir George
Somers' letter written three weeks after reaching James River,
giving Lord Salisbury an account of this protracted Virginian
voyage. The hurricane " sundered " all the squadron, the *Sea
Venture* sprang a leak, and from 23rd to 28th July he had to
keep a hundred men working at the pumps night and day.

Then suddenly from the poop of this sinking ship Sir George sighted land, all sail was made, and thus they reached the uninhabited Bermudas, where the *Sea Venture* finally brought up on a rock a quarter-mile from the shore.

Not a life was lost, nor much of their goods, but the whole of their bread. Now the islands had been first discovered in 1515 by the Spaniard Juan Bermudez, who had evidently landed hogs, which in the course of a century had fortunately multiplied. Somers took possession of this territory in the name of James I, and remained here for the next ten months. The hogs were hunted, the sea was fished, the ship's stores were partaken of, and the ship's longboat decked in with hatches from the wreck. Nine men were sent in this boat for Virginia, but nothing more was ever heard of her. The passengers began to settle down to the island life, a boy was born and named Bermudas, a girl came into the world and was named Bermuda, and a marriage was also celebrated. Two small craft were built of cedar wood, rigged, provisioned and named respectively *Patience* and *Deliverance*. Leaving behind two men for their bad conduct, this couple of vessels sailed with all the other people on 10th May, 1610, crossed the Gulf Stream's turbulent waters, and reached Virginia on 23rd May. This strange island-life story at Bermudas eventually reached the ears and imagination of a dramatist in England, already middle-aged, whose name was William Shakespeare, and thus suggested the setting of *The Tempest*, which took shape in 1611. For a time the Bermudas were known as Virginiola, or Somers Islands, and the colonization began in 1612.

Now the appalling condition of Jamestown, with its sixty moribund inhabitants, clearly indicated to Somers and Gates that this was no place to settle. These two important gentlemen were entitled to risk the London Company's wrath at still one more Virginian failure, but it was certainly opportune to quit. So everyone was taken aboard for Newfoundland ; on 7th July in four pinnaces they dropped down to Hog Island and anchored at noon, caught the next morning's ebb tide, and had got no farther than Mulberry Point (in the modern Warwick County) than they were amazed to see a ship's longboat. Spanish ? Or that missing longboat that had left Bermudas ?

It was neither, but from a vessel that had just brought Lord de la Warr from England; and there rode his three ships all well furnished! This extraordinary coincidence—still another of those dramatic moments which were to give a sudden twist to America's romantic history—resulted in a complete change of plan. De la Warr persuaded them to return, and so with two hundred and fifty people whom he had just brought out, sixty of the surviving settlers, and one hundred and forty of the *Sea Venture* crowd, Virginia was to make a fresh start with about four hundred and fifty inhabitants. Luckily those sixty people (of whom all recovered save three) could now eat something better than dead snakes; fortunately, too, Gates had prevented them from carrying out the intention to burn down Jamestown on 7th June, otherwise there would have been still more deaths owing to sleeping out in the fields.

Thomas West, third Lord de la Warr, was now thirty-three years old. Educated at Oxford, knighted when he was twenty-two, he had served with distinction in the Low Countries, and in 1602 had succeeded to the peerage. He was made a member of the Privy Council, which in its origin was merely a body chosen by the sovereign to advise the Crown in matters of State and administration, but became of peculiar importance to the American colonies as time went on. For two years de la Warr had taken the keenest interest in the Virginian colony, and now devoted to it the rest of his life. In the year before leaving England he had been made a member of the London Council, so that he came out with some knowledge of the settlement's affairs.

On 10th June he at once set to work in the big effort which Jamestown needed if she was to rise from the grave. Having gone ashore, he had a sermon preached, being a strong member of the Church of England, had his commission read, made a speech to the people blaming the settlers for their pride, sloth and shortcomings, and earnestly begged them to amend their ways; otherwise he would be compelled to draw the sword of justice. The oration was well received; every man was allotted his particular duty, some to plant vines, some to work in the woods and on the ground. Captain Martin, however, was removed from the Council for his weak, cruel and disorderly behaviour.

It was patent that during these three Virginian years London had never sent adequate provisions to keep everyone alive six months. Now, in spite of all the stores which de la Warr brought out, it became advisable to have some of the pigs fetched from Bermudas of which Somers had informed him, so as to serve the colony during the whole winter. Thus, by the merest accident, Bermudas had become theoretically a means of saving Virginia. And it was hoped also to bring back fish.

It is from the correspondence among the State Papers of England that we get a good insight into the new Governor's first impressions on arrival. He had left Cowes with his three good ships on 1st April, so that he made quite a fair passage for those days. In spite of hard weather and head winds, he reached Cape Henry on 5th June, together with that previously mentioned ship *Blessing*, which had been back to England, but now came out again with Sir Ferdinando Wainman, General of the Horse. For eight weeks of the voyage the third ship was missing, but on 6th June she also appeared and anchored under Cape Comfort, "where," writes de la Warr to Lord Salisbury punningly, "I met with much cold comfort." Had it not been accompanied with the most happy news of Sir Thomas Gates' safe arrival, the fact that the latter with only thirty days' victuals was carrying the Virginian settlers away from the river would have broken de la Warr's heart. The latter confesses that when he landed at Jamestown on 10th June he found it "a very noisome and unwholesome place," but he had the town cleansed. Affairs there were never so far out of order, but he was hopeful. Sir George Somers wrote to Salisbury also that they were in good hope to plant and abide at Jamestown, for now greater care than ever was being taken.

It was Captain Samuel Argall who had brought de la Warr across the Atlantic, having returned to England in October previously with the sad news of the missing *Sea Venture*, and now Argall was to be employed simultaneously with Somers for ensuring Jamestown's food supply. Thus the new Governor was immediately alive to the weak spot of Virginia, and carried out the John Smith policy, but with a more encompassing aim. While the merchants in London could think only of sassafras worth fifty pounds a ton, sarsaparilla at two hundred pounds a ton, and such other valuable commodities as walnut oils, wine, silk grass, pitch, tar, sturgeon, caviar, beaver and otter skins, and various sorts of wood expected from the colony, the primary consideration was still that of food.

In spite of his sixty-six years, Sir George Somers offered to go himself to Bermuda in the *Patience* that he had built, while Argall took the *Deliverance*. De la Warr was much impressed by Somers' volunteering ; " the good old gentleman," he wrote " out of his love and zeal not motioning but most cheerfully, and resolutely undertaking to perform so dangerous a voyage." These cedar-built craft, drawing seven feet of water, set sail from Jamestown on 19th June, but at noon of 22nd June they had to anchor under Cape Henry to take in more ballast. It was hoped by means of these two thirty-tonners to bring back a good six months' supply and relieve all present anxieties.

Argall's voyage was to institute those important fishing trips which were to be made every summer up the north Atlantic coast from Virginia to the New England neighbourhood. Newfoundland, as we have more than once perceived, was rarely absent from the minds of any Virginians who yearned for a change ; and, indeed, it was during this very year 1610 that James I granted to the Bristol merchant Mr. Guy a patent for a plantation which, however, was not a marked success. But Newfoundland was an unruly place, full of rough fishermen of various nationalities, and five years later the Admiralty had to send Captain Richard Whitbourne, of Exmouth, to establish order. In 1622 Whitbourne wrote a discourse on the Newfoundland trade, which James caused to be distributed in the English parishes to encourage merchants. But it was not every crew who cared to go all that way, though the West-countrymen there prospered.

When Argall chose the district between Virginia and Cape Cod for his fishing he may have had in mind that incident which had happened at St. John's, Newfoundland, only fourteen years previously, and acted as a deterrent. Late in September there had happened to be in that harbour one English and three French ships. Quite courteously the French had invited the English on board to breakfast, and entertained them well.

On the following day the English skipper, Richard Clarke, of Weymouth, invited the French to dinner. Michael de Sancé, the senior of the French skippers, excused himself, but the same afternoon sent for Clarke to visit him, feigning sickness. Clarke unsuspectingly came aboard, whereupon the French made him prisoner, captured his crew, held them for nine days, and then sent them back to a ship pillaged and thoroughly " unfurnished." Now if this sort of thing could happen to such an experienced Newfoundland venturer as Clarke, it might be the fate of any other English mariner. It was Clarke who had been in command of the *Delight* during the 1583 expedition of Sir Humphrey Gilbert.

Still, the attraction of Newfoundland for Virginian settlers was always this : they knew that, while it might be too great an undertaking to cross the Atlantic in some small craft, it was a fair risk to coast up north before the favourable south-west wind, and having reached St. John's they were pretty sure to find some Devonshire fishing craft which would give them a passage back to England. Thus the proximity of Cabot's island played a silent though real influence on Virginian restlessness.

Argall and Somers in their two cedar pinnaces were delayed several days at Cape Henry after ballast had been fetched from the beach. " The weather," wrote the former, " proved very wet : so we road under the Cape till two of the clocke, the three and twentieth in the morning. Then we weighed and stood off to sea, the wind at South-West," and made off to the S.E. hoping to find the Bermudas. On the next day Argall, being a skilled navigator, got an observation of the sun, reckoned that his latitude was 36° 47′ N., and that he was about twenty leagues off the land.

But, as emphasized in a previous chapter, these ships could never sail near the wind, and it was heart-breaking when they tried to punch against a breeze. The pinnaces got knocked about by the weather, and at six on the evening of 15th July Somers hailed Argall to say he would tack no more " because hee was not able to keepe the sea any longer, for lacke of a road and water." The old gentleman, therefore, decided to make a fair wind of it, and set a course N.N.W. to try to fetch

Cape Cod, Argall following. So fragmentary was the existing navigational knowledge of the coast north of Cape Charles that this was in effect a voyage of discovery, but they knew from those few mariners, already alluded to, that Cape Cod was situated in a certain latitude and that its waters were rich in fish. It was therefore only necessary to keep a good look-out for outlying dangers, and check the noon position by observation of the sun. Argall noted on 21st July variation of the compass, and became conscious of the Gulf Stream's influence, for " there was some tide or current that did set Northward."

Gales and fogs, however, tried these mariners severely, but the two vessels managed to speak each other by firing a " peece " and answering the gun with a cornet. " With hallowing and making a noyse one to another all the night we kept company," and by heaving the lead they felt their way cautiously through shallower waters. Cod and halibut were obtained, and on 29th July a small island was sighted where they landed and killed seals. But presently they discovered many wooded islands, where they were able to fill up with more ballast and fresh water.   Having sailed as far north as 43° 41′ N.— that is to say, to what we know as the coast of Maine—Argall returned south, picked up Cape Cod again, explored the coast-line, got a bearing of the North Star, and anchored safely inside Cape Henry on the last day of August. The net result of his cruise had been not merely to establish the fact that there was a " reasonable good store " of fish and the " very nourishing meate " of seals, both of which would keep a long time when salted, and thus afford sustenance to Virginia ; but he had, so to speak, joined up this southern colony with that northern area which must be peopled in a few years' time. Knowledge is the enemy of fear, and now that more detailed geographical information was being accumulated by the hard-bitten mariners, the Atlantic shore was beginning to lose something of its mystery and terror ; Virginia was not quite so solitary and unrelated.

Unfortunately, however, during this voyage the two pinnaces got separated, but the gallant old Somers, after going north to the fogs, still battered his way down to Bermudas in spite of the weather. With his crude navigational instruments, and no means of finding his longitude except by guesswork, one can but admire the persistency which enabled him to keep beating about the boisterous ocean till at the beginning of November he finally reached Bermudas. He was evidently fatigued and hungry after five months at sea, and his death on 9th November was directly due to a surfeit of eating pig. His kinsman, Captain Matthew Somers, and the crew did not obey the dying ex-buccaneer's instructions to make for Virginia, but, having buried his heart, and marked the place with a cross, they embalmed the body and sailed with it across in the cedar pinnace to England. Thus de la Warr's people never received their pigs after all.

Meanwhile, before de la Warr had been at Jamestown a month sickness again seized the settlement, caused in part by the marshy ground and by the fact that the fresh-water well became polluted ; so "calentures " and " fluxes " once more became prevalent. But all this was aggravated by the fact that some of the passengers from their unhygienic English homes had brought with them the plague ; the cooped-up conditions of tropical ship-life became most favourable for developing any signs of illness. Thus within a few months one hundred and fifty colonists had died, including Sir Ferdinando Wainman. Unfortunately, too, there was friction with the Indians which brought about bloodshed, and the persuasive tact of a John Smith was seriously wanting to bridge over difficulties of contact with the red men.

At Kecoughtan de la Warr made two forts, named respectively Fort Henry and Fort Charles—on a pleasant plain in wholesome air, with plenty of springs and commanding a large circuit of ground containing woods, pasture and suitable for vines, as well as gardens. Here, it was intended, the newly-arrived from England should be lodged till they should become refreshed from ship-travelling, and acclimatized to Virginia's atmosphere. In July, 1610, Sir Thomas Gates was sent to England to obtain further supplies. He arrived there early in September, and succeeded in reviving the spirits of the London Council, who were inclined to abandon the whole enterprise. No time was lost, however, in spreading good news of Virginia and refuting alarmist reports. Many influential supporters withdrew from the undertaking, but Gates's influence helped to keep things alive, and new emigrants were collected for the following spring.

In August, 1610, de la Warr dispatched a punitive expedition against the Paspaheghs, burning their dwellings, as well as taking prisoners the queen and her children, whom they afterward slew. Some time later, when the Governor caused a party to visit the Falls with the old futile object of looking for gold mines, there was an attack by Indians which caused further fatal losses to the colony. But the Governor's own health was now so bad that on 28th March, 1611, by the advice of Doctor Bohun (who accompanied him) he went aboard Captain Argall's ship with the intention of sailing down to that West Indian Island of Nevis, whose good air and wholesome baths might work a cure. From his first arrival in Virginia de la Warr had suffered from ague, which had become worse with time; but dysentery, cramp, gout and scurvy also attacked him. Before leaving, he entrusted the governorship to Captain Percy until Sir Thomas Dale should arrive. The latter's career will interest us later, but it is sufficient here to say that in 1609 he had been sent out to Virginia as Marshal, and had been sent back to England for provisions and men, which should arrive that spring.

Captain Argall, who had been employed during the autumn and winter exploring the Chesapeake Bay, now found that it was no easier to reach Nevis than it had been to sight Bermudas. The southerly winds prevented the ship making good in that direction, so it was decided to turn a foul wind into fair and steer for the Azores. Here the juicy oranges and lemons, of course, did de la Warr's health much good, but he was advised to carry on and make for England, where he arrived in June, 1611. He had brought some of the sick with him, but at Jamestown he had left behind, mostly in good health, and well provided with victuals, only two hundred people. Thus Virginia in its four years of colonization proved to be some insatiable monster, greedy for human lives, but producing little in return. The arrival of de la Warr had a distinctly unsettling effect in London, both on the Council itself and on those investors who were so anxious to back out from their financial

Annapolis, Nova Scotia
From an eighteenth-century print

responsibilities. Even the great Sir Thomas Smith, who in the previous year had helped to send forth Hudson in order to discover a North-West Passage, had to incur grave criticisms in regard to his integrity as a financier. Here was a man with a finger in every exploration pie, and hitherto regarded with the utmost respect, who yet had tempted English gentlemen to underwrite their names to an apparently worthless proposition.

For the London Council these were black times, and the failure to produce the slightest sign of gold mines made their feelings still further depressed. It was to stem all this ebbing tide that the convalescent de la Warr got up in the Council on 25th June that same year, 1611, and made the following important speech :

" My Lords, being now by accident returned from my charge at Virginia, contrary either to my own desire, or other men's expectations, who spare not to censure me, in point of duty, and to discourse and question the reason, though they apprehend not the true cause of my return, I am forced (out of a willingness to satisfy every man) to deliver unto your Lordships and the rest of this assembly (but truly) in what state I have lived, ever since my arrival to the colony ; what hath been the just occasion of my sudden departure thence ; and in what terms I have left the same : the rather because I perceive, that since my coming into England, such a coldness and irresolution is bred in many of the adventurers that some of them seek to withdraw those payments which they have subscribed towards the charge of the plantation."

After informing his listeners concerning his ague (cured by Dr. Laurence Bohun through " blood letting "), and having related his other illnesses, he gave an account of the condition in which he had left Virginia, stating that the latter possessed ten months' food in addition to other supplies obtained by Argall's trading with the Indian chiefs. De la Warr told the Council about the two forts near Point Comfort, and a third at the Falls, but they possessed only two boats and one barge. This deficiency had hindered the fishing, which in turn had caused want in respect of fish food. But what they really needed was men.

M

"The country," he emphasized, "is wonderfully fertile and very rich, and . . . the cattle . . . thrive exceedingly." Dale and Gates were now taking out thither a hundred kine, and de la Warr prophesied that success in the colony would "give no man cause to distrust that hath already adventured, but encourage every good mind to further so worthy a work, as will redound both to the glory of God, to the credit of our nation, and to the comfort of all those that have been instruments in the furthering of it."

He referred to the "goodly river called Patomack, upon the borders whereof there are grown the goodliest trees for masts, that may be found elsewhere in the world ; hemp better than English, growing wild in abundance ; mines of antimony and lead without our Bay to the northward . . . an excellent fishing bank for cod and ling as good as can be eaten . . . there are many vines planted in divers places, and do prosper well." Finally, he stated deliberately, "I am willing and ready to lay all I am worth upon the adventure," rather than it should fail, and he was willing "to return all the convenient expedition I may."

But not even this eloquence was wholly successful in quieting men's minds ; and many English gentlemen who had been persuaded to underwrite their names as adventurers, at a time when the Virginia boom was at its highest, now flatly refused to pay up. The result was that they were sued in Chancery and made to fulfil their contracts to the extent of about four thousand pounds.

CHAPTER XIV

DISCIPLINE AND DESPOTISM

DURING de la Warr's sojourn in Virginia had arrived a little ship from England named the *Dainty*, bringing a dozen men and one woman to settle. A fortnight after his departure another vessel, the *Hercules*, landed thirty more with provisions, and it was on 12th May that Sir Thomas Dale with three ships, three hundred people, cattle and a supposedly year's supply of provisions arrived. But, says a contemporary, the latter were " for the most part such as hogs refused to eat."

Dale was one of those highly-efficient but ruthless officers who are generally more useful in military matters than as Governors. His life was typical of so many Virginian rulers, for about the year 1588 he had entered the service of the Low Countries, where he was regarded as a valiant, trusty soldier. Having been knighted during a visit to England, he returned to Holland, and was sent as Marshal to Virginia in 1609. On his second arrival at Jamestown in 1611 he took over the duties of Governor, and began with a heavy hand to crush anarchy, restore order and promote industry.

That which met his eyes displeased him intensely. There were only three months' provisions in the store, the settlers had been too lazy to plant corn, so he set them sowing at Forts Charles and Henry. Other idlers he caused to fell timber and repair the ill-conditioned houses, and he also chose a site for a new town on the " Narrow of Farrar's Island, in Varina Neck, upon a high land, nearly invironed by the main river." Now stern Sir Thomas Smith, weary of all the Jamestown lawlessness, sent over a printed book of articles and laws chiefly translated from the martial laws of the Low Countries. These severe and—as many people at the time regarded them—" most tyrannous and cruel " regulations were really *ultra vires*, for they had not been sanctioned by the London Council. But, harsh as they were, Dale had good reason to enforce them, since to preserve the colony from itself it was necessary to be cruel. Such men as Price or Jeffrey Abbot, who were plotting against Virginia's government through this year, and such rascals as Cole and Kitchens, who were planning to run off to the Spaniards and give away valuable colonial secrets, had to be dealt with in no kindly manner.

On the other hand, this direct-acting Dale might have used more discrimination and attained a similar end. Some of the Virginian veterans had already suffered more than any man could be expected to endure through muddle, famine and misfortune. Abbot was one of these, and Captain John Smith (no panderer to the mutinous) had the highest respect for him. The man had put in excellent service in both the Netherlands and Ireland, while in Virginia (Captain Smith related) " hee was a Sargeant of my Companie, and I never saw in Virginia a more sufficient souldier, lesse turbulent, a better wit, more hardy or industrious," or less likely to "abandon the countrie." But the introduction of the Dutch articles was another of those incidents which gave to Virginia's Governors a despotic power quite unsuitable for dealing with men bred to liberty. Admittedly the circumstances were difficult, but this excessive counter-action created an ugly impression which would be remembered at a later date.

Writing that same August to Lord Salisbury from Jamestown, Dale " as a true lover of God " and a patriot appeals for more emigrants. If only by next April he could be sent two thousand men, he would in a couple of years settle a colony to answer all expectations, overmaster that subtle, mischievous Powhatan, and through him the Indians generally. In the meanwhile Dale recommends that all offenders out of the English jails condemned to die should be sent for three years to the colony, as the Spaniards send their criminals to the West Indies. The three hundred " disorderly " persons he took out from England with him were so profane, riotous and full of mutiny that not many of them were Christian except in name, while their bodies were so diseased and " crazed " that not sixty of them could be employed to work.

But there was another grave danger which threatened Virginia, and that came from Spain. The danger of this ill-protected colony was a source of anxiety in England during the next two years especially. In April, 1612, for instance, Sir John Digby wrote to Salisbury from Madrid giving warning that many consultations had taken place for supplanting the English in Virginia. The Spaniards, indeed, were most indignant that this colony should have sprung up. They regarded it as " a company of voluntary and loose people," yet extremely inconvenient to the King of Spain. While the latter believed, with the inspiration of hope, that Virginia would soon die out, yet the Spanish Ambassador in London was instructed to demand that the plantation be removed. Don Pedro de Zuñiga in 1612 was sending his sovereign full details as to what was going on in London for the obtaining of ships, money and settlers. And the Spanish Ambassador Don Diego Sarmiento de Acuña (who was appointed in 1613 and became Count de Gondomar in 1617) used to send home such tit-bits of news as that the head of the Virginia Company in London had authority to dispatch any criminal prisoners to Virginia, but some had preferred hanging to transportation.

By 1613 England was expecting another Spanish invasion up the Channel, Virginia being the bone of contention. Diplomacy endeavoured ineffectually to obtain the colony's overthrow; but though this effort failed, there was always uncertainty as long as disgruntled men managed occasionally to slip out of the colony and spread unfavourable reports. Ten fellows, for example, sent out from Jamestown to fish made their way across the Atlantic and filled all London with upsetting rumours.

But in the meanwhile Sir Thomas Gates with six English caravels was being sent to relieve Dale, and was bringing out three hundred more people, besides one hundred cattle, two hundred pigs and provisions. Before Gates sailed from Cowes de la Warr was able to have an interview and give him the latest news. Newport, who had been conducting Virginia voyages ever since 1606, and is referred to in 1611 by Dudley Carleton as " the Admiral of Virginia," now transferred his services to the East India Company, and before his death in 1617 commanded vessels running to the Orient, doubtless owing to the influence of Sir Thomas Smith.

Gates sailed out by the " unneedful " route, taking his wife with him, but at the West Indies Lady Gates died : another of those post-tropical deaths. It was in August that Gates reached Jamestown and took over his duties, which he was to continue for nearly three years. He had brought with him also his two daughters, but these were sent back with Newport in the following December. Dale did not leave the country, but continued his previous duties as Marshal, and in September, with three hundred and fifty men lent by Gates, he went to get on with the building of his new town. This was to be known as Henrico—another reminder of James I's eldest son—and first the area was palisaded all round, then were erected a church and store-houses, with watch towers at each corner of the town, and finally houses for himself and his men. Henrico was situated on the James River, some seventy miles above Jamestown but ten miles below the Falls. Enjoying a temperate and agreeable climate, stretching from river to river on a plain of high land, with very steep and inaccessible banks, it had the security of an island ; and here, eventually, from its three streets was to rise up a little community of people superior to the rest. It was, so to speak, a colony within a colony, while about two miles from the town " into the main " extended another palisade two miles along, stretching from river to river and protecting from Indian attack large quantities of growing corn. As a further protection from surprise onslaught a trench was made, while a palisade on the south side of the river kept the pigs within.

In spite of his unpopularity among many of the slack settlers, Dale was certainly an astute and far-sighted organizer, who was able to put his finger on Virginia's weak spots. A friend of Prince Henry, he had on leaving Holland married as recently as February, 1611, Elizabeth, daughter of Sir Thomas Throckmorton, this lady being a relative of Sir Walter Raleigh's wife. We can thus understand some of the influences at work which caused Dale to be lent temporarily from the Low Countries to " attend the plantacion of Virginia." One of the excellent achievements which he brought about was a guest

house on a high, dry situation in wholesome air, where sick
people had a real chance of winning back health ; and it was
on the same side of the river that Henrico's chaplain, the Rev.
Alexander Whitaker, was settled in a " fair parsonage," named
Rockhall, with a hundred acres of land staked off.

This cleric was another instance of the family patronage
at work in colonization.   The son of the Rev. Dr. William
Whitaker (a celebrated Puritan divine and sometime head of
St. John's College, Cambridge), Alexander's mother was a
Miss Culverwell, a relative of Sir Thomas Smith's first wife.
Henrico's padre was about twenty-six years old, and after
taking his degree at Cambridge he had been in charge of a
parish in the north of England.   A man of means, he was
inspired with the desire to go as missionary to Virginia, had
arrived in May with Dale's party, and was to remain till his
death came by drowning six years later.   Like the self-sacrificing
Hunt, he had felt a moral responsibility in regard to the New
World, and there were others like him in that respect.   That
man-of-affairs, distinguished sea officer and expert in piracy,
Sir William Monson (1568–1643), well summed up the educated
Englishman's attitude, with one eye on religion and another
on commerce, when he affirmed that " God gave a new light
of a new world by the discovery of America, now daily known
and frequented by us of Europe, and whose soil yields benefit
to the Christian world."

Dale, in pursuance of his active policy, determined to teach
the Appamatuck tribe a severe lesson.   These were the people
whom John Smith had first discovered, but recently they had
been guilty of treacherous murders ; so about Christmas, 1611,
Dale assaulted and took their town without the loss of a single
white man.   This Indian town stood at the mouth of the river,
five miles by land from Henrico, and Dale now named it
New Bermuda, annexing many miles of rich woodland divided
into several "hundreds," such as Rochdale Hundred, Shirley
Hundred and Digges Hundred.   He also erected across this
new property a paling which extended for two miles from river
to river, thus securing an enclosure for growing much needed
corn, while presently fifty " fair houses " were to spring up.
Rochdale Hundred was also enclosed and many houses erected,

and there was a twenty-mile circuit where in full safety the settlers' cattle and pigs could feed and fatten. Thus, with Jamestown well palisaded, while Gates was trying hard to make religion the basis of Virginia's orderliness, and endeavouring to carry out an administration with discreet providence, the colonial venture seemed at last to have taken a definite turn for the better.

Meanwhile Sir Thomas Smith and his colleagues were busily planning to obtain more capital for the furtherance of additional expeditions from England, and in the spring of 1612 a lottery was already in hand, which moved Don Pedro de Zuñiga to write to the Spanish King that by this means the English hoped to raise twenty thousand ducats and send out six ships to Virginia with all the people who could be procured ; while about the same time there was a rumour being spread that both Gates and Dale were " quite out of heart " with the colony, and that its failure was assured. But, as a fact, England was extending rather than withdrawing her overseas territory. The information which Captain Matthew Somers, on arriving in England with his relative's body, had brought concerning Bermudas' wonderful climate, had created immense interest, so that some of the Virginia Company in London conceived the idea of Bermudas becoming colonized as an auxiliary to Virginia itself. Seeing, however, that the present charter did not allow this, they procured a new one which gave them all the islands within three hundred leagues of the Virginian coast between the latitudes of 41° and 30° N. The Spaniards had never taken advantage of Bermudan original discovery ; for, dismayed at the frequency of the hurricanes, they preferred to let this neighbourhood alone, and give it the name of Devils' Island (*Dæmonorum Insula*).

This new charter was granted by James I to the Treasurer and Company for Virginia on 12th March, 1612, being an enlargement of the previous letters-patent. Not merely did the third charter extend the Company's limits by including " those islands whatsoever, situate and being in any part of the Ocean Seas bordering upon the coast of our said first colony in Virginia, and being within three hundred leagues of any of the parts heretofore granted to the said Treasurer and Company," but it gave an encouraging strength in other respects. There were to be held the " Four Great and General Courts of the Council and Company of Adventurers for Virginia " in Hilary, Easter, Trinity and Michaelmas terms, and they were to have full authority to set forth and publish lotteries with a view to obtaining the money necessary for Virginia's plantation. Indeed, there were so many, both Spanish and English, who were hindering progress that the utmost royal help must be afforded.

" Divers lewd and ill-disposed persons, both sailers, soldiers, artificers, husbandmen, labourers and others, having received wages, apparel and other entertainment from the said Company, or having contracted and agreed with the said Company to go, or to serve, or to be employed in . . . Virginia, have afterwards either withdrawn, hid, or concealed themselves, or have refused to go thither." Others had been mutinous, or escaped to England without licence from the Governor and been insolent to the London Council, and even spread slanderous reports of Virginia and its government, thus discouraging potential planters from going out.

Ever since May, 1609, all commodities shipped for Virginia had been allowed to go free of Customs or other duties, but it was presently decided to separate the Virginia venture from the Bermudan. The London Company sold the Bermuda Islands to about one hundred and twenty of their own members, who thus became a distinct body known as the Somers Islands Company, Sir Thomas Smith still, however, continuing as its Treasurer in England. In 1612 Richard More was sent out as first Governor, who found that three Englishmen, previously left behind, were still alive. By August the Company in London received the glad news that the ships sent out had safely arrived, and already some amber as well as seed pearls were being sent home. The overseas enterprise of Sir Thomas Smith is indeed one of the most important features of Jacobean England. His was the greatest colonial mind of the period, and whatever faults he possessed were the defects which belong to a great founder of empire. The fact that England was able to maintain a secure tenure in America and India, that during the most depressing days the Virginian settlement was still kept going, that money and ships and men and royal enthusiasm

were always obtainable, must be credited to the energy and
imagination of this master intellect. Next year he was, in
association with others, to send seven ships up the Arctic, and
for many years he acted as the Muscovy Company's Governor.
By 1614, besides finding time for his duties as Member of
Parliament, he was not merely the founder but the head of
practically every English company engaged in sea-borne
commerce, and the patron of scientists. Over men and matters
he kept a firm hand with his dominating personality, and at his
house in Philpot Lane were retained all the documents of these
various enterprises.

During the year 1612 several ships were sent over from
England to Virginia, including the *John and Francis*, the
Sarah and the *Treasurer*. The latter had been named evidently
after Sir Thomas Smith, and in her came Captain Argall once
more. She sailed from home on 23rd July with fifty settlers
and provisions, and made a quick passage (for those days) of
fifty-one days. Argall arrived in Virginia with instructions to
remain there and drive out all foreign intruders ; his ability
as a man and a mariner would be valuable if the intended
Spanish attack should materialize. Actually he was employed
till the following June up and down the waters of Virginia
doing valuable work. The following interesting letter which
he wrote from America to Master Nicholas Hawes gives an
impression of Argall's activities :

" I fell with the coast of Virginia, in the Latitude of fortie
degrees, the twelfth of September, with all my men in good
health, the number being sixtie two, and all my victualls very
well conditioned, my course being fiftie leagues to the
Northward of the Azores. The seventeenth I arrived at Point
Comfort, where by the discreet and provident government of
Sir Thomas Gates, and great paines and hazard of Sir Thomas
Dale, I found both the countrey and people in farre better
estate there, then the report was by such as came home in Sir
Robert Mansfield's ship. From my arrivall untill the first of
November, I spent my time in helping to repaire such ships and
boats as I found heere decayed for lacke of Pitch and Tarre ;
and in pursuing the Indians with Sir Thomas Dale, for theire
corne, of which we got some quantitie."

Then, about the beginning of November:

" . . . by the advice of Sir Thomas Gates, I carried Sir Thomas Dale to Sir Thomas Smith's Island[1] to have his opinion of the inhabiting of it ; who, after three dayes march in discovering it, approved very well of the place : and so much the better, because we found abundance of fish there, and very great cod, which we caught in five fathome water."

But it was in order to increase the somewhat scanty provisions of the colony that on the first day of December he was sent on one of those foraging expeditions which Captain John Smith had been compelled years previously to inaugurate. " I fitted my ship," Argall wrote, " to fetch corne from Pato-womeck,[2] by trading with the Indians, and so set sayle from Point Comfort the first of December," entered the Pembroke River, and arrived off the King of Pastancie's town, " and there built me a stout shallop, to get the corne aboord withall." Actually he was able to bring back eleven hundred bushels to Jamestown, where it was deposited into " the serverall store-houses, according unto the direction of Sir T. Gates : besides the quantitie of 300 bushels reserved for mine company." For the fear of winter's famine was now too firmly established not to take the fullest precautions.

Argall was full of breezy activity, and next set his men felling timber for the building of a " frigat, which I left halfe finished in the hands of the carpenters at Point Comfort, the 19 of March." There was in him something of the John Smith character, with the same relish for exploration yet with a lingering optimism regarding precious minerals. Argall went exploring in his ship to the Pembroke River, " which is about 65 leagues into the land," and navigable for any ship. Having landed, he found and killed cattle which turned out to be very " wholesome meate." He discovered also a " myne, of which I have sent a triall into England, and likewise a strange kind of earth . . . the Indians eate it for physicke, alleaging that it cureth the sicknesse and paine of the belly."

[1] That is to say Smith Isles (up Chesapeake Bay), first discovered by Captain John Smith.

[2] That is, Potomac.

It is at this stage that, after several years, our attention is again centred on the romantic Pocahontas. The Great Powhatan, her father, in his treacherous and unstable conduct toward his enemies the English, had not merely retained some cf the planters' valuable tools and arm., but was still keeping as prisoners a number of colonists. There in April, 1613, Argall, learning that the princess was staying with her uncle, the Chief of Potomac, resolved to abduct her as a hostage. Argall's action was less an infamous bit of trickery than a stratagem necessary for winning back the lives and liberties of Englishmen from the hands of untrustworthy savages. The end justified the somewhat questionable means. Certainly it brought about peace, and the girl (who had always been so well-disposed toward the Virginian white settlers) regarded her capture and carrying away by Argall as the happiest event of her life. She was well treated and, with feminine delight in a strange and thrilling adventure, she would not have missed the experience which was to end in a manner that even she could scarcely have foreseen. The taking of this nineteen-year-old maiden may be best told in Argall's own words :

" Whilst I was in this businesse, I was told by certaine Indians, my friends, that the Great Powhatans daughter Pokahuntis was with the great King Patawoneck, whether I presently repaired, resolving to possesse myself of her by any strategem that I could use, for the ransoming of so many Englishmen as were prisoners with Powhatan ; as also to get such armes and tooles, as hee and other Indians had got by murther and stealing from others of our Nation, with some quantitie of corne for the Colonies reliefe."

So, having anchored off the town, " I manned my boate and sent on shore for the King of Pastancy and Ensigne Swift," who had been left on a previous visit as a hostage.

Argall, somewhat in the John Smith manner, persuaded the Chief (with a threat of cancelling their existing friendship) to influence the Potomac King in delivering up the Princess. The King " concluded rather to deliver her into my hands than to lose my friendship, so presently he betrayed her into my boat, wherein I carried her aboard my ship." By one of the Indians

Argall then sent to Powhatan the information, saying, that while he had taken his daughter prisoner, he would restore her, provided Powhatan sent home the English prisoners with such arms and tools as the Indians had stolen, together with " a great quantitie of corne." On 13th April Argall with his craft sailed off and "repayred with all speed to Sir T. Gates," where he reported and delivered Pocahontas. This somewhat drastic reprisal so grieved Powhatan that within a few days he returned to Jamestown seven of the prisoner colonists now " freed from the slavery and feare of cruell murther, which they daily before lived in." They also brought with them three pieces of ordnance, one broad axe, a long whip-saw, as well as a canoe full of corn. Thus freed of this woman, the masculine, seafaring Argall was able to get on with his shipbuilding job. " I beeing quit of my prisoner, went forward with the Frigat which I had left at Point Comfort, and finished her."

While Pocahontas during the next few months remained captive, she was well treated and contented, but her father had not given back more than part of the property which belonged to the settlement; her stay, therefore, seemed likely to be of indefinite duration. She became popular and a source of great interest to the Jamestown people. Mutual curiosity bred mutual confidence. The Governor, conscious of his duty, had her instructed in the Christian religion, in which she made such good progress (at the hands of either the Rev. Mr. Buck or the Rev. Mr. Whitaker) that she finally made a public renouncement of her native idolatry, "confessed the faith of Christ, and was baptized." Her heathen name of Matoaka was at this ceremony changed to Rebecca.

With the spring had come the time for further exploration, for increased transportation along the rivers and bays, for the hurrying on of shipbuilding, and for a sea voyage north through those cold waters where good fishing could be relied upon. So first of all we find Argall setting one gang of men to work fitting out the *Treasurer* under the supervision of her Master; for in the winter it was customary to unrig such vessels, send down yards, and secure them in readiness for the strong gales as well as the high tides. Another " ginge " of Argall's men were labouring ashore under " my Lieutanent," felling timber for new spars and cleaving planks to make a new fishing-boat, while yet another " ginge " was being employed under " my Ensigne " taking the recently-built frigate into the local waters fishing, or carrying supplies up the river to Henrico. A fourth gang, however, accompanied Argall when he sailed out of James River in the shallop on the first of May in order to make further exploration of Chesapeake Bay, " which I found to have many small rivers in it, and very good harbours for boats and barges, but not for ships of any great burthern . . . so, having discovered along the shore some fortie leagues Northward, I returned againe to my ship the twelfth of May, and hasted forward my businesse left in hand at my departure ; and fitted up my ship, and built my fishing boat, and made readie to take the first opportunitie of the wind for my fishing voyage, of which I beseech God of his mercy to bless us."

It was soon after 28th June, 1613, that he was able to start. But either Argall was a humorist, or (more likely) he was anxious to disguise the immediate duty on which he was sent. We have seen that the reason why he came out from England to America was to get rid of intruders, and now he took the *Treasurer*, equipped with fourteen guns, up the Atlantic coast to smash up the newly-established French settlements off the coast of Maine, as well as St. Croix on an island of that river which to-day separates the United States from New Brunswick, and to reduce also Port Royal (six miles from the Annapolis of modern Nova Scotia), on the opposite side of Fundy Bay.

These Gallic colonies were regarded as distinct infringements of the Virginia charter, and aroused no little jealousy in the minds of the London company. We must, however, bear in mind two points : first, that the English in America were interlopers not less than were the French ; and second, that in fixing the latitude of 45° N., the navigating instruments of this age were none too accurate. But the plain truth was that Sir Thomas Smith and his colleagues were not going to suffer Frenchmen to profit by American colonization if that enterprise could be prevented. And in this attitude we have the germ of a trouble that must inevitably later on develop into such a clash of international wills as could be decided only by war. Indeed, without their realizing it, those responsible for the first period of English pioneering in America were (to change the metaphor) sowing seeds which would grow up as prickly thistles, requiring to be handled with the utmost care.

Argall succeeded in destroying the Jesuit colony on Mount Desert. This mountainous island, some fifteen miles long by eight miles broad, is in the modern Hancock County, Maine, the limits of Virginia, while the French regarded it as part of Nova Francia. Within a few weeks Argall had returned with French prisoners to Jamestown, but was sent back by Gates to make a more complete destruction of Mount Desert's buildings and fortifications, as well as at St. Croix and Port Royal. This he did, and there is unsubstantiated reason for believing that during this voyage he called at the Dutch settlement on the Hudson River and compelled its Governor, Hendrick Christiansen, to submit to the Crown of Great Britain. The important historical result of Argall's two coastal voyages was that New England was to be kept exclusively for future colonization by the English.

In December, 1613, Argall was again in the James River, and continued to be employed actively till the following 14th June, when he sailed for England with his French prisoners, arriving there by the end of July. In October of 1613 the ship *Elizabeth* sailed from England with thirteen colonists for Virginia, and it was in this craft that in April, 1614, Sir Thomas Gates, leaving the government in Sir Thomas Dale's hands, proceeded to England. Gates did his best to revive and strengthen the weak and falling hopes of the London Virginia Company's shareholders, and then crossed to the Netherlands, where he sought and obtained his arrears of pay as a Captain. Gates had certainly done well in Virginia, and laid the foundations for the prosperity which could not be indefinitely delayed. The colleagues of Sir Thomas Smith certainly felt they needed some encouragement, for already in the previous summer a ship from Virginia had arrived with no commodities but only " fair tales and hopes," besides the welcome information that Pocahontas, daughter of their greatest enemy, had been captured. Incidentally this same ship had called at Bermudas, whence she had brought nine hundred pounds' worth of pearls and ambergris, together with the inspiring news that the colonists there were now settling down splendidly. True, the Spaniards threatened to remove them next year, but the English planters (relying on the difficulties of approach and the Spanish fear of hurricanes) were not excited to nervousness.

None the less, there was what Sir John Digby, writing to Sir Dudley Carleton, called a " hot dispute " with the Spanish Secretary of State concerning these English plantations. The latter complained angrily of James I giving permission to plant in Virginia and Bermudas when by right they belonged to the Spanish King, whose title to those lands was indisputable by the conquest of Castile, and by the Papal Bull of Donation. On the other hand, the English contended that all countries on the east side of America from Lat. 32° to Lat. 72° N. had never been planted by the Spaniards, but belonged to the Crown of England by right of discovery, as well as by actual possession taken on behalf of Queen Elizabeth by the deputies of Sir Walter Raleigh, " and by the two English colonies thither conducted, whereof the later is yet there remaining." Gates, on his return, besides extending support to drooping spirits, did not omit to add the serious warning that unless Virginia were soon furnished with supplies the plantation would succumb ; yet, he emphasized, there were wonderful commodities to be had if with patience and cost they were brought to perfection.

Early in 1614 Sir Thomas Dale had taken Pocahontas, with one hundred and fifty men in Argall's ship and some of the other Virginian craft, up the Werowocomoco River to parley with Powhatan, and after some hostilities a peace was made. Two of the big Chief's sons came aboard and saw for themselves that the Princess was well. But long before this, and as result of a friendship developed during her Jamestown captivity, there had sprung up mutual affection between Pocahontas and Master John Rolfe. The latter was a man of twenty-nine, and came of an old Norfolk family. He had married a woman in England during 1608, with whom he sailed bound for Virginia in 1609 aboard the ill-fated *Sea Venture*, in which the reader will recollect were also Gates, Somers and Newport. It was after being wrecked at Bermudas that a daughter was born to Master and Mistress Rolfe, who was baptized on 11th February, 1610, by the Rev. Mr. Buck, and Captain Newport himself acted as one of the sponsors. It is hardly surprising that this infant, ushered into the world amid such strange circumstances, should die ; nor is it a wonder that, after crossing the Gulf Stream in the little thirty-ton cedar pinnace, the mother should pass away on reaching Virginia. Indeed, one marvels at and sympathizes with these Jacobean women who had the pluck to make the Atlantic voyage in such foul ships. Only the very hardiest and most lucky could survive the discomforts that killed such as Lady Gates and others not bred to adversity.

John Rolfe remained a widower during the next four years, in which he gained everlasting fame by becoming the first Englishman who learned how to cultivate and cure tobacco in Virginia. And then came the captive Pocahontas, who captured his heart. Women were rare in the colony at this time, and spinsters were fewer still ; while, amid the settlers, the labourers, artizans, prisoners, spies and officers, men were in a great majority. Pocahontas with her kindly and pleasing personality readily enough won admiration, and when Rolfe in a letter to Governor Dale announced the love-pact, Sir Thomas Smith gave it his full approval. Her father Powhatan also approved, and was flattered by the idea. The marriage is reported to have taken place on 1st April, 1614, in the church at Jamestown, the officiating minister being either the Rev. Mr. Buck, or Rev. Mr. Whitaker of Henrico, and there were present both the uncle and two of the Princess's brothers. It is, however, only right to say that there are some critics who deny the certainty of a marriage having ever taken place. And Rolfe, having claimed that it was "for the glory of God" that he wedded her, has won for himself the accusation of having been a colossal prig and humbug.

As to the girl's persistently friendly attitude toward the English colonists there is no possible doubt, and in September, 1610, Argall found that young Henry Spelman [1] in the Potomac country had been preserved from Powhatan's fury by the good offices of Pocahontas and other Indians. An exchange of prisoners and a state of amity with the natives eased a situation that had been more or less tense ever since the first settlement

[1] See Chapter XV.

N

of Jamestown. The colony was now well past its critical era, though not yet in the most satisfactory condition. There were times when want and scarcity caused some of them to go hungry. On one occasion this created a mutiny, but it was discovered and six men were executed. And there was a lack of self-sacrificing clerics, which was surprising at this moment, seeing that there was a Protestant wave passing over the English Church ; for, after Bancroft's death in 1610, George Abbot, a Puritan, had been Primate of all England. " Master Whitaker their Preacher complaineth," wrote a correspondent from Virginia in June, 1614, " and much museth, that so few of our English Ministers, that were so hot against the surplice and subscription come hether, where neither is spoken of."

Nor did anxiety as to the Spaniards lessen just yet. In the year 1616 a Spanish ship appeared off Point Comfort and sent a boat ashore for a pilot, who was dispatched in all innocence, three of the visitor's men being left ashore, while the boat kidnapped the pilot and made off to sea. It was presently discovered that several Spanish ships were in the offing and that one of the three alleged Spaniards was a renegade Englishman who had piloted the Spanish Armada up the English Channel in 1588. There had come out to Virginia again the *John and Francis* with twenty settlers, and in February, 1615, Argall had once more been sent with the *Treasurer* carrying another score of passengers. She waited at Jamestown till May of the following year, when she took Sir Thomas Dale home at the end of his official period. With him travelled also Rolfe, Pocahontas, and their infant son who had been born in 1615, together with some native attendants. On the voyage Dale caused one of the Spanish spies to be hanged, and another had already died.

On 12th June, 1616, Dale's party reached Plymouth. The landing was certainly historic, for here came the first Virginian woman that ever learned to speak English or had a child in marriage by an English father. Mindful of what he owed to one who had saved his life some nine years before, Captain John Smith wrote to Queen Anne (consort of James I) this year beseeching " your Maiestie to take this knowledge of her." The beautiful savage was indeed received by the King and Queen ;

she was introduced about London by Lord and Lady de la Warr, taken to the masques, and generally made an excellent impression. Captain Smith went to call on this little Princess of short stature. She had imagined all this time that the man whose life she had saved was now dead. Unfortunately as Pocahontas was about to leave Gravesend on 21st March, 1617, on her return to Virginia, she died. The raw English winter had evidently been too much for this young woman, but several of her attendants were tubercular. The son Thomas was then brought up by his uncle, Henry Rolfe, in London, until in 1640, being twenty-five years old, the former returned to Virginia, where he married Frances Poythress.

As to John Rolfe, he proceeded to Virginia, in 1619 became a member of the Virginia Council, married Jane Pierce, and died in either 1622 or the year following. His will was witnessed by the Rev. Richard Buck.

CHAPTER XV

VIRGINIA'S REFORMS

CAPTAIN GEORGE YEARDLEY had been left behind by Dale as Deputy-Governor. The son of a London merchant-tailor, Yeardley was a man in the early forties, who after service in the Low Countries had sailed to Virginia as captain of Gates' company in the 1609 supply, being one of those shipwrecked in the *Sea Venture*.

Dale's vigorous good judgment had been an inspiration to the colonists. Before his period every emigrant who had " adventured " his own person, or had caused others to be brought out at his own expense, was entitled to one hundred acres of land for each person. But, after the Dale régime, Virginia had become so flourishing that only half this amount could be conceded. At the end of a man's service to the company or colony a grant of not more than two thousand acres could be made ; and every person who paid twelve pound ten into the Company could obtain his one hundred acres. And so careful had Dale been to have plenty of corn planted, that there had been no scarcity, but on occasions the Indians came to buy this grain.

At this stage the cultivation of tobacco, however, with the increasing use of narcotics in Europe, became overdone, so that corn crops were neglected. To counteract this danger, Dale had a law preventing any tobacco being set till enough corn ground had been prepared and planted. After Dale's departure Yeardley relaxed the severe system of government, and while showing firmness toward the Indians, he and the colonists were so tempted by the ready remuneration of tobacco that they neglected the planting of corn. It was thus that the colony once more became in difficulties, so that Yeardley had to send to the Chickahominies, and even cause bloodshed, before corn could be obtained.

This had a chastening effect, and the colony was again moderately happy, but unfortunately by a stupid error of judgment Yeardley taught one or two natives how to use fire-arms. It was not only contrary to the London Company's wishes, but was eventually to accelerate a terrible massacre some five years later. During Yeardley's brief reign there had arrived at Michaelmas that well-known ship *Susan*, this time with the first magazine consisting of necessary clothing. And with the stage of development reached where colonists were no longer bound by service but were free, and able to exercise individuality in trading, Virginia was well on the way to prosperity.

In May, 1617, Captain Argall arrived as Deputy-Governor and Admiral. He was to succeed Yeardley, and brought a hundred more settlers. John Rolfe came too, having been made Secretary and Recorder-General because of the London Company's approval of his having effected good relations with Powhatan by marriage. This continual change of governors had the bad cumulative effect of preventing the colony from enjoying a settled policy, as may well be seen by comparing the condition of Virginia after Dale left with its state when Yeardley finished his period. So mad on tobacco-growing had the latter allowed Jamestown to become, that even the market-place, the streets and every piece of spare ground were thus planted, while the buildings were so neglected that the church was down, a store-house being used for God's worship, the palisades in pieces, and the colonists dispersed all over instead of being concentrated.

Rolfe's son was to grow up into a person of fortune and to found a fine family tradition in America, but the death of Powhatan in 1618 prevented the Chief's longing to have seen the boy ever being fulfilled. In this year occurred a terrible drought and a storm of hail which damaged the crops, yet the best tobacco fetched three shillings per pound. In October, just as Virginia was rising to life from the grave of failure, that greatest of all Virginians, Sir Walter Raleigh, went down into his grave one cold morning by way of the scaffold. And it is sad to relate that Argall, who had shown himself so excellent when playing an up-hill game, so regular in his service at sea, so ably carrying out orders to him entrusted, now became tinged with corruptness when he took over a shore job.

He sought his own ends, and even the impartial Stith accused him of pushing on his " unrighteous gains by all imaginable methods of extortion and oppression," converting to his own use that which belonged to the public. Among Argall's edicts were : No trade was to be made with the savages ; no Indians were to be taught how to shoot, under pain of death to teacher and learner. No man was to shoot, except in his own defence against an enemy, until a new supply of ammunition arrived. (Penalty one year's slavery.) No one could go aboard the ship then at Jamestown without the Governor's leave; no master of a ship was to allow his crew to go ashore or talk with the people at Kecoughtan. Every person must go to church on Sundays and Holy Days " or lye neck and heels that night, and be a slave to the colony the following week."

While there were good points in such regulations, yet the man who had distinguished himself preserving discipline aboard Atlantic ships, and wiping out French settlements, became as a colonial Governor ruthless, harsh, wasteful and even extortionate. Meantime his friend, that hypocrite John Rolfe, was writing home to England in June, 1618, that " concerning the state of our new commonwealth, it is somewhat bettered, for we have sufficient to content our selves, though not in such abundance as is vainly reported in England," yet the fact was that whereas Dale had established a yearly rent of corn from the Virginian farmers, Argall in addition employed over fifty of the Company's servants for his own personal profit. Thus it was that " some private differences happened betwixt Captains Bruster and Argall."

Now this Captain Edward Brewster was manager of Lord de la Warr's property, and felt justified in ordering his men away from work assigned to them by Argall. But one of them refused, was accordingly threatened by Brewster, and then complained to the Governor. The latter thereupon had Brewster seized, court-martialled, and condemned to death ; for among those articles sent over by Sir Thomas Smith was one which originated in the Low Countries and decreed that no man should resist or disobey his commander, or do any act which might tend to breed disorder, the penalty being death. We thus have here a vicious circle. The Virginian colonists had been so ill-chosen as to comprise a majority of lawless men. Mismanagement had made their conditions worse still, causing a general chaotic anarchy, which in turn demanded drastic and determined measures toward establishing order. But these, when enforced with excessive severity, created that reaction which inevitably follows a blatant display of force.

The point here requires stressing, for it was one of those steps that would ultimately lead to the Great Revolution and Independence, though no eye could as yet visualize such a possibility. One of the unforgivable sins committed by England against her American colonies has been the uninspired, and frequently downright unsuitable, choice of her Governors. The fact that the roots of this trouble were concealed in the lack of sympathetic respect for humanity and suffering was a mitigation of the offence though not a justification. Argall, the hard-bitten skipper and tough explorer, could not (with his violent individualism) forget himself in his official position as colonial officer. His provocative treatment of Brewster was unjustified and unlawful, and the man Argall was employing a powerful machinery which belonged only to Argall as Governor. Here was no suggestion of mutiny, but a personal dispute over a private right.

While it is true that martial law at this time was the existing Virginian law, this Dutch-begotten interference with the liberty of the people threatened to jeopardize the whole system of colonizing. It was the defect of militarism painfully manifest. Argall, fine intrepid mariner and warrior, of course knew well how nervous was the London Company of further outbreaks, and the risk of repealing these stern laws ; yet a more tactful, a more diplomatic, official would have let Sir Thomas Smith's articles become dead documents. In these twentieth-century days of rapid transportation and quick interchange of messages over the Atlantic, the whole trouble between Virginia and London could have been settled in a few days. But the weeks of intervening sea allowed a quarrel of two men to develop into a political crisis.

The members of the court-martial proceeded in a body to plead for Brewster, and with the support of clergy finally prevailed on Argall to save Brewster's life. Argall, however, made it a condition that Brewster should take a solemn oath not to utter any words or do anything in Argall's disparagement, and never again return to Virginia. Now Brewster sailed off to England in an ugly mind, appealed to the London Company against the sentence imposed, and did his best to expose Argall's tyrannical administration. This created a situation of some delicacy. His kinsman Sir Thomas Smith was compelled to exercise great care lest the King's aid should be invoked and thus endanger the Company's privileges.

But matters now began to focus themselves toward the climax. On 23rd August, 1618, Sir Thomas Smith, Alderman Johnson the Deputy Treasurer, and others wrote a letter to Argall charging him with converting the fruits of the Company's expense to his own private use, accusing him of having become so proud and insolent as to scorn the title of " Deputy " Governor. Simultaneously they denounced him for having appropriated to himself the Indian trade, employing the old planters as well as the Company's tenants and servants on his own work ; in short, he had acted as if Virginia were intended for his personal gain.

At the same time the Company sent a letter to Lord de la Warr, giving this information, and instructing the noble lord to seize Argall's tobacco, skins, furs, and to return the cattle together with all other public property which Argall had embezzled. Now this epistle was destined never to reach de la Warr. The latter, having spent many months in England, sailed in April, 1618, as once more the Governor of Virginia, with two hundred people in the 250-ton ship *Neptune*, which he had specially built ; for the business basis was such that he paid for the emigrants' transportation and subsistence, but got back his money from the profits of these labourers after the commodities should reach England. De la Warr set forth down the Atlantic by way of the Azores, whose fruits had done him so much good on his previous visit. He landed at Terceira in this group, where he was fêted and well used.

From there he sailed to the American continent, and on 7th June died at some unidentifiable spot in New England or Canada. The fact that he, together with most of those who had gone ashore at Terceira, sickened and succumbed has been attributed to Portuguese treachery. While this is not impossible, a much more likely explanation is that the voyage became protracted and the usual bad conditions on board claimed thirty lives as a toll.

His end was a loss to Virginia, but not an irreparable misfortune. While this gallant, adventurous and kindly English gentleman, full of the old Elizabethan zeal for travel, had earned immortality by having once saved Virginia from dispersion of its colonists, and is still commemorated on America's map by the name of Delaware Bay, yet no man in the great scheme that was developing across the ocean could be regarded as indispensable. His widow in September, 1619, was rewarded with a pension [1] for thirty-one years. It was renewed in 1634, but stopped at the outbreak of the Civil War. After the Restoration it was again continued by a fresh grant, his eldest son and successor to the title dying in 1628.

It was not till after sixteen weeks at sea that the *Neptune* finally fetched up in Virginia with over two hundred survivors, but having practically run out of provisions. Thus, from the month of August she remained till November, consuming Virginia's victuals, and was of necessity to be furnished with supplies before she could cross the ocean back to England. Meanwhile the Indians were still treacherously murdering the long-suffering planters, and one Sunday morning a tragedy came to the Fairfax family. The father had gone to church, leaving his wife and family of young children at home. The time of service being ended, Mrs. Fairfax sallied forth to meet her spouse, but little time had she been gone when three or four Indians entered the house and slew the children.

---

[1] The pension was five hundred pounds a year, to be paid out of the plantation. In 1634 she based her plea on the fact that the great profits accruing from Virginia were due to the large sums of money which her husband had expended, leaving her with the burden of debts, and only ten pounds a year on which to keep herself as well as seven children. It is safe to reckon ten pounds of that date as about the equivalent to-day of ten times that sum.

As to Argall, that letter which had been intended for de la
Warr fell into the worst of hands.   The former was still in
command of the situation and even arbitrarily ordered the late
peer's men to work for the present Governor, to the neglect
of the de la Warr estate.   At the beginning of April, 1619,
arrived in Virginia a pinnace named *Eleanor*, " priuatly from
England " :   that is to say, she had been sent out secretly by
one of Argall's influential friends in London to warn him of
approaching trouble.   Argall delayed only a fortnight, entrusted
Virginia to Captain Nathaniel Powell,[1] and sailed off home.
But this hurried departure was well timed ;   a few days later
there came into the James River a vessel bearing that previous
visitor George Yeardley.

In October, 1618, the London Company received the sad
tidings of de la Warr's decease, and resolved to send over
a new Governor with power to examine on the spot all the
complaints against Argall.   They were also taking steps, in
conjunction with the City of London, to ship out to Virginia a
hundred boys and girls starving in the streets.   It was not till
1620 that these children were actually sent, and then only with
difficulty.   The intention was that on arrival in the colony they
should become apprentices, but some of them were ill-disposed
to reach America.   These were just the young people, however,
of whom the City authorities desired to be disburdened, so
eventually a warrant had to be obtained for enforcement of the
transportation, and it was hoped that by placing them under
" severe masters " Virginia might find them useful.   The cost
was not to exceed five hundred pounds.

Captain Yeardley's appointment to be the new Governor of
Virginia was made on 18th November, 1618, for a term of th ee
years.   On 24th November he was knighted by James I at
Newmarket, and this honour (wrote a contemporary) " hath set
him up so high that he flaunts it up and down the streets in
extraordinary bravery, with fourteen or fifteen fair liveries after
him."   Reading into the minds of Sir Thomas Smith and his
anxious colleagues, we can hazard the opinion that the London
Company were careful to instruct Yeardley that the uneasy

---

[1] Originally he had come out: o Virginia " a worthy gentleman "
with Captain John Smith.

planters must be handled with great consideration. The time had come to suffer them a representative voice ; concessions had to be made from a somewhat haughty attitude, and it was a gesture in the direction of caution to send over one who had previously shown his successful administrative ability, and was not by temperament too harsh.

Taking with him two ships and about three hundred men and boys, having spent most of three thousand pounds on this venture, Yeardley sailed in January, and after the usual three months at sea duly arrived. It was then that he learned how narrowly had Argall evaded him. And one more illuminating ray on the curiously twisted characters of that deceitful age is the fact that Lord Rich, afterward to become the Earl of Warwick who commanded during the Civil War a fleet against his King, was at the back of Argall's mischief and safe escape. Rich was a thorn in the side of James I, but he was an energetic and able person in any matter of seafaring, if a corrupt member of the very London Company which owed something to that King's support. Indeed, the more one studies the seventeenth-century psychology, the less comprehensible does it become to us moderns. As further sidelights, one has only to instance such a man as Thomas Gage, who may be mentioned merely in passing. This " English American," as he has been called, belonged to a Sussex Roman Catholic family, which had suffered for its faith but had not lost either all its property or its social position at Court, yet sought careers in the Spanish service and fought for the Roman Catholic cause in Flanders. While other of his countrymen went to Virginia, Gage had the same adventurous zeal for Spanish America, and finally ended up, after some doubtful deeds, as a convert to the Puritan section in the Church of England, where he was given a living in Kent and afterward served as chaplain to General Venables in the Cromwellian expedition to the West Indies. Such were the strangely-mingled careers of men in a curiously muddled and abnormal age.

Yeardley's return that spring day marked a new epoch in the history of American colonization. He brought with him constructive peace and a lasting hope. The Council being increased by the names of Captain Francis West, Captain

Nathaniel Powell, John Pory, John Rolfe and two others, he set to work with all expedition to convene the General Assembly. This was strictly in accordance with the instructions of the London Company, whose hands had certainly been forced by the Brewster crisis. Thus we come to that hot, sultry summer's day of 30th July, 1619, which is the most important date between the founding of Virginia and the final separation of colonial America from English dominion.

For lack of a more suitable building, there was convened on this day in the small wooden church of Jamestown the first legislative body that ever met on the North American continent. For twelve years the colonists had endured miseries and calamities of all kinds. Every man's letters homeward had been examined, lest the true unhappy state of Virginia should be revealed, and no further candidates for martyrdom come forth. With the fewest of exceptions, planters had not been permitted a return to England, but were kept in the colony by force. And one man who indeed was sent the King's pass had to receive it closely made up in a garter lest it should have been seized. While Dale (to quote the expression of Sir Edward Sandys, referred to later) had built " upon the foundation " of Gates, and " with great care and constant severity " the colony had been largely reclaimed from its idle and dissolute conditions, yet the twelve years had not merely cost the London Company the sum of seventy thousand pounds, but endless worry.

The General Assembly consisted of Sir George Yeardley, the Council, plus two burgesses elected from each incorporation and plantation. Thus to herald this dawn of liberty came a couple of representatives from Jamestown itself, Charles City, Henrico, Kecoughtan, Martin's plantation, Martin's Hundred, Argall's Gift, Flowerdieu Hundred, Smith's Hundred,[1] as well as the plantations of Captain Lawne and Captain Warde. They gathered together in the choir of the church arranged in order of rank, yet with so little regard for God's house, and so much respect for the custom of the English House of Commons, as to keep their hats on. After opening this historic assembly with prayer, the oath of supremacy was administered and they

[1] Called after Sir Thomas Smith, but afterwards changed its name to Southampton Hundred.

got down to business. It was ordered to levy a tax of one pound of tobacco on every man and man servant above the age of sixteen, the proceeds to be distributed to the Speaker, Clerk, Sergeant of the Assembly, and the Provost-Marshal of Jamestown, for their great pains and labour.

The session continued until 4th August, when, owing to the extreme heat and " the alteratation " of the health of the Governor and divers members, it was finally resolved that this should be the last day. But during this momentous series of meetings orders were agreed upon concerning the rights of several burgesses to their seats ; committees were appointed to examine into the Great Charter, the orders and laws sent by the Governor ; and some petitions were read concerning the erecting of a University and College, as well as changing the "savage" name of Kecoughtan plantation. The price of tobacco was fixed at three shillings per pound for the best grade, and eighteen pence for the second best. Legislation was enacted for the conversion of the Indians to Christianity, the planting of corn, mulberry trees, silk flax, hemp and vines, for the general ordering of the colony, and for " every man's private conceipt." The wearing of excessive apparel was taxed, and on Sundays attendance at divine service with sermons, forenoon and afternoon, was compulsory.

And, as indicative of that barbarous age, it was decided that Thomas Garnet, servant to Captain W. Powell, should be condemned to stand four days with his ears nailed to the pillory for extreme neglect of his master's business and impudent abuse. Young Captain Henry Spelman—he who, it will be remembered, had ten years previously come out here " being in despleasuer of my frendes," but had since become a valuable interpreter of the Indians' language — was also punished. Having confessed that he had spoken to the Indians very irreverently and maliciously against the government, he was degraded of his title at the head of his troop, and condemned to seven years' servitude to the colony as the Governor's interpreter.

Thus, with the consent of Sir Thomas Smith (as wise a sexagenarian as London ever held), but without any regal ratification, these with other laws were put into force, and a self-government began for the first time in the story of overseas expansion.   Here not merely was inaugurated the principle of rule by representation, which was finally to bring about the Great Revolution a century and a half later, but was introduced the forerunner of the United States' post-Revolution form of government, not less than of the parliaments in Canada, Australia and South Africa.

During this year, 1619, no fewer than a dozen ships brought twelve hundred and sixty-one persons to Virginia, making the number of English colonists about twenty-four hundred.   There were five hundred head of cattle, besides horses and goats, together with an infinite number of pigs.   During the next three years of Yeardley's office liberty began to take the place of tyranny.   Those who had come out before Sir Thomas Dale's departure were made free ; the cruel laws were abrogated ; the settlers could choose and cultivate their own dividends of land ; the General Assembly was held every year, and altogether a grand change had taken place for the good of all.   Some inhabitants on dying had left valuable bequests.   Thus Mary Robinson gave two hundred pounds toward founding a church ; Nicholas Ferrar left by his will three hundred pounds for the College to be paid when ten infidel children were placed in it ; and one anonymous donor assigned five hundred and fifty pounds in gold for bringing up the children of infidels in the true religion.   But it was in this year that a ship brought over the first African negroes which Virginia ever received.

Great changes were being set afoot in London at this time. On 28th April, 1619, Sir Thomas Smith, after a long and one of the most successful business careers that have ever been lived —successful, that is to say, both for immediate profit and permanent, world-wide influence—declined to stand again as candidate for Treasurer of the Virginia Company.   These dozen years had been strenuous enough in all conscience, even had he not been concerned with other interests.   He had recently been made one of the Navy Commissioners ; he was still actively occupied with the far more remunerative East India Company ; and he had become extremely annoyed over a certain domestic affair, the marriage of his son John.   The latter in November, 1618, when only eighteen years old, and without his father's consent, had married Lady Isabella Rich, sister of the second Earl of Warwick. This family incident not unnaturally created in him a bitter feeling toward the man who had been intriguing with Argall.

Now, consequent on Smith's resignation, the London Virginia Company became split up into three chief factions : (1) those men who were led by Robert Rich, Earl of Warwick ; (2) those who consisted principally of the East India Company merchants and other business men, this section being led by Sir Thomas Smith ; and (3) a party led by Sir Edwin Sandys. Jealousy, let it be remembered, is one of the most frequent causes of quarrels among men and nations, but not least when it centres round worldly success. The undoubted prosperity of the East India business men had aroused such animosity that factions one and three were agreeable to concentrate and back up the candidature of Sir Edwin Sandys. Smith and his friends, however, put forward Alderman Robert Johnson as well as that other well-known shipping enthusiast, Sir John Wolstenholme. When the election results were made known, it was found that Johnson received eighteen votes, Wolstenholme twenty-three, but Sandys fifty-nine. The latter accordingly became Treasurer (with the effect of Governor) of the London Company. Appreciation of Smith's valuable services was, however, shown by presenting him with two thousand acres of land in Virginia, and he was also made President of the Somers Islands concern. The Bermudas charter had been granted on 29th June, 1615, to various noblemen and others incorporated under the title of The Governor and Company of the City of London for the Plantation of the Somers Islands, who alone had the power to make laws conformable to the laws of England.

Incidentally, one striking event showed that while those islands might cause pigs to prosper, they were probably not erroneously known as Devils' Islands. For during October, 1616, five planters of Bermudas were so convinced that famine was approaching that they resolved to quit. They therefore copied the example of the great Somers and built themselves a sea-going craft. This, however, was ridiculously small : a two-tonner, little bigger than a double wherry of the time.

Besides sail, they furnished themselves with four oars, a sack of biscuits and a barrel of water. In this crazy craft they made the passage safely to England, meeting with no bad weather. The voyage took twenty days, and the admiration for this exploit caused so great a sensation in London as to win them pardon for desertion. Nor did Count de Gondomar forget to mention this plucky escape to his Spanish sovereign. At the same time great fears as to Bermudas ever being profitable exercised the minds of Smith and his friends anew.

Let us now, however, see how Virginia under a new order of things was to work out her destiny.

The London they left behind them

This contemporary print of 1647 shows the London of Captain John Smith's time. The old London Bridge, Tower, Royal Exchange, and some of the City churches are all indicated

CHAPTER XVI

THE NEW ERA

THE outstanding personality in the London management of Virginia affairs being, for some time, Sir Edwin Sandys, it is of immediate interest to inquire into the forces which had moulded a nature that was in turn to influence the colony. He was a man of fifty-six years, and of the highest moral character, but with a strong Puritan bias ; his father, who was Bishop of London and afterward Archbishop of York, was strongly Puritan in his sympathies likewise. Edwin went up to Corpus Christi College, Oxford, where he formed a strong friendship with Richard Hooker, a man about ten years older than himself. The grave, learned and " judicious Hooker," with his simple, humble nature but erudite genius, the stout defender of episcopacy on historical grounds, a theologian with a mind noted for impartiality, appealed to Sandys' stern seriousness.

Edwin Sandys became a Member of Parliament, and was a believer in free trade rather than the privileges of the great trading corporations ; yet ever since March, 1607, he had been one of the London Virginia Company's Councillors, and ten years later had been chosen to assist Sir Thomas Smith in the Company's management. He was likewise a member of the East India Company and of the Somers Islands Company. When at length Smith's administration was called into discussion and Argall's arbitrary administration had well-nigh ruined Virginia, and the consequent discontent had cleft the London Council so that Sandys was elected as Treasurer, the choice was justified by business experience and sound uprightness. He was no respecter of persons, where the question was a matter of right or wrong. And if his outlook was narrow, it was at least straight.

o

He began his new duties by instituting a thorough examination of Virginian accounts, which had all this while been in the hands of Sir Thomas Smith, with the collateral danger of self-satisfaction and self-enrichment. Sandys had the courage definitely to accuse the mighty Smith not only of mismanagement, but of keeping down Virginia's prosperity and helping himself to the plantation's products. With wisdom did Sandys get together a committee to codify the Company's regulations, settle a form of government for the colony, appoint magistrates and officers with definite assignment of their duties. It was he who secured the exclusion from England of foreign tobacco, and thus by discouraging Spanish colonial produce assisted Virginian prosperity.

The strong individualism of Thomas Smith had indeed saved Virginia, but his overbearing nature had lulled many of his fellow-councillors into passive acquiescence. His books had been kept carelessly, he was suspected of having embezzled quite a useful amount of the eighty thousand pounds which had passed through his hands between 1606 and April, 1619. And Argall—the direct cause of Smith's downfall—evaded prosecution and punishment by going off on an expedition against the Algerines. He was discreet enough to keep in the Mediterranean during the years 1620 and 1621, but came home at length, and was even knighted in June of 1622. Such was the unstable standard of Jacobean justice.

Yeardley on arrival in Virginia made it his first care to supply sufficient corn for the colony before concentrating on tobacco. While the General Assembly's acts had to be transmitted to the London Company and read at the latter's next quarterly Court, and could there be confirmed or annulled, yet the abolition of martial law and the introduction of representative parliament had made Virginia singularly happy. During 1619 they raised the finest crop of grain in the colony's history ; nevertheless, the unhealthiness of the Jamestown locality, and the sickness brought over by ships, caused three hundred deaths that year. But matters were settling down ; husbands, wives, servants " for publike service," were all going out from England. Religion was not forgotten, worship was encouraged and " two persons unknowne have given faire Plate and Ornaments for two Communion Tables,[1] the one at the College, the other at the Church of Mistris Mary Robinson." King James had already issued letters to the Bishops of English dioceses to collect money for the erection of the Virginia college that should educate Indian children in the Christian faith, and nearly fifteen hundred pounds had been obtained.

Through Sandys' efforts ten thousand acres of land were reserved for the university at Henrico. This was intended to be the site for both an Indian college and a seminary of learning for the colonists' children. A hundred men were accordingly sent out to settle on these college lands as tenants, half the profits of their labours being given to themselves, but the other half applied to the building fund, the maintenance of tutors and scholars. A man's labour was reckoned as worth ten pounds (about one hundred pounds in modern money) a year, and labour plus land meant for Virginia the gradual creation of wealth. Thus, while every conceivable influence—ecclesiastical, regal, financial and purely personal—was being exerted to send forth emigrants from England, Sandys was portioning off definite areas of ground. He set aside three thousand acres for the Governor's revenue, and twelve thousand for the Company. It was he also who in 1619 proposed that a hundred maids, " young and uncorrupt," should be sent out as potential wives, and thus enable lonely men to rear families on the land contentedly. Sandys' management of Virginia, with his constructive and stabilizing policy and financial sense, had the double result of ensuring a future for the colony and attracting still more people from none too settled England. And by obtaining a passage for the latter aboard empty ships bound

[1] Besides the chalice " with a cover and case, a trencher plate for the bread," there were also " a damask table-cloth," and " a carpet of crimson velvet." In February, 1628, Temperance, Lady Yeardley, wife of Sir George, delivered to the Court at Jamestown the following gifts which had been sent from England for use of the college : one silver-gilt cup for Holy Communion and two small chalices in a cloth-of-gold cover ; one crimson velvet carpet with a gold and silver fringe ; one white damask Communion cloth with buttons ; four " divinity bookes " with brass bosses. Mrs. Robinson's gifts to the church at Southampton Hundred consisted of one Communion silver-gilt cup and two small chalices in a black leather cover, " one yellow & blew cheiny Damaske carpett wth. a silke fringe," one white damask Communion cloth and one surplice.

out ultimately for Newfoundland fishing, it was possible to send out planters to Virginia at a cost of six pounds each.

The interference of the Crown in November, 1619, somewhat embarrassed the Company, when the King ordered them to send out one hundred dissolute persons to Virginia. Shipowners, however, were not eager to risk their vessels through the wintry seas, but by good luck one large vessel was obtained and the mutinous crowd was dispatched in the following February at the Company's expense. And when the rapidly-approaching time came for the better-class Englishmen to seek solace in America, these were more favourably disposed toward New England than to a territory so stained by criminal characters. The practice, which existed down to the twentieth century, of parents shipping off to British colonies the unsatisfactory sons of the family, was thus four centuries old and of royal and ancient encouragement, but narrow-sighted none the less.

Another wrong conceptionof Stuart times was in regard to national finance. Of the discontent which culminated in the Civil War few causes were more outstanding than the high-handed, arbitrary proceedings on the part of the Customs officials, who were supported by royal authority. These conditions were bad about the time Sandys came into power, but they were worse in the reign of Charles I, and brought about a mighty revolution, just as in 1775 the same kind of arbitrariness, the same assault against human independence by means of taxation, created American colonial independence. The great value of history lies in the lessons which it affords to posterity in demonstrating that certain human actions will bring about particular results. Sooner or later the oppressed will always rise and overthrow tyranny, whether expressed by governor or government ; the same set of premises in different epochs will present the same conclusions as before. And we shall find that a generation not overdisposed to study the past, and draw inferences, will go on making the identical mistakes of its forefathers. Even in this twentieth century politicians have still to learn that elementary truth. But had the statesmen of the late eighteenth century been as well supplied with the principles derived from historical study, it is conceivable that the chapters following the date of 1775 would make vastly different reading.

The great struggle between the Stuart Kings and Parliament centred round this matter of finance, and especially taxation, of which the Ship Money trouble is a familiar instance. At the back of this trouble was the practice of farming out the English taxes, a system copied from the French. Sir Thomas Smith's father had himself amassed a great fortune by this farming. And while the early seventeenth-century Customs of England showed a steady increase owing to colonial expansion, especially in regard to Virginian tobacco, yet it was not until the Restoration period that the English revenue system was overhauled, reconstructed and put on a healthier basis. Notwithstanding that by the letters-patent of 23rd May, 1609, the Virginia Company was granted for twenty-one years freedom from all Customs on goods imported into England, yet the farmers of the Customs (of whom that wealthy merchant Sir Thomas Wolstenholme was another) demanded their sixpence on every pound of tobacco and thus robbed the planters of their full fruits of labour.

Excepting a few interlopers Virginia had so far kept all trade in the hands of the investing adventurers, but there was in 1620 still a shortage of clergy, with only five parsons to minister to those eleven boroughs or parishes which we have seen sending representatives to the General Assembly. Here again a more constructive policy was established by the Company ordering a hundred acres to be set off for a glebe, thus providing out of the land's produce at least two hundred pounds a year for the benefice. The Company were now in a position to ask the Bishop of London for more ministers of religion.

When at the end of May, 1620, Sandys completed his term of office, the colony was then on a substantial basis, and (writing to the Marquis of Buckingham on 7th June) he declared that in one year with eight thousand pounds he had done more for Virginia's advancement than had been achieved by Sir Thomas Smith in twelve years at ten times that expense. Indeed, the Company were so pleased that they wished to elect Sandys again, but the King sniffing sedition in the Puritan's influence vetoed the appointment, and suggested one of the following :

Sir Thomas Smith, Sir Thomas Roe, Alderman Johnson, or Mr. Maurice Abbot, a merchant.

We thus have the recrudescence of bitterness and the heralding of further trouble. For the Company took the revolutionary attitude of deliberately opposing the King's interference, and they chose that handsome middle-aged patron of poets, and friend of Shakespeare, Henry Wriothesley, Earl of Southampton. The latter, being also a personal friend of Sandys, ensured for the next year internal peace. Assisted by that eminent lawyer and man of letters, John Selden (another independent thinker, whose liberalism won him a short spell of imprisonment in 1621), a new patent was prepared, whereby the title of the Company's principal officer was to be changed from Treasurer to Governor. Sir Thomas Smith and Argall allied with the Earl of Warwick—Smith having made up his quarrel with the last mentioned—and Sandys was suspected of intending to establish a Puritan republic in America. It was even charged against Sandys that he had misused the Company's funds and issued false information concerning Virginia. On 16th June, 1621, he was imprisoned in the Tower of London, but the King released him a month later.

The pettiness and mutual mistrust among these otherwise able men still continue to surprise us. It is possible that, additional to the unsettled atmosphere of the political times, the lack of healthy athletics may be partly responsible for a significant lack of what to-day we should call sportsmanship and gentlemanly conduct. Captain Brewster, during the year 1620, brought his case into court, appealing against Argall's notorious sentence ; and it was decided that Brewster had committed no act worthy of the death penalty, and that the manner of trial by martial law in time of peace was unlawful. Nor was the Spanish danger yet passed, for the ship *Margaret and John*, after eleven weeks on her way to Virginia, had called at the West Indian Island of Nevis to refresh. Her eighty passengers, having been " pestered in this unwholesome ship," had the unpleasant experience of finding their vessel attacked by two Spanish men-of-war. Ten of the English were killed or died of their wounds, sixteen others were injured, but the *Margaret and John* (one hundred and sixty tons, armed with eight iron guns and one falcon) eventually reached the James River.

Yeardley's period of successful governing was now drawing to a close. The Company in London therefore chose Sir Francis Wyatt, who was connected by marriage with the Sandys family. Stith has wrongly referred to Wyatt as " a young " gentleman, but in fact the new Governor was forty-five years old. Knighted in 1603, Wyatt came of a good Kentish family, was like de la Warr educated at Oxford, as were so many of those leading men who helped Virginia in her early days. A man of integrity and fair fortune, just of character and noble of carriage, he represented the best type of ruler whom England could send out at this time. He sailed with nine ships, and reached Jamestown at the end of October, 1621, entering upon his duties on 18th November. With him went as chaplain his brother, Hawte Wyatt; William Clayborne sent forth as surveyor; Dr. John Pott as physician; and George Sandys, the noted poet and traveller, a younger brother of Sir Edwin. George was to act as Treasurer in Virginia and look after the Company's interests. Remuneration was made by allotting so much land and so many tenants to each official. A Vice-Admiral was also appointed, his services being required to see that Virginian shipping was well managed, and that vessels were not improperly there delayed.

But Virginia was now attracting foreigners as well. Walloons and Frenchmen were anxious to go out and plant. To this request the London Company had no objection provided the number did not exceed three hundred, that they took the oath of allegiance, and conformed to the rules of government established in the Church of England. Land would be granted to them in the principal towns, boroughs and corporations. Thus during the year 1621 more than two hundred Walloons and French promised to go. And among the State Papers in London is preserved the following document, which is written in the form of a round robin :

" We promise my Lord Ambassador of the Most Serene King of Great Britain to go and inhabit in Virginia, a land under His Majesty's obedience, as soon as conveniently may be, and this under the conditions to be carried out in the articles we have communicated to the said Ambassador, and not otherwise, on the faith of which we have unanimously signed this present with our sign manual."

It was endorsed by Sir Dudley Carleton. These people number two hundred and twenty-seven, consisting of fifty-five men, forty-one women, one hundred and twenty-nine children, and two servants. The signatures and calling of each person are appended ; the person stating whether married, and if so the number of his children. It is characteristic of the educational standard that ten per cent. could not sign their names but made their mark. All sorts of vocations were here represented. Thus there was " Mousnier de la Montagne, medical student, marrying man," " Paul de Pasar, weaver, wife and two children," " Francois Fourdrin, leather dresser, young man," " Pierre Cornille, Vine-dresser, young man," " Pierre Quesnée, brewer, marrying man," " Jacque Conne, tiller of the earth, wife and two children." There were such different occupations mentioned as apothecary and surgeon, woollen draper, porter, hatter, weaver, labourer, wool carder, musician, serge maker, student in theology, dyer, locksmith, shuttle-worker. Thus America was calling to Europe and the Old World was being drawn to the New. Of great use were the vine-dressers and the others to a young colony about to extend its productiveness, and on 8th April, 1623, George Sandys writing from Newport News reported that the " vinerouns," settled together at Elizabeth City, were being employed about the silkworms, and he hoped to send silk to England next year.

By the end of 1621 the London Company had even to suffer from its own success. The cost of sending out so many people this year, transporting Sir Francis Wyatt, officers, tenants and servants had completely exhausted the public treasury. The lotteries had brought in twenty-nine thousand pounds. But Parliament had complained that this system of obtaining money became abused, so by order of the Privy Council on 4th March, 1621, lotteries were suspended. It was therefore suggested to the London Company on 12th April by no less a person than Captain John Smith that " it could not but much advance

Philadelphia

From an early print

the Plantacion in the popular opinion of the Common Subjects to have a faire and perspicuous history compiled " of Virginia. A four-page prospectus was accordingly issued to the nobility and gentry, and John Smith thus began the compilation of *The Generall Historie of Virginia*, which appeared three years later, and was so successful that further editions were soon called for.

While Sir George Yeardley, with his gentle and sensitive nature, was content to remain in Virginia, on whose Council he continued to serve, Sir Francis Wyatt was busy carrying out the London instructions, which included maintaining the religion of the Church of England " as near as may be," and (*inter alia*) " to forget old quarrels now buried." He had brought with him a new constitution for Virginia, dated 24th July, 1621, the intention being " to settle such a form of government there as may be to the greatest benefit and comfort of the people and whereby all injustice, grievances and oppression may be prevented." By authority from the King the London Company ordered that from henceforward there should be two supreme Councils in Virginia : (1) The Council of State ; this was to assist the Governor and was appointed by the London Council ; (2) The General Assembly, which was not to meet more than once a year ; in this assembly the Governor was to have " always a negative voice." The General Assembly was to make general laws and orders for the colony's good, but not contrary to the laws and customs of England.

The establishment of the Church and Ministry of England had not taken due effect in Virginia, and it was part of Wyatt's duty now to see that this was done, that the Ministers were respected and churches decently accommodated, all gaming, drunkenness and the wearing of excessive apparel suppressed. To this end no person (other than Councillors, or heads of hundreds, with their wives and children) should wear gold on their clothes, or any kind of silk except such as had been raised by their own industry. And the people were to produce only one hundred pounds of tobacco a head. Trial by jury was secured. During Wyatt's first year no fewer than twenty-one vessels reached Virginia, bringing thirteen hundred settlers. A large hospital was erected for the sick, glass works were placed near Jamestown, and there were also ironworks. Italian workmen arrived to make beads, which were the means of trade with the Indians.

Sixty more young and handsome maids, well recommended for their virtue and upbringing, were sent out from England, each as an intended wife and bearing a testimonial. The price of each woman was one hundred and twenty pounds of tobacco at first, though it was afterward raised. The current price of tobacco being then three shillings a pound, a wife cost eighteen pounds, or the equivalent of nearly two hundred pounds in modern money. This bartering for brides seems to us strange and grossly commercial, but the Company's coffers had to be filled somehow, and this was thought a good method. Poor people in England, who were a burden to the parishes also were to arrive and swell the fast growing population. Those who subscribed to the fund for sending over the young women were known as " adventurers for the magazine of the maides." But the following record of indentures, dated 25th September, 1622, shows under what conditions a man went out to Virginia as a servant :

" To all to whom these presents shall come, greeting in our
    Lord God Everlasting.
Know yee that I Wessell Webling, son of Nicolas Webling of London, Brewer, for & in consideration that I have been furnished & sett out & am to bee transported unto Virginia, at ye costs & charges of Edward Bennett of London, marchant, & his associates, & for & in consideration that they have promised & covenanted to maintain me with sufficient meat, drinke, & apparell, doe by these presents bind myself an apprentise unto ye said Edward Bennett for the full terme of three yeares to begin the feast of St. Michaell the Archangell next after the date of these presents. And I doe promise & binde myself to doe & perform all the said terme of my aprentishippe true & faithful service . . . & to bee tractable & obedient . . . & at the end of the said terme of three yeares the said Edward Bennett do promise to give unto ye said apprentice an house & 50 acres of land in Virginia. . . ."

We pass now to the matter of John Bargrave, which was to have the effect of still more inciting royal interference and

changing the whole colonial structure. Bargrave in the year
1618 had become planter of a private section of Virginia. He
obtained a patent from the London Company for free trade, and
sent along both ships and servants. But during the régime of
Sir Thomas Smith most of his estate was violently taken by the
Company, and as a result of seized shipping, detaining of goods
and fraudulent selling of the same, John Bargrave lost sixty-six
hundred pounds. The result was that on 12th April, 1622, the
latter petitioned the Privy Council, begging that a commission
from the King might be appointed to examine, rectify and
order this colonial governing, so that it might be fixed in
a dependency on the Crown of England. While Bargrave
admitted that during the three years now ending the business
of the Virginian plantation could not have been better managed
(since Sir Thomas Smith resigned), and better results had been
effected at less cost, yet he was determined to be recompensed
for what had been suffered under that tyrannical tenure which
had brought many men to slavery and death. It was iniquitous
that while Virginia during the period mentioned consisted only
of public servants sent out by the lotteries, and of divers
private plantations, the Company should be able to dispose
of any estate.

The King's immediate reaction to Bargrave was not,
however, favourable. On 17th June, 1622, James desired the
Privy Council to dismiss the suit which Bargrave brought
against Sir Thomas Smith, Alderman Johnson and others, for
unjust practices and personal loss through mismanagement.
The King, indeed, took the line that Bargrave seemed to have
no other end in view than to blemish Sir Thomas's reputation.
Instructions were now given that if Bargrave still continued
contentious the Privy Council were to punish him. This was
a temporary defeat, nominal rather than actual. At least it
served to draw attention to the danger of colonizing on a private
commerical basis rather than on a strictly royal or national
system. Bargrave was thus preparing the King's mind for an
inevitable change. Disappointed of rewards from gold and
silver mines, the get-rich-quick London merchants had caused
Virginia to plant tobacco even excessively, and to sell much
of it on the European continent, thus depriving England of

Customs. So we find the London Company being rebuked by the Privy Council for not importing all tobacco into England, and in the latter half of 1622 the Company were advised to breed silkworms in the colony, and set up silk factories, since this " rich and solid commodity " was preferable to tobacco.

A discerner of the times could have guessed that big events were not far distant. The constant scandals which defiled the Court of James I inclined many toward Puritanism who otherwise would scarcely have been attracted, and by a curious influence united many hitherto separated by political or class distinctions. Drunkenness and debauchery are bound ere long to create disgust and an extremely narrow rectitude. The unquestioning reverence for royal rulers was gone, these people already born would live to see the day when a Stuart King would be executed in Whitehall. The Renaissance and the Reformation had passed on, but the love of liberty had increased. The sale of monopolies had become unpopular, Parliament was inclined to suppress these privileges, and there was a fight going on between Parliament and King for obtaining the greater authority, a contest for the subject's wider liberty. While the King strenuously resisted, and was as keenly opposed, it became in fact largely a fight between himself and the London Virginia Company ; for many of the principal Parliamentarians were the leading men of this Company.

Thus the atmosphere and setting were fast being prepared for that moment when the King would put his hand down firmly and take Virginia to himself, away from the men who mismanaged and made factions among themselves. Truly Sir Edward Sandys had brought about a great improvement in Virginia's affairs ; he was thinking of no sudden money-snatching tobacco deal, but of a growing concern. And his kinsman George Sandys was in full sympathy. Writing home from Jamestown on 3rd March, 1621, the latter from his well-informed official position was able to say : " If we overcome this yeere the yronworkes, glasse-workes, salt-works ; take order for the plentifull setting of corne ; restraine the quantitie of tobacco, and mend it in the qualitie, plant vines, mulbery-trees, fig-trees, pomegranats, potatoes, cotton-woolles ; and erect a faire Inne in Iames Citie (to the setting up of which I doubt not but wee shall raise fifteen hundred or two thousand pounds : for every man gives willingly towards this and other publique workes) you have enough for this yeere." But it might be almost too late. Would it not be advisable, the mind of James ruminated, to end the present unhappy Company now ?

And while the " wisest fool in Christendom " was pondering there came another of those dramatic situations which instantly gave Virginia's history another twist.

CHAPTER XVII

CHANGES AND CHANCES

IT will be recollected that the Council in London had from
the very first impressed the Virginian leaders with the
necessity of winning the Indians over by kindness ; and,
since the Pocahontas marriage, the fraternizing of red and
white people had become so developed that the natives were
often entertained in the planters' houses.

This was a foolish policy, and had to be paid for dearly. It
was on 13th July, 1622, that a ship from Virginia reached the
Thames with the devastating news that the savages had
surprised and slain three hundred and forty-seven English,
owing to the latter's supine negligence in living scattered among
straggling houses. The massacre had occurred on 22nd March ;
scores of families had been brutally murdered, the Indians
possessing themselves of the colonists' arms and weapons. But
apart from the horror which this news aroused, it created in
England a sense of disgrace and shame, and a self-accusation
that no other nation would have allowed itself so grievously to
be deceived.

According to the evidence, given after the massacre, by
Robert Poole and Edward Grindon, gentlemen, on oath, the
whole blame rested on the precedents inaugurated by Captain
John Smith, Sir Thomas Dale and others, adding that Yeardley
was most cautious. Since the death of the Great Powhatan,
Opechancanough had become the big Indian Chief, and with
him Sir Francis Wyatt had immediately confirmed existing
agreements. But it was the treacherous and subtle mind within
Opechancanough which conceived the idea that it was about
time this rapidly-increasing colony of pale-faced men and
women should be wiped out ; they were surely about to take
away the red man's territory for ever.

The Indian organization and strategy were perfect. They borrowed the settlers' boats, brought venison, turkeys, fish and fruits to the settlers' houses, and in some cases even sat down with them at breakfast. And then with the colonists' own tools the Indians slew barbarously, with no respect for age or sex, slew with amazing suddenness not merely those indoors but those working in the fields. That veteran Captain Nathaniel Powell was among the killed, and indeed no fewer than six of the Council perished. The massacre had been well-nigh universal, at Captain Barclay's plantation sixty-six miles from Jamestown, at Henrico, Charles City, Flowerdieu Hundred, Southampton Hundred, and so on. Such enterprises as the ironworks were now ruined in one action.

This terrible blow to the Company in London had the most stunning effect, and no one felt it more than Captain John Smith. The latter offered his services and begged " if you please I may be transported with a hundred Souldiers and thirty Sailers by the next Michaelmas . . . we would endevour to inforce the Salvages to leave their Country, or bring them in that feare and subjection that every man should follow their businesse securely." But there were such factions and despondency that nothing came of it. The massacre had brought to reality the weakness in having so many small plantations separated, and the unrelenting suspicion with which the native Indian must be regarded ; so all the little outlying settlements were given up, and the colony was concentrated into a few easily-defended localities, such as Shirley, Flowerdieu and Southampton Hundreds and Jamestown.

The Privy Council now allowed the London Company to send out for the colonists barrels of powder and a stock of old arms from the Tower of London, such as were unfit for European warfare but serviceable against savages. By December, 1622, notwithstanding all the deaths by massacre and otherwise, there were still about twenty-five hundred colonists, one thousand cattle, as well as goats and swine. The industries connected with ironworks, wine-growing, silks, saw-mills, salt-pans were again a healthy counter-influence to unlimited tobacco growing. And Christmas Day saw no fewer than seventeen sailing ships up the James River. Thus, in spite of everything, Virginia was still developing as a producer of wealth.

Now about this time Captain Nathaniel Boteler (or Butler), the eldest son of a Bedfordshire gentleman, and a member of the Council for Virginia, arrived up the James River. For the last three years he had been serving as Governor of Bermudas, and now on his way home to England he came to have a look at Virginia. This able and experienced sea captain, who took part in the expeditions to Cadiz (1625) and the Ile de Rhé (1627), was author of the well-known *Dialogues*.[1] He was a profligate sea-dog like many of his contemporaries, and led a high old time during the weeks sojourning in Virginian territory. But after a fortnight's stay with Sir Francis Wyatt in Jamestown, Boteler with Captain William Powell took an armed expedition against the Chickahominies, who fled in fear.

In February, 1623, Boteler sailed for England, where he immediately issued his essay entitled *The Unmasking of Virginia*, which was yet another hard blow at the colony and the cause of one more serious faction. The unfavourable report which a man of his high standing made to the King could not fail to have a baneful effect. But we must bear in mind the bias of those scheming persons, and remember that, belonging to the Earl of Warwick's faction, he was anxious to damn the existing régime. Boteler, however, was not far from the truth in stating that Virginia was mostly settled on marshes, that it was full of infectious bogs, and thus unhealthy, that near the shores it was so shallow in the James River that craft could not go alongside. (The latter statement, none the less, suggests that since the first pioneer days either the river had silted up, or the draught of Atlantic shipping had increased.) But there was some exaggeration in stating that for new-comers from England there was no guest-house (that is, hospital) or inn, and nothing charitable done, that many died under the hedges and there remained unburied, that the cost of meal and corn was too high, their houses the worst he had ever seen, and scattered by the interposition of creeks and swamps. He was convinced

---

[1] *Six Dialogues about Sea Services between an High Admiral and a Captain at Sea*, which remained in manuscript form only, till their publication in 1685.

that the colony was quite inadequately fortified, the ironworks wasted, the glass furnaces at a standstill ; Henrico and Charles City were abandoned to the Indians. A petition to the King by Captain F. West, John Brewer and other " ancient " planters, poor and distressed, was yet another means of impressing the King that something drastic must be done to alter the existing management in London.

At the same time dismal letters managed to reach England from private sources. For instance, on 24th January, 1623, George Harrison, who owned land, wrote from Jamestown to his brother John[1] in London that there were not more than ten men and boys now living in Jamestown of all those servants who had come out in the *Seaflower*, that more had since died than were slain in the massacre. God had indeed cast a heavy hand on them ; they cried for mercy on their sins. And while Harrison sent home three hogsheads of tobacco by the ship *Little James,* he recommended that his relative should send out as " a private venture " good wines, butter, cheese, sugar, soap. John Harrison did send on 16th September in the ship *Marmaduke* goods for his brother, and the invoice still exists. They arrived at Virginia in good condition, but in the following April George had a duel with Richard Stephens, another colonist, and received a small cut in the knee. This became fatal, yet the jury at the inquest after the post-mortem examination affirmed that George died of a natural disease. Finally, in August, 1624, power of attorney was given by John Harrison of London to James Carter, master of the ship *Anne* to dispose of the unexpired time of George's seven servants in Virginia, as well as his effects generally.

In the meanwhile the Governor, Council and Assembly represented to the King that Boteler's statements were slanders and notorious untruths, that Boteler's spleen arose through his not having been admitted to the Council, that " more than Egyptian slavery and Scythian cruelty " had been exercised on the colonists by those laws written in blood during the period of Sir Thomas Smith's government. The people breathed execrable curses on Sir Thomas. Ministers of religion there

[1] John Harrison was a wealthy London citizen, who was knighted in 1641. His daughter married a nephew of Sir Thomas Smith.

P

were, but not in orders. Rather than live under the Thomas Smith kind of government, the Assembly preferred to be hanged.

We mentioned in a previous chapter the anonymous gift of five hundred and fifty pounds. Actually nothing very definite had resulted from this. The Council, in accordance with that strange Stuart mentality, used this sum together with other money in employing eighty labourers to set up ironworks, the profits therefrom to be applied to the education of thirty Indian children, but the truth was that the suspecting Indian parents were reluctant to have their offspring so educated. And what added to the irony of the Virginian situation was the fact that only a month after the massacre, and before the news could reach London, a thanksgiving sermon " for the happie success of the affaires in Virginia this last yeare " was preached at the London Company's desire by the Rev. Patrick Copland, in the Church of St. Mary-le-Bow, Cheapside. Mr. Copland was to have gone out to Virginia as Rector of the intended college for the conversion of Indians, but the massacre stopped this project. It is another instance of the brave women of this time that when Lady Wyatt heard of the wholesale murders she did not hesitate to sail out from England to be at the side of her husband, the Governor, and duly reached Jamestown by December in that well-known ship *Abigail*, which brought over not merely arms to repel Indians but unfortunately also fever, and bad beer made by a man named Dupper, which went " stinking " bad and caused the death of two hundred colonists.

It is possible from contemporary documents to get an accurate and composite picture of what the emigrants saw with their own eyes on the way from England till they settled down on Virginian soil. Some of these ships, apart from being fertile with disease, were so badly built and trimmed that they were positively dangerous. The *Tiger*, for instance, could sail only with the wind on her port side, for she " would not woorke uppon her starr boorde tack," and when caught in a gale she " wold not woorke but laye under the sea," to the ill-health of her passengers outward bound, and the ruination of her tobacco cargo sent to England. A master of any of these ships made himself fairly comfortable at the start, with a clean pair of sheets on the bed in the " great cabin," with a chest for personal property, and a thin deal partition separating him from the boys' cabin. The crew would begin drinking beer at breakfast. Each mess of five men had three small cans of beer and upward at each meal, together with three pounds of bread daily. There were three days a week on which meat was eaten, but sometimes when the voyage became lengthened these had to be restricted to a couple.

Such ships were known to leak so badly as to be compelled to hurry into port and there wait as long as nine weeks, with the loss of forty baskets of bread ruined by sea-water. Engraved in the imaginations of these long-suffering passengers were such vessels as the *Black Bess*, one hundred tons, and the *Elizabeth* of London. The former was commanded by Captain John Powell and called at Cowes for Southampton passengers. Here is a bill of lading in connection with *Elizabeth*, dated 17th December, 1625 :

" Shipped by the grace of God in good order and well condicioned by me Richard Wake in and uppon the good shipp called the " Elizabeth " of London wherof is Mr under God for this present vioage Laurence May and now ridinge at anchor in James River and by God's Grace bound for London in England, To say one Butt one cheast, one hogshead . . ."

No one can envy the shipmaster his task of keeping any sort of discipline among those scalawag crews. The runlets (or round casks), which were sent out, nominally each containing twenty gallons of aqua vitæ and Canary wine, not unusually reached Virginia with nothing but an alcoholic perfume. The sailors had drunk every gallon and replaced the peg ; so an unfortunate planter would presently express his intense disappointment with selected Stuart oaths. And we know that those monotonous, protracted voyages would suddenly be enlivened by quarrels and fights between decks, when a culprit would find stout hands seizing him by the collar of his doublet and thrusting him on to the main deck.

The *Bonny Bess*, which reached Jamestown in September, 1623, brought such a varied collection of passengers that we can see how universally was the colony appealing to England in general. There arrived in her gentlemen, joiners, chandlers, bricklayers, haberdashers, carpenters, husbandmen, vintners, grocers, tallow-chandlers, students from Christ Church, Oxford, goldsmiths, coopers, tailors and others. They came not merely from London and Portsmouth, but also from the counties of Worcestershire, Berkshire, Lancashire, Leicestershire, Hampshire, Somerset, Wiltshire, Surrey, Bedfordshire and Yorkshire. And all, of course, had to take the oath of supremacy and allegiance.

Actions are the outward expression of character, and it is obvious enough that many of these emigrants were an extremely drunken, lascivious lot who slandered with their tongues, cheated with their intellects, and stole one anothers' cattle. Such a " drinkinge and committinge of a ryott " went on at the colony as in England. Scarcely had the ships anchored in the James River and a lighter come off to land the stores, and the passengers gone ashore to recruit their delicate health, than they would begin spreading their disease and bad behaviour imported from England. The drunk and disorderly cases were much the same. In the merry month of May one Robert Ffitts was fined by the colony forty shillings for that he was " disordered in drinke, not beinge able to goe home contrary to the proclamation made againste drunkenness."

The employed would work in the fields till evening, usually protected by some watchful sentinels, while by night the guard would keep vigil at James City for the stealthy Indians. From the open doorways of the rude houses we might have seen shining a candlelight, as a family would be observed seated, supping, with the pewter on the table, the pot of butter, bread and whatever tit-bits had been obtained from a newly-arrived English ship or the colony's actual products. One of the family perchance was dying of dropsy in the next room, having just made his will bequeathing to the church so many pounds of tobacco—the only coinage in existence. In another house the owner would be playing painfully on his viol, with which he had amused his fellow-passengers on the way out. Some, such as Simon Tuching, had been banished and could never see England or Ireland again. " I come of a good kindred," this man used to inform his neighbours. " I dare not show my face where I was born, and I care not if all my kindred were hanged." But it was this very man who had been suspiciously busy getting soundings in the James River and making eager inquiries as to the channels of the other rivers. Spy fever was not the least virulent of Virginia's maladies.

Some of the men who could not endure ill-treatment fled to the savages, but were usually retaken, and then hanged, shot or broken on the wheel. One man for stealing corn was punished by having a bodkin thrust through his tongue, and he was chained to a tree till he starved to death. Officers were punished with suitable severity, as when Captain Richard Quaile not merely had his commission cancelled, but his sword ceremoniously broken ; he was sent out of James City with an axe on his shoulder and brought in again as Richard Quaile, carpenter. With this humble rank he was then placed in the pillory, and his ears nailed thereto. He could afterwards either have his ears cut off, or redeem them by paying a fine equivalent to one thousand pounds of to-day's money.

Similarly Richard Barnes for using " base & detracting speeches concerning " the Governor of Virginia was ordered to be disarmed, his arms broken, his tongue bored through with an awl, and he was then made to pass through a guard of forty men and be " butted " by every one of them till he came to the head of the troop, where he was to be kicked down and footed out of the fort, banished from James City. The whipping-post played an important part, and servants who escaped from their masters but were afterward caught had to receive sometimes as many as five hundred lashes, which almost brought about death.

Among this immoral crowd there was plenty of trouble with the women, whose backbitings and jealousies, lyings and other offences could be fierce. Joan Vincent, wife of William Vincent, slandered Mrs. Alice Boyce by saying the latter had given birth to a bastard. Joan therefore was summoned to appear at the monthly Jamestown Court, and was ordered the penalty of standing in a white sheet and asking Mrs. Boyce's forgiveness in the presence of the church's congregation. But, with feminine pride, Joan refused to accept such humility. And so the wicked tongues in parochial narrow-mindedness went on wagging. No person's character was safe, and of

the fourteen female members belonging to the church seven
were crudely accused of being " Thomas Harris's whores."
Mrs. Margaret Jones, who struck a man with a tobacco stalk,
was condemned to be towed or dragged at the stern of a boat
in the James River from the shore as far as the anchored ship
Margaret and John, and thence to the shore again. Such was
the laxity in regard to weddings that a proclamation had to
be published against marrying without a licence from the
Governor, or being three times asked in the church.

And Eleanor Spragge caused Virginia anxiety by her breach
of promise. Robert Marshall once asked her affectionately :
" Eleanor Spragge, art thou mine ? " " Yes," answered the
woman, " with all my heart. And thou art mine, art thou
not ? " Marshall also said " Yes," whereupon they took each
other's hands and began talking about their wedding apparel,
and having the banns asked. But the unfortunate part of this
romance was that she made a similar engagement to another
man. This led to her appearance before the Court, when she
acknowledged her offence of being committed to two men
simultaneously. It was ordered that on " the next Sabath day
in the tyme of devine service " she should " publickly before the
congregatione acknowledg her offenc . . . and penetently
confessinge her falte shall aske God and the congregatione's
forgiveness. And to prevent the like offence in others, it is
ordered that every minister give notice in his church to all his
parishioners " whenever any man or woman should use words
amounting to a contract of marriage, " though not precise and
legall ; yet soe as may intangle and brede scrouple in their
conveyences, shall for such offenc under goe either corporall
punishment as whippinge or other punishment by fine."

Among other social cases was that of Mr. Ferrar and Mrs.
Jordan living " skandelously " together ; drunkenness, too,
was already a grave evil in America. While such husbands as
Joseph Johnston were made to enter a bond of the equivalent
of four hundred pounds to be of good behaviour, after
continually squabbling and ill-treating his wife, others of more
exalted rank shocked convention by their boisterous conduct.
Captain William Epps, in charge of the Accomac district, and
therefore one who should have set a good example, on a certain

occasion came ashore at Martin-Brandon about eight o'clock in
the evening. He then passed the time till midnight consuming
two or three gallons of wine with six of his friends, and went
to bed intoxicated. And there are not lacking records of those
who after supper would indulge too freely in " a bottle of burnt
clarett wine conteyning five pints," and end up by a violent
altercation, in which everyone called the other a rogue and
knave. So proclamations were made against drunkenness and
swearing, and two men were chosen in every plantation to give
information against such as should offend, and no person of evil
habits was to buy any great quantity of wine. In this wise was
introduced into America the first kind of modified prohibition
against alcohol. But a subsidiary reason was the desire for
economy ; the tipplers were so apt on these carousals to waste
valuable gunpowder. It was further ordered that whereas great
inconvenience had been caused by the hoarding of wine and
drink by certain unsuitable men—in other words profiteering
—thus leaving most of the colony unprovided for, every
plantation must now choose one man as merchant to purchase
for all the plantation ; and no person should go aboard a ship in
Virginia without leave of the Governor or any two Councillors.

The repetition of slanderous males' misdeeds well indicates
how contentious was Virginian life. A man named Capps
called Adam Thorowgood a rogue and thief, and threatened
to have the latter burned with a mark on the shoulder ; men
like Luke Eden did not evade being " laid neck and heele in the
market place " or paying a fine of two hundred pounds of
tobacco for " lewd behavior and unreverent speche used " in
the Council Chamber ; and John Heney, for accusing Captain
Tucker of murder, was condemned by the Court to be whipped
sixty stripes and to ask Tucker's pardon in open Court, as well
as in the public congregation at Elizabeth City.

But still human nature went on in Virginia as everywhere
else in the world. Thomas Hatch had the temerity to say that
a certain colonist had been wrongly put to death. Hatch was
sentenced to be whipped all the way from the fort to the place
where the gallows stood outside, and thence whipped all the
way back. He was then to be set in the pillory, forfeit one of
his ears, and instead of his seven years' service to Sir George

Yeardley ending, the period was to begin afresh. Hatch was one of those so-called " Duty " boys who had been sent over by the London Company in 1619 in the ship of that name. Another of that shipload, Henry Carman, was also just completing his seven years' apprenticeship when he committed a criminal offence and thus had to commence service all over again. But the Court at James City was strict in regard to misdemeanours likewise. Thomas Farley, gentleman, was fined one hundred pounds of tobacco for that he " contrary to ye late Act of the Generall Assembly hath absented himself from cominge to church uppon the Saboth day for the space of three moneths." This negligence caused frequent fines and may seem unreasonable. But no one will deny the justice of punishing the owner of any dwelling who had failed to have his house palisaded against the Indians after a certain date.

These and other examples are quoted to show the domestic side of the growing colony, whose human character was not to be altered when very shortly its official character was changed. No intending emigrant set forth from England lightly if he were a person of standing, high moral character and some wealth. What he thought is of less immediate importance to us, in our reconstruction of the past, than what he actually took with him. And the following is the inventory of goods which Thomas Clark packed up when he went as passenger on board the *Elizabeth* of London. Clark was destined never to sight the James River, for he died at sea on 9th May, 1625. Here is the list of his property, which may be taken as fairly representative : One bed, two pillows, one pair of coarse sheets and one old rug, one suit of clothes and a cloak, two old suits, three hats, three old shirts, two old pillow " bears " and a pair of drawers, one " ruffe," one Turkey sash, five falling bands, three plain handkerchiefs, one old pair of stockings and one pair of silk garters, six pairs of Irish stockings, five pairs of shoes, one pair of pumps, one pair of boots with spurs, 30 lbs. of cheese, 2 gallons of aqua vitæ, 15 lbs. of powder, 2 gross of tobacco-pipes, one sword, 4 dozen fishing hooks and lines, 4 weeding hoes and one other hoe, 4 cakes of soap, 3 lbs. of starch, 1 lb. of sugar, one Bible, 2 axes, 2 knives, one powder-bag and horn, one tobacco box and glass, one small pair of " stillers that will

Scene in Carolina

End of seventeenth century, showing fort, pinks, ocean ships and smaller craft;
Indians, carts, settlers, well, guns, houses

waighe 6 lbs. at a draught," one pewter porringer and an " aquevity " measure, a spoon, a nutmeg grater, an old stocklock without a key, two old masks, a shoeing horn, a small chest, a barrel and a runlet of vinegar.

A settler who died that same year left behind " one case of bottles, 1 fether bedd and two ruggs, 12 pownd of pewter," and " 2 barrells for peeces." Various punitive expeditions were made against the Indian tribes after the massacre, but the precaution was instituted whereby the Commander of every plantation was to exercise and drill his men in arms that " they be made the more fitt for service uppon any occasione." Every male above sixteen years had to pay the minister of religion so much ; at Elizabeth City the sum was ten pounds of tobacco and one bushel of corn from the present crop. In the same way shipbuilding was being carried on. A shallop measuring eighteen and a half feet along the keel, six and a half feet in beam, with mast, yard, oars and rudder was constructed at the price of one hundred and twenty pounds of tobacco.

The James River with its strong currents was gradually becoming a busy waterway, and it was ever a welcome sight when the tall three-masted vessels arrived from England. The country needed more and more families, and it was impossible to send to Virginia too much in the way of stores of all kinds. But in October, 1626, an order had to be made that ships were to come straight up to James City, and not break bulk or make sale of goods before there arriving, but to deliver up an invoice of their goods, then bring them ashore and not sell anything for ten days, so that the whole colony should have notice of the same and send a representative to get supplies for the family.

The treacherous mud of the James River was responsible for occasional deaths, and a boy servant named Thomas Savage who had been sent to fetch a canoe got stuck in the mud and was drowned. But the danger of Virginia's invasion by means of this river still continued as a veritable possibility. Preparations were still made against the arrival of a " forreine enemy." So at Elizabeth City, once known as Kecoughtan, that most likely of all places where the invader would anchor and land, the Commander of the plantation was ready for surprise. If he should see sailing in a number of ships whose nationality he suspected, then he was to assemble the ablest men, draw them up to their colours and prevent by force any of the strangers from coming ashore. Meanwhile the plantation's children and unserviceable people, together with the cattle, were to be sent to Matthews' Manor.

Such then was the internal life of the Virginian community which planted and toiled, drank and quarrelled, loved and hated, but by sure foundations was gradually building up a young American nation.

CHAPTER XVIII

THE ROYAL COLONY

THE cumulative effect of the massacre, the baneful results of the Thomas Smith régime belonging to the past yet not quite wiped out, the unfavourable Boteler report on his visit to Virginia, and the tiresome factions within the London Company itself, with the possibility that Spain or Holland or France might make a sudden advantage out of all this disunity, brought it about that the King must exert his own authority. The colony needed above all things a knitting and centralizing control, freedom from partizan profiteers, with fixity of purpose, so that in peace and industry plantations might go on developing, towns might spring up, and the flow of emigrants across the Atlantic proceed uninterruptedly. The day had long since passed when this American enterprise was just a commercial venture. And while the change over to a royal master must inevitably mean a threat to liberty, with the certainty some day of revolt for the acquisition of independence, yet it was the only way out of the difficult situation which had evolved by the year 1623.

The meetings of the London Company became explosive. Personalities were exchanged, bad tempers and bad manners were uncurbed, the word " lies " was hurled backward and forward, insults came tumbling out freely. Sometimes these unpleasant assemblies would last till 10.0 p.m., when one faction would withdraw to the fireside apart, and in a loud, objectionable fashion speak their indignant minds, till presently the rival group, weary and angry, would go yawning home to bed. Warwick complained of Sandys' conduct of affairs, Alderman Johnson finally presented a petition this year (1623) to the King showing that the Company was all discord, that Virginia itself was on the brink of ruin. It was suggested that his

Majesty should nominate a commission who could inquire into
the colony's condition, its finances and its needful reforms.

At the back of this apparently disinterested movement was
the real truth that the " old brigade," consisting of Thomas
Smith's friends, had become embittered by having been thrust
out of power and exposed by the Sandys faction.   Johnson,
being himself indebted to the Company, was gladly planning
to have the corporation dissolved, and there were so many
members who were also influential Members of Parliament that
there was a good deal of wheels working within wheels.   On the
Sandys side were such men as Sir Edward Sackville, Sir John
Ogle, as well as Lord Cavendish and the Earl of Southampton,
while on the other were the Earl of Warwick, Sir Thomas
Smith, Sir Nathaniel Rich, as well as Alderman Johnson.   It
was on 14th April that these appeared before the King with
their accusations and allegations, when Sackville carried himself
so insolently that his Majesty " was fain to take him soundly
and roundly " for his impertinence, wrote Sir Dudley Carleton
at the time.   Three days later, the grievances having been
heard, came the Privy Council's order that the King was
appointing a commissioner to inquire into the true state of
Virginia and Somers Islands, the moneys that had been
expended, the abuses and grievances, and how they might be
prevented hereafter.   At the same time the Company were
commanded to send " general letters " to Virginia requiring
the inhabitants to live together in concord and amity.

On 13th May the Privy Council ordered Lord Cavendish,
Sir Edwin Sandys, Nicholas and John Ferrar, being the chief
instigators in " penning an impertinent declaration " against
the Earl of Warwick and others, to be confined to their
respective houses.   Meanwhile private letters intercepted from
Virginia indicated that the planters were in need of supplies
consequent on the massacre, so in obedience to the Privy
Council stores were now sent out " for the relieving of the poor
souls."   " Relieved they must be," insisted Lord President
Mandeville, " and that presently."

Nor was that the only problem which now confronted the
Privy Council.   We mentioned in the last chapter the incident
of Eleanor Spragge.   That was the second breach of promise

case in Virginia. The first had happened just a year previously. Cicely Jordan, a few days after the death of her husband Captain Jordan, went through a form of marriage with the Rev. Greville Pooley, which seems to have been of doubtful validity. She then engaged herself to Mr. William Ferrar, disavowed the former contract, and was eventually married to Ferrar before the Governor and Council, who were so perplexed at the problem that they referred it to the London Company desiring the opinion of the civil lawyers.

Actually conditions were improving in Virginia, though it took months for the latest news to reach London. In the spring of 1623 the Indians' big Chief had sent Sir Francis Wyatt a message that blood enough had been shed on both sides, and the savages shortly returned a number of English prisoners. But Wyatt in a letter to John Ferrar expressed no confidence in the existing temporary peace ; trouble with the Indians was not yet over. " Without doubt," added Sir Francis, " either we must drive them or they us out of the country." But now that ships from Canada and Newfoundland were bringing fish to Virginia, there was little likelihood of starvation, and in fact the colony had gathered in its corn before the supplies from England arrived. The sum of thirty-three hundred pounds had been subscribed in England between April and July, 1623, and in August the ship *George* had left Gravesend with part of the meal and other victuals thus paid for, another instalment of provisions following in the *Truelove*.

King James by this time had certainly taken the problem of Virginia very much to heart, and realized that there was only one solution. In July, 1623, the Attorney-General having been ordered to examine the London Company's letters-patent, reported to James that the sovereign might justly resume government of Virginia, and recommended that James should issue a proclamation if the Company did not voluntarily yield up their privileges. On 8th October the Privy Council informed the London Company that by reason of that colony's distressed state, occasioned by miscarriage of the government thereof, the King had resolved by a new charter to appoint a Governor and twelve assistants resident in England, dependent on the Privy Council and to be chosen by his Majesty at first. These thirteen men were to govern the colony and company, who should nominate a Governor and twelve assistants that should control affairs and be resident in Virginia. And it was explained that should the London Company not now submit, then all their previous charters would be recalled.

This was like pressing a pistol at the head. The Company were astounded at this royal ultimatum, and a week later, in Court assembled, replied that they must have time to consider such a weighty matter and proposed delaying till 19th November. But the representative heads of the Company were now directed to appear before the Privy Council at once, and deliver their final answer as to whether they would surrender the old charters and accept the new. The Company's reply on 20th October was that having put their Lordships' proposition to the vote, there were only nine hands raised in favour of surrendering the charters, while the rest (numbering about sixty) voted to the contrary. It is significant that Sir Samuel Argall, the immediate creator of the Virginian crisis, was leader of the nine. The London Company thus flatly opposed the Privy Council, and in this we see on the one hand an increasing insistence on democratic liberty, and on the other the King's nervous suspicion of any such tendency toward independence. King and Company were at loggerheads, and the former being the whole fountain of authority could thus in due time cause the venture to dry up. But what neither James nor his successors could perceive was that a colony must essentially be a merely temporary affair in the development midway between discovery and autonomy, that it was useless to imagine planters and others would tolerate being mismanaged from a distance of three thousand miles indefinitely.

James was clever enough to keep the Virginia problem out of Parliament's hands, and to rely on legal force. At the same time there was a good deal of common-sense method employed. On 24th October the Privy Council ordered John Harvey, John Pory, together with Abraham Peirsey and Sam Matthews as Commissioners to go out to Virginia, there to inquire into its present state, the number of its plantations, the fortifications, arms, provisions, boats, barges, bridges, public works and intercourse with Indians. Later on Captain John Smith was asked seven leading questions with regard to Virginia's improvement. He answered that idleness, carelessness, "the oft altering of Governours," the lack of martial discipline and the multiplicity of diverse opinions were root causes of the trouble.

While all this was going on the Courts of the London Company were still marked with lively incidents which were repeated even outside. Thus at the beginning of 1624 Thomas Keightley brought an action against William Canning (one of Argall's supporters) because Canning struck Keightley one day while on the Exchange as a result of a quarrel the day before, and the jury awarded Keightley twenty pounds' damages.

In Virginia there had recently been hostilities against the Indians, whose corn had been cut down, houses burned, and many of their people slain. While the colony had erected many more buildings for new-comers to recuperate in, yet there was still serious mortality caused by the pestilent ships reaching the James River with musty bread and bad beer. No one in the colony had lately died of famine, and abundance of corn was being sown. The following list is valuable as giving Virginia's settlements and population on 16th February, 1624:

SETTLEMENT	POPULATION	
At College Land	29	persons.
Neck of Land	41	
West and Sherlow Hundred	45	
Jordan's Journey	42	
Flowerdieu Hundred	63	(including 11 negroes)
West and Sherlow Hundred Island	24	
Chaplain's Choice	24	
James City	182	(including 3 negroes)
In the Main	88	
James Island	39	(including 1 negro)
Neck of Land	25	
Over the river	33	
At the plantation over against James City	77	(including 1 negro)
At the glass house	5	
Archer's Hope	14	

SETTLEMENT	POPULATION
Hog Island	31
Martin's Hundred	24
Warwick Squeak	33 (including 4 negroes)
At Indian Thicket	11
Elizabeth City	319 (including 2 negroes)
Buckrow	30
Bass's Choice	20
At the Eastern Shore	76

TOTAL   1,275 persons, including 22 negroes.

But three hundred and seventy had recently died, including fifteen killed and two lost. Among those killed was Captain Spelman previously mentioned. The clear fact emerges that in spite of all the shiploads of arrivals from England, Virginia was not being peopled as rapidly as it ought ; death was far too busy, and the cost of the Indian hostilities had put a heavy burden on the colony. The action of the King, however, in remitting threepence in the shilling Customs duty on tobacco, and his granting Virginia the sole right to export tobacco, was a most encouraging incident. Early in 1624 the Commissioners reached Virginia, and in February the General Assembly met, expressing a desire that the Governors to be sent over might not have absolute authority, but be restrained as hitherto by the Council. The latter title the Assembly requested might be retained, and not be converted into the suggested name of Assistants. And (very significantly) reference was made to the inconvenience found in the strict limitations of the Governor and Council to the instructions sent from England.

We thus here note the foreshadowing of ultimate revolution, for practical experience had shown that the brevity of a Governor's tenure was disadvantageous to the colony. In the first year he was engaged learning his job, in the second year he had just begun to get a grip on the country's affairs, while during his third year he was preparing to return home. Emphatically the Council and Assembly begged the Privy Council permission to retain the important liberty of their

General Assembly. " Nothing," they wrote, " can more conduce to our satisfaction or the public utility."

On 2nd March the General Assembly met again and answered the four Commissioners as to the most suitable places for fortifications, but now came another firm stand in the slow yet certain march toward independence, and it was caused by a sheer attempt on the part of the Commissioners to bluff the unsuspecting colonists. Captain John Harvey and colleagues presented a document to the Assembly and invited the latter's signatures. The Assembly, however, firmly declined ; for this form testified thankfulness for the King's care of the colony, and consented to the revocation of the old patents and to acceptance of a new charter. While the Commissioners considered this " very fit to be subscribed to by the whole Assembly," Sir Francis Wyatt, Council and Assembly replied that already they had given thanks to the King for his tender care, and now intimated that when the colony's consent to surrender of the patent was required, it would be the proper time to answer. Furthermore, they conceived that the King's intention to change the government had proceeded from misinformation, which they hoped might be altered upon their own more faithful declaration.

We can well sympathize with the rising of indignation. The Virginians had every reason to feel infuriated that the blackguard Boteler had been able to influence the King and unsettle the settlers. During his few weeks' stay among them, this ungovernable ex-Governor of Bermudas had been guilty of " riots and lascivious filthiness with lewd women purchased with rials-of-eight and wedges of gold, the spoils of the distressed Spaniards in Bermudas." Virginia, notwithstanding all its reverses, was gaining strength internally by its own reforms. Most of the plantations were now situated on high ground ; quite big ships could come alongside the banks on each side from half flood to half ebb ; most of the houses were now well palisaded against the Indians ; at James City there were mounted four demi-culverins, at Flowerdieu there were even six. Three more pieces were at Newport News, two at Elizabeth City, two at Charles Hundred, seven at Henrico, while several planters had provided themselves with their own

Q

ordnance. Everywhere mulberry trees for the silkworms, and vineyards, were being planted. In short, Virginia was not in the bad way that the misinformants had slandered. In every plantation there was a house or room set apart for the worship of God ; absence from divine service was punished by a fine of fifty pounds of tobacco ; 22nd March (the anniversary day of the massacre) was to be kept holy ; no minister was to absent himself from his cure for over two months, men were not allowed to go to work unarmed ; and generally Virginia was setting her own house in order.

But this did not prevent the King's purpose from being proceeded with. In spite of the London Company's resistance, its representations to his Majesty, and the Virginian General Assembly's expressed wishes, Sir Thomas Smith's party won the day. On 16th June, 1624, the Company had met their final defeat by the legal process of *quo warranto*. This was a King's Bench writ by which persons were called upon to show by what warrant they held an office. The Company of English merchants trading to Virginia had their authority declared null and void, and the charter came to an end. Thus the colonial government passed from being a trading concern to a royal undertaking, though the sound representative institutions continued as a model for future American colonies. And future royal Governors who endeavoured to deny the established representative rights of the General Assembly did so to their own peril. This amount of free government remained so firmly implanted in the American mind, that interference only brought about revolution in succeeding generations.

While the oppressive methods of disestablishing the London Company were open to criticism, yet it was (for the present) better that the adolescent colony should spend the rest of its tutored days under royal care rather than under the profiteering hands of proprietors. From the King's point of view all those discords and factions were too dangerous and self-centred. Moreover, the negotiations for the marriage of Charles I to the Spanish Infanta had failed, and the fear of Spain proceeding with a demolishing expedition against Virginia now had become more real. Apart from other results against English prestige, the loss of Virginia's tobacco crops would have been a very serious depletion in the Crown revenues. The great peril now involved was that the all-powerful Privy Council might so exercise its strength in the future as to bring about collisions with the very people who were sending all this wealth to England. That singularly restrained and impartial historian and resident of Virginia, the Rev. William Stith, Rector of Henrico, writing in 1746, thirty years before the greatest and final Revolution, could already foresee this danger developing.

After the return of the four Commissioners, the King by a proclamation dated 15th July, 1624, ordered the Courts of the Company for the present to meet at Sir Thomas Smith's house in Philpot Lane every Thursday afternoon, and a Commission of Privy Councillors was appointed to advise on a fit new patent together with the most suitable course of government. Even in the forming of this Commission there were the usual jealousy, factions and mutual mistrust ; for the seventeenth century had not yet acquired that high standard of public opinion which insists on fair play and tolerance. Sir Edward Conway (who had been in Essex's Cadiz expedition of 1596, became in 1623 one of his Majesty's Secretaries of State, and was one of the commissioners appointed on 15th July, 1624, for the winding-up of the Virginia Company) received a letter about this time from Sir Thomas Coventry, the Attorney-General, explaining that the name of Mr. Robert Bing was intentionally not included in the commission. The business, he wrote, is weighty and serious, but Bing is light and " a mere good fellow, a man of no estate, who for saucy conduct before the Council table, and offensive behaviour to Lord Southampton, had been committed to the Marshalsea " prison. And while this was going on, Sir Francis Wyatt, the Council and General Assembly, were anxiously petitioning the King for his tender compassion not to allow the colony to fall again into the hands of Sir Thomas Smith or his confidants.

But one more of those well-timed incidents occurred to save Virginia from those fears. On 4th September, 1625, ripe in years, and very wealthy, Sir Thomas Smith, who had already been a widower twice, died. He left behind a widow and numerous bequests, the latter being to this day annually distributed by the Skinners' Company. In that same year passed away also his supporter, James I. Thus were removed two powerful influences which might have so changed back Virginia's newly-won representative freedom to her former " Nubian slavery " that a revolutionary crisis would have been hastened. But, as it was, royal Virginia was given a dignity and position, a recognized approval and protection, which would exalt her in the eyes of the Spaniards.

On 13th May, 1624, was issued from Whitehall the royal proclamation to the effect that James I, having repealed the letters-patent of the London Company, had undertaken the government of Virginia, Somers Islands and New England, which should form part of his Empire ; that the government of Virginia should immediately depend on himself ; that Councils should be established for that colony's affairs—one in England and the other subordinate and resident in Virginia—and that all public officers and ministers should be maintained at the King's expense. During the previous year Sir Francis Wyatt had gained a great military victory over Otiotan (brother of Opechancanough) and the Pamunkeys with their confederates numbering eight hundred bowmen. This fight had lasted two days, in which many of the Indians were slain, and as much corn burned as would have sustained four hundred men a year. The colony was, in the Governor's words, wearing away the scars of the massacre, but during the summer of 1625 the scarcity of supplies and desperate condition of the colony caused great numbers of planters to resolve to leave for England. It was to prevent these clamours developing into serious trouble that Sir George Yeardley, who had remained all this time in Virginia, was unanimously chosen as spokesman. He duly came over to submit a petition with these grievances, which were heard during October.

What the colony especially needed were munitions, clothes, tools and provisions, as well as more settlers and some soldiers. For this reason a supply ship of one hundred and twenty tons was sent from London, as well as another from Plymouth. But a further anxiety was created about this time owing to the boldness of the Moorish pirates, who came up from the Mediterranean to the Atlantic approaches of the British Isles. On 8th August, 1625, the Mayor of Poole complained to the

Privy Council that unless measures were taken the Newfoundland fishing fleet of two hundred and fifty sail, having on board about five thousand men from the West of England, would be surprised by these corsairs ; and the Mayor of Plymouth wrote that they had great fears also for the homeward-bound vessels from Virginia. Within ten days twenty-seven ships and two hundred persons had been taken by such enemies.

And now came the time for Sir Francis Wyatt's departure from Virginia. His Governorship had been popular, and he had steered his people through anxious years. But his father had died and Wyatt had private affairs requiring attention at home. Before sailing, however, he wrote informing the Privy Council that the supplies had arrived, "though not answerable to our great wants." Five hundred soldiers would be required annually to suppress the Indians, man the fortifications, explore the land and sea. And again he bluntly wrote on 17th May, 1626, informing the Privy Council that " the slow proceeding of the growth of the plantation " was due to the government being divided between England and Virginia. Tobacco was their currency, he added, but they did not possess it all the year round for paying their workmen ; Virginia badly required public stock to be subscribed to enable them to carry on this big work. At present it was being supported almost exclusively by private adventurers.

To succeed him was appointed again Sir George Yeardley. The instructions to him were dated 19th April, 1626, and warned him that the possibility of Virginia's invasion was still not unlikely ; in fact " you may daily expect the coming of a foreign enemy." He was to suppress drunkenness, cause the people to raise more staple commodities than tobacco, plant corn, strictly forbid any planter from receiving Indians into the houses, " to avoid the treachery of the savages and prevent such dangers as heretofore have fallen." Francis West, John Harvey, George Sandys, John Pott, Roger Smith, Ralph Hamor, Sam Matthews, Abraham Peirsey, William Clayborne, William Tucker, Job Whitaker, Edward Blandy and William Ferrar were appointed as the Council, William Clayborne being Secretary of State in the colony. Some of these names are already familiar to us, others will come up again. Hamor was much experienced, having been in Virginia from 1609 to 1614, and he sailed out again in 1617.

Tobacco was a constant centre of trouble, radiating in three separate directions. The London adventurers, who, after Sir Thomas Smith's death, used to meet in the house of Sir John Wolstenholme, that other wealthy merchant, resisted " with one voice " the Privy Council's attempt to regulate how much leaf should be brought into England and at what price. The planters in Virginia also preferred free trade, but hated the " avaricious and cruel men, whose exorbitant and wide consciences project and digest the ruin of this plantation, for profit and gain to themselves." King Charles was annoyed that so much attention was given to the growing of tobacco, and that it might truly be said " that this plantation is wholly built upon smoke, tobacco being the only means it hath produced." Therefore he insisted on their taking special care to produce pipe-staves, pitch, tar, soap-ashes, potashes, iron, salt ; to search for mines and plant vines.

Before the end of 1627 Sir George Yeardley died, and Francis West was elected by the Virginia Council to succeed him. Yeardley left behind an estate in the colony valued at six thousand pounds, and his body was buried in Jamestown church. By February, 1628, Virginia had increased its population by a thousand, but the planters still suffered by not being allowed to export sufficient tobacco. With about three thousand people, and every master of a family raising two hundred pounds of tobacco and every servant one hundred and twenty-five pounds, this amounted to only four hundred and twelve thousand five hundred pounds, a quantity inadequate for their maintenance. Such was one of the bad effects of being so closely controlled under royal dominance. It was as if the youthful colony could not be trusted to know its own business. The very least amount exportable should have been five hundred thousand pounds at three shillings and sixpence or four shillings a pound delivered in England, and to this the colonists would have consented.

CHAPTER XIX

THE ROAD TO REVOLUTION

CAPTAIN WEST, having finished his period as Governor, sailed for England, and October of 1629 saw Dr. John Pott elected by the Council instead. The times were anxious, for on 7th September some thirty-six Spanish ships had captured, in the West Indies, Nevis (that favourite island of refreshment for Virginian emigrants) and St. Christopher ; there was no telling whether this fleet would come north into the James River.

Doctor Pott was a notorious physician and surgeon, who had been guilty of loose living and other offences. In the meantime John Harvey in England had been chosen by the Privy Council as Yeardley's successor and been knighted, though there was some delay in his sailing forth. He was to proceed in the *William and John* of London, and the mariners were afforded protection against impressment. Before starting he requested six " grave and conformable " ministers of religion to be sent to Virginia, a fort to be erected at Point Comfort, forty barrels of powder and twenty more barrels yearly, a competent sum of money to cover transportation of himself and retinue, an allowance of forty thousand pounds of tobacco, and that the City of London send at its own expense a hundred poor boys and girls.

Sir John Harvey reached Virginia in the spring of 1630, after a long and tedious voyage by reason of the ship leaking. This compelled them to put in at the Cape Verdes, where he found about forty Dutch west-bound ships. The hot weather caused great sickness aboard Harvey's ship. On arrival up the James River he found the people engaged in a necessary war with the Indians which exhausted all the colony's powder. He summoned an Assembly a week before Easter and found the colonists " miserably perplexed " for want of corn which they had neglected to plant. An act was therefore passed to augment the quantity of corn and prevent the excessive growing of tobacco.

He found also serious accusations against his temporary predecessor, Dr. John Pott, who was alleged to have pardoned a wilful murderer and reinvested that criminal with his estate after a legal condemnation. Harvey accordingly confined Pott to his plantation at Harrope, seven miles from James City. But a ridiculous situation followed. Although Pott had been found guilty of various capital offences and his estate had become forfeit to the King, yet his life was too valuable to be taken away. The colony was always being attacked by disease, and Pott was the only physician skilled in epidemics. Harvey thus gave the man a respite, and a petition was sent to the King, supported by Governor and Council ; they would rather Pott lived than that they should be felled by fever. Mrs. Elizabeth Pott, the accused's wife, also took the long journey to England with a similar petition, pleading that the family had been residing in Virginia for over ten years. Months went by, and finally in July, 1631, the King wrote to Governor Harvey that in consideration of Pott's penitence, the necessary need the King's subjects had of his services, and the fact that he was the only physician in the colony, he was to be pardoned and restored to his estate

Let us for a moment turn our attention away from Virginia to Newfoundland, where Devonshire fishermen and planters from England were quarrelling about rights and fees ; and the Devonians told the latter that they knew a great deal better how to manage the fishing than any planters could teach them. By 1621 Newfoundland had become a hopeful English colony, employing three hundred ships a year and ten thousand English seamen, thereby maintaining twenty thousand more poor people at home, and assisting the English Customs by ten thousand pounds a year. But then it was desired by James I to make a more settled plantation there ; for it was infested with pirates, and between 1612 and 1621 damage to the extent of forty thousand eight hundred pounds had been done in that area, besides the loss of men and guns.

View of Baltimore, Maryland
Showing covered wagon

So on the last day of 1622 we find the whole country of Newfoundland granted to Sir George Calvert and his heirs, but in the following year James granted him by letters-patent that region known as Avalon, which is Newfoundland's south-east peninsula. After the failure of the Spanish match was definite, Secretary of State Calvert resigned office, and was created Baron Baltimore in 1625. Being a Roman Catholic, his popularity was not increased, and we find him writing " From my lodging in the Savoy " (not far from the site where many modern American tourists sojourn when in London), hurrying the warrant for his 160-ton ship *Ark of Avalon* and the 140-ton *George* of Plymouth. By this means he went to visit his colony, but by September, 1629, having spent twenty-five thousand pounds thereon, and no longer able to stand its climate, he sailed the following month to Virginia in search of less vigorous winters.

He wrote to the King saying that, his strength being much decayed, he desired a grant of a " precinct " of Virginia land, whither he might move himself and forty people. Charles I replied that men of Lord Baltimore's condition and breeding were fitter for other employments than the farming of new plantations, and advised him to return to his native country. But in the meantime Baltimore had arrived in Virginia (during Governor Pott's period), and at first seemed anxious to reside in James City. There arose an immediate difficulty, for this new party of emigrants being " of the Romish religion " firmly refused to take the oath of supremacy and allegiance. It was not till 1632 that the King promised him a charter conferring lands to the north and east of the Potomac River. Before this charter was through Lord Baltimore died, but the rights were transmitted to his son and heir Cecil, the second Baron, in June of that same year. The territory was named Maryland by Charles I, in honour of Queen Henrietta Maria.

" Now if I would be rich," wrote the amusing Aubrey (1606–75), " I could be a prince. I could goe into Maryland, which is one of the finest countrys of the world ; same climate with France ; between Virginia and New England. . . . Plenty of all things : ground there is 2000 miles westwards. I could be able I believe to carry a colony of rogues ; another,

of ingeniose artificers ; and I doubt not one might make a shift
to have 5 or 6 ingeniose companions, which is enough."

But it was Maryland which was to be the direct cause
of another revolution, though it is but fair to remark that
practically from the first Harvey, who had been accustomed to
hard seafaring, failed in the more diplomatic duty of governing
with a gloved if firm hand.   As early as April, 1631, he wrote
complaining to the Privy Council of the waywardness and
opposition of the Council in Virginia, who disputed his authority,
averring that he had no power beyond a casting vote.   And
he begged that the King might strengthen his commission,
distinguishing the duties of Governor and Councillors.   But
Harvey was always trying to screw the last farthing for himself
out of those in authority.

Harvey busily had those settlers prosecuted who were
stirring up sedition, but on 20th December of this same year,
and because of the approaching festival of Christmas at James
City, the Governor and Council silenced by a temporary period
of peace those " unhappy differences which have interrupted
all good proceedings."

It was under Charles I that a commission of distinguished
men was formed in 1631 to advise upon the future of Virginia,
and Harvey was requested to send a map of the colony " with the
exactest description he can make to represent it to their knowledge ; who can not view it otherwise."   The Commissioners
recommended, in effect, that the government be carried on
in the manner laid down by James I in 1624.   All tobacco had
to be landed in no other port than London, which made it very
awkward when a freighted ship sprang a leak in the Atlantic
and wanted to make for a Devonshire harbour.

During the next year Virginia was planting vines and
English grain considerably, and building ships.   But the colony
was in great need of shoes as well as other necessities.   Harvey
again asked the Commissioners in England for means wherewith
to support his great expenses, pleading that he might just as
well be called the host of Virginia, for there was no other house
but his for hospitality in James Island.   Relations between
Harvey and his Council were becoming strained owing to this
Maryland affair.   In plain language, the Virginians resented the

intrusion of other colonists in this territory ; and, in particular, because it was a crowd of Papists arriving where hitherto strict oaths had been exacted as to orthodoxy in religion and politics. Further complications were caused by the fact that Councillor William Clayborne had, by the King's commission dated 16th May, 1631, been given permission for himself and his associates to make discoveries up the Chesapeake Bay for the increase of trade in America. It was thus that the Isle of Kent had been found and purchased from the Indians.

Therefore when Lord Baltimore's settlers came over in the spring of 1634, it was a bitter annoyance to Clayborne that this Kent Island should be claimed as part of Maryland, and the Councillor refused to acknowledge the new jurisdiction, rightly and properly claiming an earlier title. The King requested Harvey and the Council in Virginia to give Baltimore friendly assistance, which made the situation more delicate still. Clayborne and others petitioned the Privy Council that as great expense had been incurred settling the island, Lord Baltimore might settle somewhere else. The Virginia Council were in sympathy with Clayborne, but Harvey, in obedience to superior orders, was giving every aid to Lord Baltimore in opposition to what the latter termed Clayborne's " malicious behaviour and unlawful proceedings." Harvey's action was officially approved at London headquarters, and he was reminded by letter " that it is the duty of good subjects to obey and not to dispute their Sovereign's commandment " ; the King would be very sensible of any disobedience " presuming of impunity by their far distance from hence, or some other silly hopes here," and Harvey was even further instructed to continue against Clayborne's malicious practices. As if to leave no possible doubt in the matter, Charles I, on 8th October, 1634, wrote from Hampton Court to the Governor, Council and officials in America, ordering them to assist the planters in Kent Island, that they might peaceably enjoy the fruits of their labours, but forbade Lord Baltimore or his agents to do the planters any violence.

Sir John Harvey was admittedly in a difficult position. He realized that his own actual power was limited at the Council table. Many of the Councillors, he wrote, were so averse to the

Maryland plantation " that they cry and make it their familiar talk that they would rather knock their cattle on the head than sell them to Maryland." And Captain Sam Matthews, " scratching his head and in a fury, stamping cried " out a curse upon Maryland. Secret meetings followed, and on the night of 27th April, 1635, one was held at a house in York plantation, where Captain Francis Pott, William English and others arrived to hear " a writing " read by the former complaining of a tax Harvey had imposed, and that the latter would bring a second massacre among them. The Governor ordered these ringleaders to be arrested, and demanded the Council's help to suppress these mutinous meetings. On 28th April Captain Matthews and other Councillors all armed, and with about fifty musketeers, surrounded the Governor's house where the Council was about to assemble. Another of the Councillors, John Utie, struck Harvey violently on the shoulder and said : " I arrest you for treason," and told him he must get ready for returning to England and there answer complaints against him. Dr. John Pott, who was in charge of the musketeers, then ordered the latter to retire " until there should be use of them." Pott, English and Martin were released, and thus a bloodless revolution had taken place.

On 7th May the Assembly met and approved of this action, Captain John West (twelfth child of the second Lord de la Warr) being elected Governor. While Harvey imagined that this revolt had been caused partly by personal reasons (such as that Dr. John Pott had been superseded in the government, and that his brother Francis Pott had been relieved as Captain of the Fort at Point Comfort), the culminating act had been brought about when Clayborne had as usual sent his pinnace *Long Tail* to trade with the Indians that spring, and this was seized by the Marylanders on 23rd April. The indignation meeting four days later followed naturally. Matthews wrote to inform Sir John Wolstenholme that Harvey had done infinite injuries to the colony, usurping power without any respect to the Council's votes, and making a dangerous peace with the Indians. Matthews believed that Sir John's return to England would be " acceptable to God, not displeasing to His Majesty, and an assured happiness unto this colony."

With Harvey sailed also Captain Francis Pott and Thomas Horwood, who were to present the Assembly's case to the Privy Council. It was on 14th July, 1635, that the ship reached Plymouth, whereupon ex - Governor Harvey informed the Mayor of what he called a mutiny and rebellion in Virginia. The Assembly's letters, sealed up in a trunk, were sent up to London by Thomas Horwood, and the Mayor wanted to know what should be done with Francis Pott. On this same July day Harvey sent a letter to Sir Francis Windebank, Secretary of State, apologizing for returning from Virginia without license. Three days later the letter reached London.

Early in December a meeting of the Privy Council was held over which Charles I himself presided, and the whole matter was investigated. As a matter of principle the King, with due respect for deputed authority, deemed it essential to send Harvey back to Virginia, if even the latter should remain in the colony but one day. If he should clear himself, then Sir John should remain there longer. In any case it was an assumption of regal power to have sent the Governor to England. Finally Harvey was exonerated, and in February began making arrangements for a ship to carry him back to Virginia. Francis Pott was sent up to the Fleet prison, and his letters taken away from him. But by May, 1636, he was so weary of captivity as to express himself "truly sorrowful" and prayed for liberty, whereby he might be preserved from infection "in this dangerous time of contagion." In the spring of 1637 West, Matthews, Utie, Menefie and Pierce were sent as prisoners to England.

But eventually all these revolutionaries were able to receive their freedom and get back to Virginia. It was no welcome news to the colony that Harvey was returning, but this rebellion had shown most clearly that unsuitable and high-handed Governors, supported by an imperfect policy in England, could quickly undo the good work of predecessors and foment the spirit which insists on a revolution to free from oppression.

But the ignoring of history was to create the same sort of crisis later on. It is sufficient to bear in mind that already a revolutionary tradition had been installed in America.

Meanwhile, America was doing a great deal to build up the British Mercantile Marine. Already three hundred British ships were being employed sailing to Virginia, New England, Nova Scotia and so on, though the French and Dutch interrupted them. But it was no easy matter to leave England for Virginia without taking the necessary oaths. When in October, 1633, Baltimore's party were sailing in the two ships *Ark* and *Dove* there were several evasive incidents. Before getting under way from Gravesend the passengers for Maryland were billeted in the local houses for three days at twelvepence each per diem. Unfortunately these four hundred men and women were taken aboard without payment being first made for their lodging, so that an action had to be brought against Lord Baltimore, and both ships had to be delayed when it was found they had left Gravesend without the passengers taking the oath.

But the most hopeful sign was that corn was so plentiful in Virginia by February, 1634, that, notwithstanding the arrival of twelve hundred new-comers into the colony, it had been possible to export ten thousand bushels for the relief of New England. " Virginia," wrote Harvey that summer, " is now become the granary of all His Majty's northern colonies." There were plenty of beeves, goats, hogs, all sorts of poultry ; and oranges, lemons, vines, as well as all kinds of fruit, were being grown. By the summer of 1635 Virginia's population had reached over five thousand, and such was the progress that during the first five months of the next year another 1,606 persons had been added to the colony.

There was, however, an amusing series of incidents in regard to Harvey's return voyage to Virginia which made it seem as if Fate were purposely delaying him. In February, 1636, he particularly desired that his arrival in the James River might be in a King's ship, that is to say, a man-of-war. This honour, he suggested, would much " animate the boldness of the offenders " in the colony when they see his Majesty " takes the business so to heart." He therefore asked the Admiralty for the loan of the *Mary Rose* for six months, furnished with munitions and ready for sea, but Harvey himself would pay for victuals and wages. (He was already being sued for a seven-year-old debt due to some ironmongers.) Harvey did not care for a merchant ship, and just at this period his successor for the time (Captain John West) was complaining that the merchants of England " pester " the colonial ships with passengers that bring infection to Virginia. " The most pestered ships carry with them almost a general mortality."

Harvey was still a genius at bargaining, and having been assigned a vessel, he requested that he might have the benefit of the freight out and home. He knew what he was asking, for this spring twenty-one ships had reached James River and all of them were returning freighted with tobacco, the King's Customs on one of them alone (the *John and Barbary* of Ipswich) amounting to the sum of three thousand three hundred and thirty-four pounds. On 2nd April Harvey's new commission as Governor was issued to him, and in the following month he was allotted the *Black George*. This was a prize ship, with eighty mariners. He then bargained again—intentionally to reduce the wages bill, but under the pretence of being able to carry more passengers. Fifty men, he said, " are sufficient to sail her," so that modification was conceded, and May had nearly run out. The *Black George* now began fitting out at Portsmouth, and it was agreed that he should have the freight both ways.

But by August *Black George* was still being unloaded of her guns, cables and heavy gear to search for a mysterious leak, " she being a most crazy old ship," as Lord Wimbleton designated her. Meanwhile the Portsmouth authorities were longing to see the last of Harvey, for every day there kept arriving so many of his emigrants by road from London that it was feared Portsmouth might receive an " ill,"[1] of which as yet the town had been free. But weeks slid by, and *Black George* was no farther than Portland, waiting for seamen and carpenters. Pump-boxes were here made, and at last she really started off down-Channel. She then leaked so badly that after sailing less than a hundred miles she had to put in at the Scillies, where she waited a fortnight for a fair wind back to Portsmouth. With great difficulty the tiresome old tub was back in the latter on the last day of October, when Harvey returned her to the port authorities. Finally he took passage in

[1] *i.e.* the plague.

a smaller ship, leaving his goods and company of settlers behind.
He landed at James City on 18th January, 1637, summoned the
Council, read his commission and instructions at the church of
Elizabeth City, and then published the King's pardon to those
who had aided and abetted in the rebellion of nearly two years
ago. High-handed and unpopular as ever, Harvey resumed
his office, and continued till he was succeeded two years later
by that very different official Sir Francis Wyatt, who once
more acted for Virginia's great good.

Putting to Sea from Portsmouth (England)

Roysterers bidding good-bye before sailing

CHAPTER XX

NORTHERN COLONIZATION

NOW that we have witnessed Virginia passing through every crisis, short of actual invasion, that could conceivably afflict a young community, and have seen Maryland created as the first English colony where liberty in matters of faith was eventually to be established by law, we may pass north along the Atlantic coast to contemplate those other ventures. It has been our privilege to study Virginia's evolution in detail, for that plantation was not merely the pioneer of all other American settlements, but the creative inspiration, the encouragement and model. Virginia, in its slow and painful advancement through dragging difficulties, was blazing the trail of all other comers to the New World. Had the Jamestown settlement been allowed to fizzle out in the régime of Captain John Smith or Lord de la Warr, a future English-speaking America would have become impossible under the influence of French, Spanish or Dutch ideals. Furthermore, the fact of Virginia's success was an enormous incentive to English overseas expansion elsewhere.

Of the two original separate Virginia Companies we have noticed that the Plymouth undertaking, after the temporary Popham effort, merely lingered on with memories of Maine tucked away in the mind's archives. But human curiosity, and eagerness to wrest from Nature its geographical secrets, was very much alive. Henry Hudson, armed with John Smith's map of Virginia, went to sail under Dutch support in 1609, when he was to explore what we now call Hudson River as far up as Albany, thinking to find that elusive passage to the South Seas. And this discovery could not fail to make a lasting impression on the enterprising minds of Holland's splendid merchant-seafarers. There is reason to believe that in that autumn of 1613 Captain Sam Argall, when he sailed from

R

Jamestown up the Atlantic to wipe out the French encroach-
ments on the Virginian grant, called at Hudson River on the
way back and compelled the little Dutch settlement on
Manhattan Island to surrender. But it was not long before the
Hollanders had returned and were busy trading.

The early voyages to those parts, of which Cape Cod was
the natural centre for mariners, have already been considered.
There followed the interval when England's few available
ocean-going merchant ships not employed on the Indian route
were required either for Newfoundland fishing or for carrying
persons as well as supplies to Virginia. But always there existed
a feeling that even if the Gosnold family had been swallowed up
in the Virginia project, the Cape Cod vicinity contained great
possibilities. Imaginations and events moved sluggishly in
those days, but after he had been home from Virginia five years
and recovered from his accident, Captain John Smith was sent
out by Captain Marmaduke Royden, Captain George Langam,
Master John Buley and Master William Skelton, with two ships
and orders to sail to that part of the North American coast lying
in " 43½ of Northerly latitude to take whales . . . make
trialls of a mine of gold and copper ; if those failed, fish and
furs were then our refuge." Thus the old lust for precious
metals was again at the back of voyaging.

Smith, therefore, sailed from London, left the Downs on
3rd March, 1614, and was lucky to complete the quick direct
Atlantic passage by the last day of April to the Isle of
Monahigan in the latitude just mentioned. While most of his
men fished in open boats, Smith with eight men went " ranging
the coast " of what we know by the name of New Hampshire
and Maine. He explored the bays and inlets, bartered furs and
skins from the Indians, " tooke a plot (*i.e.* made a map) of what
I could see," having found that the charts which he brought
out from England " did mee no more good then so much waste
paper." So excellent, indeed, was Smith's cartographic work
that for many generations this map held a supreme place.
And it was his idea that this territory which he investigated
during a period of May, June and half of July should be known
as New England. In the following March Smith set out again,
this time from Plymouth, the intention being " to beginne a

Plantation " in New England. But bad weather compelled him to return into Plymouth. One ship, however, from that port and four from London reached New England and profited by the fishing.

In 1616 John Smith published *A Description of New England*, that territory which " is betwixt the degrees of 41 and 45," and in it was a glowing account of its rivers, islands, gardens, soil, healthy climate. " I would rather live here then any where," he wrote of that new country. The book created such European interest that it was afterwards translated in Frankfort and abridged in Leyden. In 1620 was printed a further volume by him entitled *New England's Trials*. The departure of the Pilgrim Fathers and those who followed created a great demand for the book.

The permanent colonization of New England begins only with the *Mayflower*. On 3rd March, 1620, the Plymouth Virginia Company petitioned the King for the same privileges which had been granted to the London Company, and desired their territory to be called New England and the bounds settled from Lat. 40° to 48° N This patent was granted exactly eight months later, though the actual warrant for preparing the charter was issued on 23rd July, 1620. Now one manifestation of the unsettled condition following the Reformation was the disregard of the old faith, together with much respect for private judgment in matters of religion. The result was that in Stuart England there was an extraordinarily diverse sectarianism, and any Act of Uniformity not unnaturally had the opposite effect of creating Nonconformists. Separatists— that is to say those who attended services other than such as were prescribed by law—morally rebelled against Jacobean compulsion, and in order to obtain full freedom in religious expression would logically be inclined to seek another country.

Thus we find a sect of Separatists taking their wives and children to Holland, but proceeding thence back to England *en voyage* to the now much-discussed New England. Seventy-four English Nonconformists with twenty-eight women of John Robinson's church at Leyden formed the historic Pilgrim Fathers expedition, which sailed from Plymouth on 6th September, 1620, in the *Mayflower*, which was under the command of Captain Christopher Jones. The latter was a Rotherhithe man, and the register of St. Mary's Church, Rotherhithe, shows that he was buried there in March, 1622, letters of administration of his estate being granted to his wife Joan the following August. Besides Jones, his crew were Rotherhithe men, and this famous Atlantic ship used to sail from Greenland Dock, Rotherhithe (now part of the Surrey Commercial Docks). For at least eleven years her captain had been living there. This Pilgrim trip to New England was one of his last voyages, and eventually (it has recently been discovered), the *Mayflower* came back to be sold at Rotherhithe to a man named Gardener, her timber being re-erected to form a barn.

John Smith was willing to lead this party of emigrants, but his services were declined, partly because he was a firm member of the Church of England, and partly because they wished to save expense. The dark, sober-visaged and dignified Edward Winslow, a man of better birth and breeding than his shipmates, stands out conspicuous among the *Mayflower* Pilgrims. He had left his salt-boiling business at Droitwich in 1617 and joined his co-religionists at Leyden, whence in July, 1620, he sailed, accompanied by his wife and three servants. He crossed from Delfthaven to England in the *Speedwell*, being at this date just twenty-five years old. A few months after reaching America his wife died, but in May, 1621, he married a widow named Susanna White, who became the mother of Peregrine White— the first English child to be born in New England. The latter did not die till 1704, so in Peregrine we have a unique link between the earliest and the later chapters of New England.

The *Mayflower* was a vessel of one hundred and sixty tons, quite small enough for winter work in the Atlantic, yet not unduly small as compared with the average ocean-going ship of the time. The first start had been on 23rd August, when she sailed with a vessel of seventy tons. The latter sprang a leak, so both ships returned to Plymouth, where the seventy-tonner was paid off and her twenty passengers joined the *Mayflower's* one hundred and two. According to John Smith, the *Mayflower* herself was a " leaking unwholesome ship." She sighted Cape Cod on 9th November, and then for six weeks longer they were

" for want of experience ranging to and again " before they found " a place they liked to dwell on."

They had come out from England with no charter but merely a licence from the Plymouth Company. They had intended to pick up the land farther south, within the Company's jurisdiction, but the hard winds, dangerous coast, and the unhandiness of the ship interfered with their navigation. With fifteen weeks of knocking about the wintry Atlantic " lying wet in their cabbins, most of them grew very weake, and weary of the sea." And when they landed they were " forced to lie on the bare ground without coverture in the extremitie of winter." So " fortie of them died : and 60 were left in very weake estate " at the time the *Mayflower* on the following 5th April sailed off to England. We thus have the same sad experiences of the Virginian settlers repeating themselves ; but the attractive feature was that, even if a ship could not get a fair slant of wind across the Atlantic, it was a shorter distance to New England than having to go through the Tropics to Virginia. And it was an advantage that the food would be less likely to go bad.

Cape Cod was like a guide-post which pointed the *Mayflower* to that spot which is now known as Plymouth, but was marked on John Smith's map of New England (engraved in 1614) as New Plimouth. Here, then, the Pilgrims came ashore to a place that Smith had surveyed and named.

It was on territory not belonging to the London Virginia Company but to the Council for New England, who subsequently were to confirm the tract of land to these pioneers, corresponding with the south-east section of Massachusetts State. But, before landing, the *Mayflower* Pilgrims drew up and set their signatures to a compact of government.

The *Mayflower* sailed back to England in a thirty-one-day voyage, and on 21st July, 1621, a supply ship of fifty-five tons carrying thirty-seven passengers was sent out. Head winds delayed her, and she was not clear of the English Channel till the end of August, nor did she reach New Plymouth till 11th November. She found that only six of the *Mayflower's* people had died since April. The supply ship was now reloaded with timber, beaver skins and sassafras, but on nearing the English

Channel she was captured by a Frenchman, though eventually the Master and crew were released and got back to England. Piracy, indeed, was still a grave menace to Atlantic vessels, and only in 1617 Sir Ferdinando Gorges had remarked that during the last few years Britain had thus lost three hundred ships, their goods and their seamen.

First impressions are always valuable, and it is worth while to quote from a letter sent home from New England in this captured ship, written about 13th December, 1621, by William Hilton, who had gone out in her as one of the thirty-seven passengers :

" Loving cousin, at our arivall at New Plimmoth in New England, we found all our friends and planters in good health, though they were left sicke and weake with very small meanes, the Indians round about us peaceable and friendly, the country very pleasant and temperate, yielding naturally of it self great store of fruites. . . . Better grain cannot be then the Indian corne. . . . We are all free-holders, the rent day doth not trouble us ; and all those good blessings we have, of which and what we list in their seasons for taking. Our companie are for the most part very religious honest people ; the word of God sincerely taught us every Sabbath : so that I know not any thing a contented mind can here want. I desire your friendly care to send my wife and children to me, where I wish all the friends I have in England, and so I rest

" Your loving kinsman
" WILLIAM HILTON."

Such were the beginnings of this northern planting of America by the English. It was no sudden effort, for Captain John Smith ever since his own visit had been trying to tempt West-countrymen to finance a settlement in New England. In 1618 he even approached no less a personage than the great Francis Bacon (who had been made Lord High Chancellor of England), though unsuccessfully. John Mason of King's Lynn, a naval officer who in 1616 was sent as Governor of Newfoundland and surveyed it, also explored the New England coast in 1617 But it is Sir Ferdinando Gorges who has been called the father of New England's colonization. Here was a typical English gentleman of the Elizabethan - Jacobean type. He belonged to a good West-country family, was about twenty-two years old at the time of the Armada campaign, and devoted himself to the profession of a warrior, serving afloat in various expeditions. He was that interesting soldier-sailor, explorer-patriot, churchman - anti - Spaniard, and plantation - promoter species of adventurer which was the logical Stuart development of an Elizabethan training.

His interest regarding American colonization continued to his death, and he was very jealous even of the London Virginia Company using the Cape Cod fisheries. Closely associated with Plymouth (England), where for some years he was in command of the fortifications, he had taken charge of those five Indians whom Captain George Weymouth had brought back in 1605 from his voyage to North America. And as in course of time these natives learned sufficient English to describe their country, there had been born in Gorges' mind a desire that England should colonize it. To that end, but with slight success, did he send out various expeditions for discovery or settlement. After the Plymouth Virginia Company of 1606 had finally been dissolved in 1619, Gorges then formed the new company incorporated on 3rd November, 1620, under the name of " The Council established at Plymouth, in the County of Devon, for the planting, ruling, ordering, and governing of New England." The territory was to extend from sea to sea, and the Council could number forty members. Of this first Council naturally Sir Ferdinando was an important member, whose meetings he attended with regularity. Before he died he expended on North America quite twenty thousand pounds (or the modern equivalent of ten times that amount).

But with all the unattractive poverty at this time in England and the high rents previously indicated, with Virginia rather tightly fenced against unauthorized visitors, but the colonial enthusiasm at home fast extending, it was not easy to prevent interlopers from reaching New England. Already farther south some private persons from Amsterdam had inaugurated an American trade. During the year 1621 Gorges, Sam Argall (another member of the New England Council) and others protested indignantly against the Dutch settling in certain parts of America. Official complaints were that year made to Holland, but the reply given through Sir Dudley Carleton, Ambassador at the Hague, was that the Dutch were aiming less to plant a colony than to continue a trading station. Actually the Dutch West India Company, on the site of what one day should become New York, was establishing New Amsterdam in a locality at Manhadoes (or Manhattan) known as New Netherland. But against the dissolute English interlopers who had injured New England by ruining the woods, damaging the harbours, trafficking with the Indians, selling the latter weapons and teaching the savages how these arms could be used, a proclamation had to be issued in November, 1622. This prohibited such trading and inter-meddling, unless first a licence had been granted by the New England Council. At the same time youths of high character were encouraged to be sent out thither and apprenticed.

The problem of intruders was not easy, and another six years had to pass before the New Plymouth colony was permanently settled. But the difficulty of the fisheries was eased, though not solved, by the settlement's proximity to Cape Cod. On 10th August, 1622, the New England Council granted to Sir Ferdinando Gorges and John Mason a tract of land on the sea-coast between the Merrimac and Sagadahock Rivers called the province of Maine ; but already in March Mason had obtained a grant on the coast between Naumkeag and the Merrimac called Mariana, which is now the north-east corner of Massachusetts. In this same year Gorges was about to send his son Robert, with a large patent for lands, to "Messachuset " ; it was on 30th December that the Council granted to "Robert, son of Sir Ferd. Gorges and to his heirs and assigns for ever " all that part of the mainland called "Messachustack " situate upon the north - east side of "Messachuses Bay," in consideration of the payment of one hundred and sixty pounds.

Robert Gorges went out in 1623 as Lieutenant-Governor of the New England territory ; two new pinnaces were assigned by the King for the protection of New England fishermen, and Sir Sam Argall was appointed Admiral of New England, while Mason was sending a party of emigrants to settle on the west bank of the Piscataqua. Captain Francis West, as Captain of

South-east View of New York

Showing old English church, City Hall, French church, North River, Staten Island, and prison as they appeared in the middle of the eighteenth century

Savannah, Georgia, in 1734

This shows the land already cleared and laid out, with public mill, guest-house, public oven, well, public store, fort, parsonage, palisades, and houses beginning to be built

the Plantation, and Captain Thomas Squibb were also going out. The Privy Council's orders for settling the New England trade were printed and affixed by the Admiral to the mainmast of every ship. Meanwhile the New England Council, which used to hold its ordinary meetings in the New Exchange, London, was sending directions to the Governor for managing trade with the Indians, and was also writing to the Lord Mayor of London asking for a hundred children to be shipped out. Contracts with merchant shipowners were made to transport men with victuals for a couple of months. Arthur Champernoun was given permission for his vessel *Chudley* to fish off the New England coast ; and the *Little James*, commanded by Captain Emmanuel Alchem, used to sail between old England and New. But it was exceedingly annoying that crews of these merchantmen were being pressed for the King's ships. At Whitby a new ship was being built by a syndicate for the New England trade, and all sorts of people from tailors to distillers were anxious to go out.

The Council made contracts with merchants who wanted to fish or trade in those waters, and while it was forbidden to barter either provisions or " furniture of war " with the Indians, yet the Council was anxious for it to be known that they had no wish to hinder people going out provided the latter conformed to the orders. Of course, there were tiresome people like the master of a certain English vessel who, after robbing the Indians of furs, took some of these natives aboard as prisoners. Unfortunately the ship then ran aground and the savages escaped, who " made great exclamations " against the New England planters, to the colony's great harm. But the Council had power to make its own laws, and was anxious to set north-eastern America well on the road to prosperity. A certain unity in American colonization was effected also when in July, 1624, Sir Ferdinando Gorges was made one of the Commissioners for the winding up of the London Virginia Company, and was wisely afterward made a member of his Majesty's Council of Virginia.

During the year 1623 the King urged the Lord-Lieutenants of Cornwall, Somerset, Devon, and the cities of Bristol and Exeter—that is to say the whole of the West Country—to

move " persons of quality " to join in the advancement of New
England plantation. What the Council for New England
especially required just then was that four thousand pounds
should be expended to obtain for the colony two hundred men
of three distinct classes : (a) gentlemen to bear arms and attend
on the Governor ; (b) handicraftsmen of all sorts ; (c) husbandmen to till the ground. But various merchants and others were
being admitted as patentees, and the Council decided that the
seat of New England's plantation for the public was to consist
of forty square miles, to be settled on the River Sagadahock
and called the State county. While the Council was very
strict about no men or goods reaching New England without
a licence, yet a steady trade was developing. An English
ship, for instance, could make a profitable voyage by taking
out barrels of meal as well as planters themselves, and then
for the return cargo filling up with skins, Cape Cod fish and
other commodities. Southern Catholic Europe was always an
excellent market for the fish especially. Sir Ferdinando Gorges
owned the ship *Katherine*, with Captain Thomas Squibb in
command, but the West-countrymen by the spring of 1624
had become very anxious. It was all very well for Gorges to
want the complete fishing rights of these valuable waters, but the
Mayor and citizens of Plymouth pointed out that the English
western ports had little means of livelihood except in ships,
and most of the latter were employed off north-eastern America.

But excellent propaganda work, which was much to be
desired, could now be carried on both in New England and old
England by Edward Winslow. This pioneer Pilgrim had been
selected by his fellows to visit the Sachem (or Indian Chief)
Massasoit at Pokanoket. He was able to cure the Chief of an
illness in March, 1623, and thus gained the Indian's valuable
good will toward settlers. It has been said by an American
cynic that the Pilgrim Fathers, having landed, " fell first on
their knees and then on the aborigines." The attitude of the
white man with his Bible, his missionary zeal for Indian
conversion, his zest for trade, and presently his reliance on
soldiers, was to the red man incomprehensible. While the
newly-come English had a pitying but disrespectful regard for
such human expressions of heathenism, the natives found

Christian ethics of civilization more than perplexing. This misunderstanding had the obvious tendency to create in the primitive mind that distrust and suspicion which would untimately lead to wars.

In September, 1623, Winslow sailed for England in the *Ann* to act as New England's agent, and it was while there that he followed John Smith's excellent example in publishing *Good News from New England*, being the colony's history from 1621. In the following March he went back to America in the *Charity*, taking three heifers and a bull, which were the first meat cattle England sent to New England, though Ireland became valuable to Virginia in this respect. During the summer of 1624 Winslow revisited England as colonial representative to the adventurers, and during his absence was elected one of the five assistants to the Governor. In the latter capacity he continued annually till 1647, except during the years 1633, 1636 and 1644, when he was made Governor.

Miles Standish, a Lancashire man, who had joined the Leyden community and set sail with the *Mayflower* Pilgrims, embodied the military determination of the settlers against the Indians, as also later on against the French intruders. But while various small settlements were now being made to the north of New Plymouth, it was not always the highest characters who came over. The month of June, 1622, for example, saw the landing of Thomas Morton, an able lawyer of Clifford's Inn who had been practising chiefly in the West of England. So pleased was he with New England that he came home after three months, bought a partnership in Captain Wollaston's adventure in 1625 and again sailed for Massachusetts Bay. His plantation was at Mount Wollaston (now Braintree) on the coast. Morton was a thoroughly unprincipled person, who was ever smart enough to perceive opportunities and to grasp them, whether legitimately or otherwise. And there was good reason to suspect him of having conveniently murdered his wife. Now after Wollaston (whose name is for ever connected with Boston in Wollaston Heights) presently departed for Virginia with most of his servants, Morton during the summer of 1626 established himself in control at " Mary Mount " (Merry Mount), where in the following spring he erected a maypole. The festival of dancing round a may tree or pole was the ancient European way of symbolizing the triumphant joy of summer over winter. But Morton's carnival in company of the Indians was an occasion of mere indulgence, to the horror and disgust of the strict-faced Plymouth seniors. Nor did Morton's folly end with this.

Contrary to all rules, he traded guns and ammunition to the Indians, instructed them how to use them, and established commerce with the Indians on the Kennebec. Merry Mount became a home for pirates ; the Plymouth people determined that it must be suppressed, and Captain Miles Standish arrested Morton at Wessagusset (now Weymouth). Morton escaped in the night to Wollaston, where he was retaken, and in 1628 was sent back to England with letters informing Sir Ferdinando Gorges and Council that the culprit must answer for his delinquencies. In the meanwhile John Endicott, Governor of the chartered new Massachusetts Company, ordered the maypole to be cut down, and the name of the place to be changed to Mount Dagon. This extreme caution in New England's dealings with the Indians was justified doubly, since the news of the 1622 massacre in Virginia reached the younger colony. More wary than ever was it necessary to be, and the building of a strong fort was a natural care. But the acres of planted corn, the rich harvest of the sea, the plentiful fruits of the trees, the valuable skins, gave to these increasing settlements a firm confidence with courage.

Thus it was that all these more northerly settlements were to be embraced under a new charter, and men of a higher social grade than the Plymouth Separatists were to come out. It was the political and religious unrest in England which now created the new colonial development. " The vigour of the Puritan and Roman Catholic attacks upon the Church of England threw Englishmen back upon first principles. . . . They had to justify alike their treatment of Puritanism as a system of religion incompatible with that of the Church, and of Roman Catholicism as a tyranny fastened upon the religion of the Church."[1] Hooker had shown where the intellectual basis of

[1] *An Introduction to the History of the Church of England*, by H. O. Wakeman. London, 1898.

Puritanism was wrong. A reaction against Puritanism set in strongly. Philosophers like Bacon rebelled against its mental narrowness, and Laud stood out against its attitude even unskilfully and forcefully. In 1628 he was appointed Bishop of London, the most Puritan diocese in England. And his energetic reaction against all complicity with Calvinism was a clear opportunity for a Puritan exodus.

In March, 1628, Captain John Endicott, a man of about forty years of age, joined with five other " religious persons " in purchasing a patent of the territory of Massachusetts Bay from the New England Council. Having been given full powers to take charge of a plantation at Naumkeag (afterward called Salem), he sailed with his wife and about twenty emigrants from Weymouth on 20th June, the selected ship being that well-known Atlantic carrier *Abigail*. The voyage was a lengthy one, and he did not reach Naumkeag until 6th September. There established, Endicott in his honest, tactless, courageous but bad-tempered manner began zealously, with his Puritan Council, the Massachusetts Bay venture in a set objection against any cultivation of tobacco, which was considered not merely injurious to health but hurtful to morals. He would have as little to do with the Book of Common Prayer as with Morton's merry maypole, where the wicked lawyer had been wont to publish anti-Puritan satires. It was on 27th February, 1629, that at Westminster the grant made by the New England Council was confirmed to Sir Henry Roswell, Sir John Young, Thomas Southcote, John Humphrey, John Endicott, Simon Whitcombe, their heirs and associates, with a further grant of incorporation under the name of The Governor and Company of the Massachusetts Bay in America. The Royal Charter was issued to them on the following 4th March.

Morton managed to ingratiate himself with Gorges, so that in August, 1629, the former arrived back in New England with Isaac Allerton, went to Mount Wollaston, encouraged the old planters against the new Massachusetts Bay Company, defied Endicott's authority, continued to trade with the Indians (though not in fire-arms), till in the following year he was arrested, placed in the stocks, again sent home to England and his house burned down. After imprisonment in Exeter jail, he was freed in 1631, and began intriguing with Gorges for the overthrow of the Massachusetts charter. The results of that conduct will appear presently. In 1629 Gorges and Mason increased their property, procuring from the New England Council a grant on the coast between Merrimac and Piscataqua Rivers which was designated New Hampshire, and also a patent , for a tract embracing Lake Champlain with its vicinity, called Laconia. Mason had been busy during the period 1624–29 as Treasurer and Paymaster of the English forces during the war with Spain, but now in 1630 he sent out some more colonists to Piscataqua, and in the following year formed a partnership with Gorges, as well as others, for trade and settlement there.

CHAPTER XXI

THE NEW ENGLAND NUCLEUS

CAPTAIN JOHN SMITH died in London on 21st June, 1631, but a few months before passing away he wrote an interesting summing up of those principal colonial founders who took out parties between April, 1629, and October, 1630, and in a few sentences we see the general character of this Puritan (Massachusetts Bay) endeavour as distinct from the Pilgrim Fathers' (New Plymouth) proposition. Of the former he remarked : " Those which are their chiefe undertakers are Gentlemen of good estate, some of 500, some a thousand pound land a yeere, all which they say they will sell for the advancing this harmlesse and pious worke ; men of good credit and well-beloved in their Country, not such as flye for debt, or any scandall at home ; and are good Catholike Protestants according to the reformed Church of England, if not, it is well they are gone. The rest of them men of good meanes, or Arts, Occupations, and Qualities, much more fit for such businesse, and better furnished of all necessaries if they arrive well, than was ever any Plantation went out of England."

Having got together a large sum of money as capital, six good ships in the spring of 1629, containing three hundred and fifty men, women, children, one hundred and fifty cattle, horses, goats, household provisions, clothes, six guns for a fort, and fire-arms, set sail from the Thames for Massachusetts Bay, into which flowed the Charles River, the name which Charles I had given to it when Smith had submitted for royal approval the first New England map. The ships were the *George Bonaventure, Talbot, Lion's Whelp, Four Sisters, Pilgrim,* and one which (in accordance with prevailing custom) kept up the name *Mayflower.* The people reached Salem, and found that Endicott's people from Dorchester (England) had already erected houses. At Charlton, where a northern suburb of the modern Boston was eventually to rise, some hundred and fifty people settled also. During the next year many people were anxious to settle in New England, if the means could be provided to take them, the intention being to further " the conversion of the savages." And long discourses, interspersed with Scriptural quotations, were put forward by such applicants. Thus the early days of New England were more fortunate than those first years of Virginia ; good class families of volunteers were likely to make better colonists than expelled criminals.

Now in the year that witnessed the coming of the Armada there was born, in the county of Suffolk, John Winthrop whose grandfather had been a well-established clothier. John went up to Trinity College, Cambridge, and afterward married Mary Forth, who died in 1615. Here was a man of keen religious instinct, but of an introspective and strictly Puritan type. Wild-fowl shooting over the Essex marshes he gave up because he conceived it to be a sinful thing ; the use of tobacco and the popular Stuart practice of drinking a man's health he condemned likewise. One angle of his character reveals a somewhat morbid, lonely mind, intensified by domestic events. He was a widower for only six months, and then married Thomasine Clopton, who died after a year, but in 1618 he wedded Margaret Tyndal, who did something to curb his self-accusing religiosity. There was a time in his life when he contemplated receiving Holy Orders, but in 1628 he was admitted to the Inner Temple.

Men or women in this uncertain world searching for sadness not unusually find it. The loss of his mother, the political unsettlement, the growth of luxury, the increased cost of living and educating children, a general impression that the world was rapidly drifting to perdition, so affected him that by the spring of 1629 he was considering leaving his native country. The Company of Massachusetts was originally intended to be governed, after the manner of Virginia, from England, but in July, at a meeting held in the house of Deputy-Governor Thomas Goffe in London, it was suggested by Governor Cradock that the government (with a view to obtaining the utmost freedom from royal control) should be transferred from London to Massachusetts. A month later there was a meeting in

Boston, Massachusetts

As it appeared in the eighteenth century

Cambridge, when John Winthrop, Sir Richard Saltonstall, Increase Nowell and nine others pledged themselves to sail with their families and remain in New England, provided the government and patent of the Massachusetts Company be first legally transferred to " us and others which shall inhabit upon the said plantation."

When it was announced on 20th October, 1629, that this transference had been decided upon, Winthrop by reason of his social standing and high character was elected Governor by vote for the ensuing year. Five months' preparations followed, people and cattle were collected, and shipping obtained. Out of the eleven vessels chartered four were ready by 22nd March, 1630, and on that day Winthrop, Richard Saltonstall and others embarked in the *Arbella* at Southampton. Winthrop's wife, being about to have a child, did not sail till a year later. But among the party were three of Winthrop's sons, five of Saltonstall's children; the wealthy Isaac Johnson, with his wife Lady Arbella, daughter of the Earl of Lincoln; and in honour of this woman Winthrop's flagship had changed its name from *Eagle*. Winthrop was the founder of one of the most famous families in all American history, which later on gave to the new country distinguished governors, soldiers, scholars, mathematicians, scientists, orators, statesmen, barristers and men of letters. The Saltonstalls of Boston to this day are another illustrious historic family, whose history is rooted in these early Anglo-American colonization ventures. Sir Samuel Saltonstall was a close friend of Captain John Smith, and to him the first President of Virginia made important bequests. Captain Charles Saltonstall, son of Sir Samuel, is mentioned by Smith in his *True Travels*, and Wye Saltonstall translated Hondius's *Historia Mundi*. Other persons of good family and standing who sailed were the Earl of Lincoln's brother; Thomas Dudley, his wife and six children; William Coddington and wife; the Pinchons; and the Vassalls. The first Earl of Lincoln had been interested in Frobisher's voyages; the second Earl was a member of the Virginia Council, Lady Arbella being his granddaughter. And it is worth mentioning that a descendant of that family, Sir Henry Clinton, was commander-in-chief of his Majesty's forces in America during the Revolution.

S

But westerly winds delayed the Winthrop ships off the Isle of Wight during a fortnight, which gave the leaders time to write their letters of farewell, and while still under the shelter of Cowes roadstead Winthrop began that valuable diary which continued till the close of his career, and was the basis of all future histories concerning the young New England colony. The actual voyage took thirty-six days, part of the time being beguiled by Winthrop in writing his work entitled *A Model of Christian Charity*, the manuscript of which was eventually to come into the hands of the New York Historical Society.

Owing to bad Atlantic weather seventy of two hundred cattle died and many of the passengers became ill. It is significant that, having anchored off Salem in mid-June, Isaac Johnson died on 30th September, at Boston, but Lady Arbella had already predeceased him in August at Salem, two notable additional instances of the heavy toll of lives which these terrible ships demanded from American pioneers. On arrival it was learned by Winthrop that the Salem people had lost sixty persons by death, that there had been idle negligence in providing houses and corn. In preference to Salem, Winthrop chose to settle at Charlton (or Charlestown) on the Charles River. Endicott had been acting-Governor, but now Winthrop took over the office as the first regularly-elected Governor, and the friendship of the two men continued till death. To a colony of about three hundred people Winthrop brought about another ten hundred. A church was started at Charlton on 30th July, but lack of good water compelled them on 7th September to shift to the neighbouring Shawmut peninsula, which now was given the name of Boston, though what we know to-day as York farther up the coast appears in John Smith's 1614 map of New England as Boston also.

Winthrop needed all his abilities to control this crowd. Many of those who followed were ill-provided, and there were so many women and children as to cause a heavy strain on supplies. The Puritan selectiveness was also a difficult problem. " Some," wrote John Smith, " could not endure the name of a Bishop, others not the sight of a Crosse nor Surplesse, others by no meanes the booke of common Prayer." Those of the Brownist sect Winthrop let go to New Plymouth to join the

Pilgrim party, but about two hundred departed for England, disgruntled with the country and its rattlesnakes.

Already there were preachers in New England ; the Lord's Day was observed, and catechizing diligently carried out. How did this compare with the early Jamestown life ? Smith himself will answer the question :

" When I went to Virginia, I well remember wee did hang an awning (which is an old saile) to three or foure trees to shadow us from the sunne, our walles were rales of wood, our seats unhewed trees till we cut plankes, our pulpit a bar of wood nailed to two neighbouring trees. In foule weather we shifted into an old rotten tent ; for we had few better, and this came by the way of adventure for new. This was our church, till wee built a homely thing like a barne, set upon cratchets, covered with rafts, sedge, and earth ; so was also the walls : the best of our houses of the like curiosity ; but the most part farre much worse workmanship, that could neither well defend wind nor raine. Yet wee had daily Common Prayer morning and evening, every Sunday two sermons, and every three moneths the Holy Communion, till our Minister died : but our prayers daily, with an homily on Sundaies, we continued two or three yeares after, till more Preachers came."

With some interruptions Winthrop remained Governor until his death in 1649. Massachusetts was seething with sectarian narrow-mindedness, jealousies and intolerance. When he was re-elected Governor at the General Court on 18th May, 1631, it was decided that in the future no man should be admitted to the freedom of " the body politic " except such as were members of the churches within the limits of the same. In that year also the Massachusetts village of Watertown indignantly declined to pay a tax levied by the Massachusetts Board of Assistants, the reason given being that she was not represented on that body. This led to speedy stabilization of self-government, two deputies being sent from each settlement to advise the Assistants. Next the colonists elected deputies and representatives to a General Court. Representative government in Virginia and New England could not be gainsaid.

In consequence of the ships during 1630 having carried out more persons than expected — " many poor people pressing

aboard "—and little or no corn having been planted by their
immediate predecessors, the necessary supplies had to be
imported for carrying on till the end of the next summer. But
during the next year further grants of land were being made
by the New England Council to John Stratton, Walter Bagnall,
George Norton, Robert Rainsford, Robert Trelawny, Moses
Goodyeare and others. The proclamation forbidding the
sale of arms to the New England Indians had a salutary
effect, and the Council did not hesitate to deport to England
anyone found guilty of this deed. For every person brought
from England who remained in Massachusetts three years an
additional hundred acres were earned by their master.

A map of Salem and Massachusetts Bay was being made in
1632 for the New England Council by Mr. Saltonstall, but of
the forty permitted Councillors only about half had been so
far elected. Hitherto the Council had held its meetings at
Warwick House, Holborn, but these now took place in Captain
John Mason's house in Fenchurch Street. Settlers were anxious
to settle Long Island, whose position was described vaguely as
between James City and Cape Cod. But the island was reported
as excellent for building and launching ships, with springs of
drinking water as good as small beer ! Winthrop in July, 1632,
wrote to the Rev. John White of Dorchester, England, saying
that after spending about three hundred pounds he owned only
some cattle and old kettles. He asked for cod-lines and fish-
hooks to be sent out, and feared that his own brother and sister
were dead, as they had not written. There is a delightfully
human touch when Winthrop marvelled that Mrs. Galopp
preferred to live miserably with her children in England, when
she might be so comfortable with her husband in Massachusetts.
White's colonial philosophy was typical of the best - class
Puritans : New England was a magnificent chance for doing a
solemn work on behalf of God. Young people and skilled
artificers should be encouraged to go out, but great and funda-
mental errors had been made by placing profit as the chief aim
and not the propagation of religion. Indeed, it was Mr. White's
opinion that the very scum of the earth had been sent over.

And yet, in that selfsame year, at one of the New England
Council's meeting in Fenchurch Street, steps were being taken

Salem, Massachusetts

From an old engraving

for " the poorer sort " of people to be carried to this new
territory. But it was good to receive such information as
was brought by Captain Thomas Wiggin, who had been on a visit
to these English plantations and described Massachusetts as
" the largest, best and most prospering in all that land," adding
that the country was well stored with timber and would yield
cordage, pitch and tar, that the two thousand inhabitants had
done more in three years than others in seven times that space,
and at one-tenth the expense. (This was a criticism of Virginia.)
Winthrop he regarded as a discreet and sober man, wearing
plain apparel, assisting in any ordinary labour, but ruling with
much mildness and justice. Even the Indians so greatly
respected and loved him that they came to the Governor when
it was justice they sought. In September, 1632, we find
Winthrop paying a ceremonious visit to the New Plymouth
planters.

In the personal troubles that were boiling up Edward
Winslow was not the least significant figure. While he rightly
accused the notorious Morton of having been twice sent home
in disgrace, and even alleged that Dixie Bull was only a pirate,
and that Sir Christopher Gardiner was a Jesuit, Winslow himself
got into hot water. In 1635 he became agent in England for
both the Massachusetts and Plymouth colonies. He was called
upon to answer complaints made by Morton, and was further
accused that, being only a layman, Winslow had publicly taught
in church and celebrated marriages. For these offences he was
in July committed to the Fleet Prison by the orders of Laud,
and from this jail he petitioned the Privy Council as follows :
He admitted having exhorted the people in American and per-
forming the marriage ceremony, but the inhabitants had been
seven or eight years without a minister, and had he not carried
out these religious actions " we might have lost the life and
face of Christianity." The colonists had left England " disliking
many things in practice here in respect of Church ceremony,"
and choosing rather to quit the country than be accounted
troublers of it. He mentioned the valuable supplies which could
be exported to England if the King would only continue their
liberty of conscience, afford facilities to new settlers, and grant
them a free commission for displanting the French and Dutch.

This petition secured Winslow his release, and he returned to New Plymouth, where he was made Governor in 1636. Now there are two important matters which stand out from the above document. We have seen the theme of discontent which was running through the whole of Virginia's story, and must some day be heard in the final symphony of Independence. Not less discernible is the motif which from the first begins in the primitive New England music, and must at the finale mingle with the clashing Virginian notes. The people of New Plymouth and Massachusetts Bay sailed out as protestors against certain established English principles that had been made to seem, in the light of ephemeral episodes, harsh and unbearable. Thus, besides planting corn in New England, there was sown something more permanent still : the seeds of discord, the grains of distrust, the germs of revolution which would keep springing up and never die. Or, to omit all metaphor, each generation passed on its grievance, its inheritance of oppression, till the great chance came of rising with the other colonial communities against the originating country of their forefathers.

There was raised by Winslow this serious matter of the foreign interlopers. In February, 1631, John Mason, in the year before he became a member of the great Council for New England and was soon afterward chosen its Vice-President, had detained at Plymouth that celebrated ship *Eendracht* of Amsterdam, belonging to the Dutch West India Company. She was bound from the Manhattan (Hudson) River and brought American products to Europe. Sir Ferdinando Gorges, writing to Mason in approval of the latter's action, insisted that they must stand upon the just title of the King to those American territories, by virtue of first discovery, actual possession and their own rights by several patents. Gorges further called to remembrance the fact of the British Ambassador (Sir Dudley Carleton) to the United Dutch Provinces having had orders to question the Dutch arrivals in America, and the answer given that these were solely private traders ; the King had granted certain parts of north Virginia, " by us called New England," to particular persons, and Gorges was clever enough to request Mason to obtain from the *Eendracht* all possible information as to the strength of the Dutch in

America, where they lived, how fortified, where were their friends and enemies, and what trade was there besides furs.

In 1632 the *Eendracht* was released at the earnest request of the Dutch Ambassador, but the King made it perfectly plain that his Majesty had the right to the territories whence this ship's merchandize had come; and declared that if the Dutch remained there without his licence " they shall impute it to themselves if hereafter they suffer." The English attitude was well summed up in Mason's letter to Secretary of State Coke, reminding him that in 1621 certain Hollanders had begun a trade on the New England coast between Cape Cod and Delaware Bay in Lat. 40° N., a region granted to Sir Walter Raleigh in 1584 and afterward confirmed and divided by King James in 1606; that the Hollanders had come as interlopers between Virginia and New England, and had published a map of the coast between Virginia and Cape Cod with the title of New Netherlands, calling the river upon which they were planted Manhattan, and giving Dutch names to other places discovered by the English; that Sir Sam Argall with many English planters was about to settle in those parts; that in 1622 under a pretended authority from the Dutch West India Company these interlopers had made a plantation on Manhattan, fortified themselves, and built ships there, including one of six hundred tons. The English of New Plymouth had warned them neither to trade nor to make settlement, but the Dutch with proud and contumacious manner answered: " We have commission to fight against such as should disturb our settlement." Thus the Dutch settlement went on, the English were vilified to the Indians, and in the year 1632 alone fifteen thousand beaver skins and other commodities were exported into Holland.

The French attitude in regard to the New England settlements was that the former claimed the country by right of first discoverers, that Jacques Cartier had called it Nova Francia, though he had never attempted to plant there; and in 1603 the French King had granted to Monsieur de Monts a patent of that area between Lat. 40° and 46° N. The French certainly made three unsuccessful attempts to discover Massachusetts Bay. In 1623 about one hundred and twenty emigrants had set out to plant in Delaware Bay, but had been forced by cross winds to land about twenty-five miles south of Massachusetts Bay and there begin a colony.

But the Dutch settled also on the Quonektacat (or Connecticut) River in 1633 ; where Hartford now stands, however, and elsewhere there presently came companies of people from Massachusetts in 1634–36, whom the Dutch failed to get rid of. John Winthrop, able son of that other Winthrop, became Connecticut's Governor in 1635. In Boston ship-building, as on the Dutch Manhattan Island, was going ahead. One William Stephens, who built the 600-ton *Royal Merchant*, was supposed to be no less skilled than the best shipwrights in the United Kingdom. Hundreds of settlers continued to reach New England, but the Privy Council were not too pleased that so many emigrants were thus earning the title of being religious just because they hated the ceremonies of the English Church and its Book of Common Prayer. Such " giddiness," as Commissioner Henry Dade of Suffolk called this protestation, suggested alarming future trouble in New England.

But already there were beginning certain differences in the New England Council itself, and a petition was presented at the end of 1632 praying the Privy Council to inquire into New England's affairs. The affidavits of Morton and others were largely responsible for this new development. It was felt by Sir Ferdinando Gorges and his party that discontented people settling in Connecticut as neighbours to the Dutch, disaffected " both to the King's Government and to the State Ecclesiastical," created a new situation of danger. Uniformity of control was now needed for New England. The authorities at home were being careful that no more passengers (except those under age) should be allowed to sail, until they had taken the oath of allegiance. This interference with the flow of people and supplies, and, further, the prohibitive Customs tax in New England, annoyed the planters considerably.

The frenzy of Massachusetts Puritanism during the year 1634 reached such a point that it is difficult for us nowadays to comprehend all this anger. In September Endicott heard of a rumour that the King was about to demand their charter and compel obedience to the ceremonies of the English Church as interpreted and enforced by Laud. Endicott, whose religious conventions were the exact opposite of Laud's, now publicly cut out the red cross of St. George from the banner used by the Salem train band, under the curious conception that the symbol of Christian salvation was the emblem of Popery. The matter was brought before the General Court ; Endicott was admonished and prohibited from holding public office for a year. But by the " irregular, inconformable fugitive ministers " of religion who had gone out to Plymouth, Boston, Dorchester, Charlton, Salem and elsewhere, considerable feeling had been roused among the people. While the Salem inhabitants had (as James Cudworth wrote home) " cut the cross in the flag or ancient [1] that they carry before them when they train," the militia even went as far as to refuse service until that should be done ; so, in respect for such bigotry, the military commissioners had finally to order the cross to be omitted.

Just as in 1624 Virginia had surrendered its charter and become a royal colony, so in 1635 the Great Council of New England surrendered theirs. It was Sir Ferdinando Gorges' own idea that this three hundred miles of coast-line should be divided into several provinces, with a Governor and assistants assigned to each, and a Lord-Governor or Lord-Lieutenant to represent the King. The territory was divided, Gorges receiving a new charter four years later confirming to him the province of Maine with vice-regal powers, and to this region he devoted the rest of his life. A royalist, member of the English Church, and no Puritan, he served during the Civil War in England and died in Somerset during the year 1647, being then over eighty years of age.

The manner of this change in the affairs of New England was as follows. On 3rd February, 1635, the New England Council at the house of Lord Gorges (an Irish peer and relative of Sir Ferdinando) in St. Martin's Lane, London, agreed upon the surrender. On 22nd April they granted the Province of New Hampshire, with an additional ten thousand acres (to be called Masonia), to Captain John Mason ; and certain other grants were made also. It was on 25th April that the New

---

[1] " Ancient " was a time-honoured word used by Tudor soldiers and sailors when referring to the national ensign.

England Council assembled in the Earl of Carlisle's chambers, Whitehall, when the charter was formally resigned in the presence of Lord Gorges, and a number of distinguished noblemen and knights, who drew up an important declaration. By long experience they had found that their endeavours to advance the New England plantation had been attended with frequent troubles and great expenses ; they had been assaulted by sharp and litigious questions before the Privy Council by the Virginia Company, who complained that New England was a grievance to the Commonwealth ; they were disheartened by the claims of the French ambassador. These crosses left only a " carcass in a manner breathless." The first foundations of the colony had been rent in pieces ; new conceits on matters of religion and forms of ecclesiastical and temporal government framed. Thus—but with reservation of their lawful rights— the patent was surrendered, the physical act taking place on 7th June. Mason was appointed Vice-Admiral of New England, his area being from 40° to 48° N., and (amusing to mention) this should include the South Seas "where lyeth California and Nova Albion." But before this patent could be drawn up Mason died.

By this year 1635 over forty sailing ships were trading to the English plantations, and hundreds of people were crossing to New England as well, men, women and children. Among them now sailed Henry Vane, eldest son of that statesman, ambassador and Lord High Admiral Sir Henry Vane. The young Henry was in some respects another Winthrop. " I was born a gentleman," Henry, Jr., wrote of himself, " and had the education, temper and spirit of a gentleman as well as others, being in my youthful days inclined to the vanities of the world, and to that which they call good fellowship, judging it to be the only means of accomplishing a gentleman." Born in 1612, he was converted to Puritanism at fifteen, and a year later went to Oxford, later studying in Protestant Geneva and Leyden.

He grew up a man of courage, quick-minded, astute, incorruptible, unorthodox, and a curious mixture of sectarian fancies allied with extravagance. Somewhat obscure in his actual religious faith, he was essentially opposed to any ordained and settled ministry, in favour of a free conscience, and opposed entirely to the Church of England's ceremonial expression of faith. So, like the rest, he set out for the freedom of New England, obtained the King's licence, and sailed on 3rd October, 1635, in the *Abigail*, duly arriving at Boston. This friend of John Winthrop, Jr., was well received in Massachusetts as " a young gentleman of excellent parts," who had forsaken the honours of the Court to pursue his religious instincts. On 1st November he was admitted a member of the Boston church, and on the following 25th of March became Massachusetts' youthful Governor. Immediately he arranged with the ship-masters for the better control ashore of the wild seamen, but his stay in New England was not long.

"A wise and Godly gentleman," as Winthrop described him, Vane had the impetuosity of a youngster, the introspective character that is super-sensitive, irritable, headstrong, and the temperament easily roused to suspiciousness, jealousy, controversy and irritation. At this period Massachusetts was divided into rival factions concerning such theological subjects as " grace," " sanctification " and " good works," and it was his misfortune to become associated with the smaller faction, to gain unpopularity in dealing with problems that his inexperience did not suffer him fitness for solving. So on 3rd August, 1637, he sailed for England. The rest of his life, his knighthood, his three thousand pounds a year bequeathed by his father, and his execution on Tower Hill in 1662 for high treason concerned with the death of Charles I need not here concern us. But it is interesting to note how his departure from home in 1635 had been regarded in England. Thus, on 18th September, G. Garrard writes to Lord Conway that Sir Henry Vane has as good as lost his eldest son, who has gone to New England for conscience' sake ; for he likes not the discipline of the Church of England. None of our ministers, continues the correspondent, will give him the Sacrament standing, and no persuasions of the Bishops, nor authority of his parents, will prevail with him.

During Vane's sojourn in America he found that the French were continually encroaching and arming the natives, who killed and stole whenever possible. In 1638 New Haven was settled, but in the following year the Connecticut planters were in great distress for want of provisions through improvidence.

They had come here because of hardships endured in Massachu-setts, and now three thousand transmigrants were without butter, cheese and shoes. The Privy Council refused to help them.

In New England's young life theological controversies went on with as much vehemence as in old England. Individuals were admitted into the congregations by making a confession of faith, giving glory to God, and, in the case of notorious sinners, first making a penitent confession. So many men were now selling their lands and going out that there was a veritable danger of English parishes becoming impoverished. In March, 1638, for example, fourteen ships were about to sail from the Thames, and so much corn was being carried to New England that there would hardly be enough in the old country till next harvest. In that year it was proposed to establish a post office in New England and allow twopence a letter—that sum being the smallest coin there.

The better-class emigrants took out corn and provisions with which to land, but " the poorer sort " were impoverishing New England by having brought merely enough for the voyage. Old Sir Ferdinando Gorges made a caustic remark in comparing Virginia's and New England's factious colonization with that of other nations. " Romans, Spanish, and Dutch did and do conquer ; not plant tobacco and Puritanism only—like fools." Many people " conformable to " the Church of England were also coming out, however, especially from Bristol. Morton, after a varied career, was starved out of England, arrested in Boston during 1644 for libelling the colony, fined one hundred pounds, and eventually died in poverty.

Sooner or later it could have been discerned that the several New England colonies must, without loss of individuality, form some sort of union, some connecting bond. Nothing so tends toward alliance as the danger from a common foe. And it was the persistent peril from the Indians that in 1643 brought about that important confederacy of Massachusetts, New Plymouth, New Haven and Connecticut. This union was historic because it was the inauguration of a new colonial conception, and created a precedent for that more comprehensive confederacy which over a hundred and thirty years later was to carry on the Revolutionary War. We thus have a strengthening and stabilizing of the Puritan policy of independence at the time when the executions of Archbishop Laud and Charles I were not far off, and the Commonwealth period was to give Puritanism in England supremacy of place. Those who had during the last twenty - odd years forsaken England as individuals of liberty now had become merged into an organization which in course of time must gain and need greater strength against that common foe of colonial America to be found in Britain's policy toward them. The struggle would undergo phases and degrees of intensity, but in the main it would resolve itself into one between the attempt to impose the will of the Crown and the determination of exiled men to live their own existence free of trans-Atlantic domination. Circumstances, accidents, personal incidents might accelerate or delay the conclusion, but the premises of the syllogism were by this mid-seventeenth century conspicuously clear. The mere fact that Maine was not included in the 1643 confederacy was simply because of the Gorgesian anti-Puritan, rather than anti-colonial attitude.

On the other hand, there was spreading into New England a disuniting force based on theological and political differences of opinion among the colonists themselves. While thus some families emigrated into Connecticut and incidentally planted an obstacle to the Dutchmen's eastern expansion from Manhattan, others had found solace in Rhode Island. In December, 1643, the Earl of Warwick in his capacity of Governor-in-Chief and Lord High Admiral of all the Plantations in America granted (in association with others) to the Governor, Assistants and Freemen of Massachusetts the whole tract of the Narragansett Bay region, extending about twenty-five English miles to the Pequot River. In the following March the same authorities in England granted to the inhabitants of Providence Portsmouth and Newport — because a newer neighbourhood was being adventured and other places were being bought from the Indians—a free and absolute charter to be known as Providence Plantation, with power to govern themselves and make laws conformable to those of England. The rise of the Quakers was a result of the preaching by George Fox (1624–90). Fox's adherents developed religious individualism with such vehemence that their arrival in New England could not fail to cause violent collisions with the equally individual Puritans. For years the peace of Massachusetts was disturbed, and intolerant laws were passed. Governor Endicott, who would flog and execute those not in religious agreement with himself, and banned the wearing of long hair, hated the Quakers above all. Winslow, too, was persistently narrow-minded. In 1646 he sailed to England to answer complaints of cruelty raised by Samuel Gorton and others, and to defend himself against charges of religious intolerance and persecution. But men like John Child and William Vassall were more forbearing, and resented Winslow's policy.

The Commonwealth Government allowed Winslow to send in 1650 to New England one hundred and fifty barrels of powder, twenty tons of shot and lead, and one hundred muskets and fowling-pieces, on condition that these should not be sold to any plantation disaffected toward the Commonwealth. On 31st May of that same year was granted the charter for Harvard College in Cambridge, Middlesex, Massachusetts Bay Colony, for the education of English and Indian youth which had been founded in 1636. There were to be a President, five Fellows and a Treasurer, Henry Dunster being the first President. New England was fast developing its own character and its own trade. In 1653 the Commonwealth decided to purchase therefrom ten thousand barrels of tar and five thousand pounds' worth of goods suitable for shipping. Two hundred youths were being sent out from England as servants to any New Englanders who would pay for such service by rendering products needed at home for men-of-war and merchant vessels. And four hundred children were being carried out from Ireland to New England and Virginia too. Indeed, so well peopled was New England by 1655 that an official offer came to remove such as " knew and feared the Lord " into Jamaica, which had recently become British. It was on the voyage to this island that Winslow died.

CHAPTER XXII

THE STRUGGLE FOR FREEDOM

WE have now reached the stage when both Virginia and New England had grown to increasing strength and fresh consciousness of a capability for independence. We next enter upon the period when this youthful exuberance and self-confidence pass into a mature desire for the fullest expression. The struggle against the Crown was the fight for self-determination, but it was aggravated by two considerations: (a) the indifferent and often totally unsuitable selection of men sent over as Governors; and (b) the isolation of North America by the physical width of the Atlantic, which in practical terms meant months.

With regard to the latter, we could find no more witty and caustic phrases than in the words used by Daniel Denison, Major-General in New England, when in the year of the Restoration, sitting in the Court of Judicature, he spoke the following scoffing words to the Quakers: "You will go to England," he said, "to complain this year. The next they will send to see if it be true. And by next year the Government in England will be changed." It was to rid themselves of all this lonely dependence, interference with internal affairs, and instability of governance that the English-Americans were now about to focus their future activities. One of the basic causes of the English Reformation had been the desire to be free from appeal to Rome ; in America the cause of separation would be found in the longing to possess its own supremacy, to become master of its own fate.

With this implied declaration on the lips of responsible, thinking planters both in the North and in the South, we can now trace the trend of events with keener clarity if we exclude all non-effective detail. Our objective in the previous chapters has been to show causes, circumstances, and counteractions in regard to overseas colonization. It remains now to connect these with final and definitive results.

Between the date of appointment and the arrival in the American colony of a new Governor there was inevitably a varying lapse of time. On 9th August, 1641, Sir William Berkeley, brother of the first Lord Berkeley, was granted his commission as Virginia's Governor, and reached Jamestown the following February. Here was another Oxford man who, after leaving Merton College, had further widened his mind by travel. A gentleman of Charles I's privy chamber, prudent, pious, sober, just and diligent, he brought to his duties as administrator a knowledge of the world and colonial zeal which Virginia recognized with appreciation. The times were difficult, and great decisions were hanging in suspense. While Virginia's settlers had now become more inclined to have good buildings, and to find permanent pleasure in their gardens and orchards, their cattle and their pigs, most of the new arrivals were in effect human merchandise, homeless vagrants whom England was glad to deport. Still, the planters could never tell, until the tobacco crop had been taken down, whether there was enough to purchase one of these servants ; and the levies for various occasions, such as repairing the Fort at Point Comfort and building a State House at James City, were first claims on industry. Ministers of religion enjoyed tithes, and this necessitated still further labour before profit could be gathered.

By 1638 the excessive purchase of wines had been restrained ; running away to the Indians had become a felony ; constables were being established to prevent disorders ; and it was forbidden to export cattle from Virginia. Only one of all Scotland's merchants had begun trading with that colony, and he was John Burnett of Aberdeen. As to the Maryland difficulty, the Lords Commissioners of Plantations, who were now the responsible colonial authorities in England, had decided that the right and title of the Isle of Kent belonged absolutely to Lord Baltimore, and no grant was to pass into the hands of Clayborne. At the same time Baltimore was informed that the Kent Island planters were not to be interfered with, but rather encouraged. And while convicts were still being transported into Virginia, emigrants from Sweden were planning to settle around Delaware and grow tobacco, having heard of the Dutchmen's profitable trade at Manhattan.

Before Berkeley's advent Virginia had begun to stabilize itself by many diverse efforts. From every ship that came up the James River to trade enough ammunition was demanded to keep Point Comfort Fort well supplied for defence. It had also been decided by the General Assembly that a fee of sixpence per poll be paid to the Captain of the Fort, who was to keep a register containing name, age and birthplace of every passenger arriving. Houses and stores of brick by January, 1639, had been built in Jamestown, and were (in the words of Secretary Kemp) " the fairest ever known in this country for substance and uniformity." While the State House was being constructed by levy, other houses of a substantial type were being erected to beautify the place in accordance with Charles I's orders that the slight cottages heretofore run up should no longer be allowed. Already by this time large contributions toward providing a brick church for Jamestown had been collected. As a badge of sovereignty an annual rent of twelvepence on every fifty acres of land was still being paid to the King.

Sir Francis Wyatt's régime had been marked by determination and drastic procedure with a view to ultimate benefit. He inaugurated his term of administration by destroying all the bad tobacco and half the good, as the only means of maintaining prices. " And," he wrote to England in explanation, " though the physic seems sharp, yet I hope it will bring the body of the colony to a sounder constitution of health than ever it enjoyed before." Now when his successor was appointed the instructions given to Sir William Berkeley well illustrated the mind that was England's. Briefly they may be summed up as follows, and are of especial interest with regard to the future history of Virginia :

The Governor was to be careful that Almighty God is served according to the form of religion established in the Church of England. Every congregation to provide its own Minister. Those who refuse to take the oath of allegiance to be sent home. Justice to be administered according to the

T

laws of England. The General Assembly to meet annually ; the Governor to have a negative vote. Quarterly Courts to be held, and all suitors to have free access thereto. Councillors are to be preceeded against whenever requisite. Inferior Courts of Justice to be established for suits not exceeding the value of ten pounds, and for minor offences. The Governor to appoint all officers, except members of the Council, the Captain of the Fort, the Muster-Master and Surveyor-General. Every Councillor and ten of his servants to be exempted from public charges and not to be assessed as contributor except for a war, the building of a town or churches, and the duties of a Minister. Probate of wills to be made. All persons above sixteen years of age to bear arms. The Captain of the Fort at Point Comfort, and ten guards, to be maintained. All but new-comers and Councillors to contribute to a war. Trade with savages forbidden without a special licence. Beacons to be erected in various parts of the country. Everyone to build a house according to his proportion of land. A Government House to be erected in a more convenient place than James-town, which place is to retain the same ancient name. Patents of land to be granted, of fifty acres, to every person transported to Virginia since midsummer 1625. No person to go on board a newly-arrived ship without leave. No ship-masters to break bulk till they reached Jamestown. The sale of wine and strong waters, the impaling and fencing-in of orchards, and the stinting of tobacco to be regulated. Staple commodities, such as hemp, flax, rape-seed, madder, pitch, tar, vines and white mulberry-trees to be raised.

But those eventful years of 1642–49, the quarrels between Charles I and his Parliament, and his departure by the scaffold, were to have the effect of lowering royal authority in the estimation of colonial America. While Virginia was for a time little affected to outward appearances, and seemed even the one royalist plantation, yet the shock was received none the less. One of the earliest measures of the Republican Govern-ment sought to establish its authority over the colonies, letters informing the latter of the change, and requiring continued obedience, being sent on 26th July, 1649. Berkeley's presence, as a loyal friend and subject of the late King, but also a popular personality in the colony, certainly prevented Virginia from becoming Cromwellian at once. But the influence of incidents, the impulse which suggests repetition of events, to other minds, cannot be doubted. A wave of suicide will sometimes sweep through a community, gathering its own force. Everyone to-day knows that, as a result of the Great War of 1914–18, thrones fell with increasing rapidity, and others soon began to shake. Not immediately did the signs of universal European unrest manifest themselves, but the ensuing ten years were to exhibit revolutionary feelings unquestionably.

So, too, it was with colonial America. The spirit of revolution had been infused; the suggestion to rebel and overthrow long-established authority had been put before them by their Cromwellian relatives in England. Seventeenth-century minds were slow to reason and form conclusions; yet the idea had been imparted sure enough, and another rebellion would ere long ripen in Virginia. But, before such an incident repeated itself, there was the recurrence of a massacre. The day selected was Maundy Thursday, 1644, and several hundred colonists were murdered by the Indians. But Berkeley himself led an expedition against the red men, which resulted in the capture of old Opechancanough, who was himself murdered presently at Jamestown. After two years of war, however, the Indian tribes were glad to have peace, which lasted for twenty years.

With the advice and assent of the freemen, the Lord Proprietary of Maryland had offered religious liberty as an attraction, and thus we get the strange result of Puritans from Virginia going to settle under Roman Catholic leadership. Laws were enacted at St. Mary's with the consent of the Upper and Lower House of Assembly for the punishment of such offences as swearing, cursing, adultery ; and Indians were prohibited from entering Kent Island or Anne Arundel Counties without notice.

For dealing with the English colonies the Commonwealth operated by means of a Committee for Trade and Plantations. When Barbados, St. Kitt's, Nevis and Virginia remained antagonistic to the new governance in England, an Act of

Parliament was passed in October, 1650, prohibiting trade with these four plantations, and any ships that did so trade were to be arrested. In the following August Sir George Ayscue was sent across the Atlantic with a squadron of seven ships from Plymouth. Proceeding via the Tagus and the Cape Verde Islands, he finally reached Barbados on 16th October, having been delayed by " little winds " and many calms. His arrival at the West Indies was unexpected, and by 12th January Barbados surrendered, after a stubborn resistance. The other two islands also submitted, so that Ayscue was able in a few weeks to return home. As for Virginia, there arrived the twenty-eight-gun frigate *Guinea* at Jamestown, which was to compel submission by force. Berkeley had been all for resisting, but, having regard to the embargo on Virginian trade, this policy seemed to the Councillors and Burgesses to spell the colony's ruin. No tobacco would be sold, and therefore there would be no income.

So on 12th March, 1652, articles of surrender were agreed upon by the Governor and Council with the Parliamentary Commissioners, of whom Clayborne was one. The terms were distinctly liberal and more likely to placate than irritate Virginians. Thus neither Governor nor Council should be compelled to take any oath to the Commonwealth, nor censured for speaking well of the King, for one year. The Governor should be permitted to hire a ship for removal of himself and goods to England or Holland. All persons who had served the King to be free from punishment. In a word, Virginia was not only the last of the colonies to surrender to the English Republican Government, but obtained terms more favourable than others had received. Maryland and New England had been the only two provinces which had not declared against the Commonwealth Parliament.

Commissioner Richard Bennett was now elected Governor to succeed Berkeley, and in spite of subterranean grumblings Virginia still presented a picture of peacefulness. On sea matters were distinctly anxious for the trading vessels running to and from England. In the summer of 1652 a further illustration of the unsettled times manifested itself when war broke out between England and the Netherlands, and this caused grave risks to emigrants and tobacco, which were the two most important considerations for the colony. Therefore ships bound to Virginia were given " commissions for private men-of-war for defense." The English Channel was not healthy at these times, and letters of marque were thus requisite. The following were some of the ships which, being about to sail for Virginia in January, 1653, were given the status of privateers : *William and John*, *John and Katherine*, *Planter*, *Honor*, *Hopeful Adventure*, *Golden Lyon*, *Charles*, *Anthony*, *Margaret*, *Seven Sisters* and *James*. This little fleet mounted between them two hundred and twenty-five guns and represented three thousand tons, so the average ship was still well under three hundred tons. But what was more important to individual Virginians was that these vessels brought out some hundreds of dozens of shoes. The passenger and freight trade between England and her western plantations—that is to say, the West Indies, Virginia, Maryland and New England —was now giving employment to over a hundred ocean-going ships. But some of these were unlawful intruders who surreptitiously carried away tobacco to foreign parts.

Royalist refugees had found an asylum in Virginia ; yet not merely were being transported children from Ireland but "lewd and dangerous persons " (as a 1656 document bears witness), "rogues, vagrants, and other persons, who have no way of livelihood and refuse to work." Two ships in that year were built for the navy for service in Virginia. These were the *Blackamoor* and *Chestnut*, each being of ninety tons, measuring forty-seven feet long on the keel, nineteen feet beam, ten feet deep, and mounting a dozen guns. The possibility of Virginia finding a prosperous peace, so essential to her immediate future, was still delayed both by further trouble with the Indians and by internal factions connected with local government. By the year 1658, as a result of English political changes and uncertainties, Virginia was in what a contemporary did not hesitate to call a "distracted state," and then on 3rd September died Cromwell.

With the Restoration there came a lull of satisfaction. Charles II arrived from his Continental exile and landed on English soil in May, 1660, but already Sir William Berkeley had emerged from retirement and been elected Governor once more. In November a Committee of the Privy Council in London was entrusted with the colonial affairs, and it was the desire of Charles II to bring about some uniformity in their rule, as well as improvement. Experienced planters and seamen were to be consulted, shipping and navigation to be encouraged, " learned and orthodox ministers " to be provided for the plantations, steps to be taken for reforming the debaucheries of planters and servants, and consideration to be made as to how natives and slaves might be invited and made capable to receive baptism in the Christian faith.

But the march toward freedom now quickened its pace over American soil. Changes in attitude, in government, in aspirations had multiplied amazingly since the Reformation had fired somnolent minds with the torch of liberty. Executions of prominent men such as Raleigh, Laud, Charles I ; big independent movements like that of the Puritans and the Cromwellians ; far - reaching influences such as General Assemblies and a growing belief in the ultimate future of American colonial strength, all had combined to create a new thought that was diametrically opposed to white slavery and indentured service. In Virginia servants were getting restive, and contemplating the use of force. Farther north, in Massachusetts, the General Court in June, 1661, published their declaration of the right to choose their own Governors and representatives, to admit freemen at their own pleasure, to choose their own officers, to exercise their own legislative, executive and judicial powers without appeal to England, to defend themselves against all aggression, to reject royal or Parliamentary imposition adjudged harmful to the colony. Since it was emphatically not the intention of Charles II to leave his colonies to their own devices, but rather to exercise control over them, we can at once see the big struggle for ultimate freedom strongly indicated. Here was the beginning of a long drama which must end in tragedy.

Changes were going on all round. The Parliamentary Commissioners had in 1652 deposed Lord Baltimore's officers and appointed a Puritan Council, but after several years the proprietary party was finally established. From the southern end of Virginia there was carved out a new colony to be called Carolina, by a grant of Charles II in 1663. Connecticut's numerous settlements had been brought under one jurisdiction, and great changes were taking place to the westward. It was in 1646 that Peter Stuyvesant was appointed Governor of the Dutch territory in North America. He was able to negotiate a settlement of the boundary dispute with the New England colonists by the Treaty of Hartford in the year 1650. The conclusion of the first Anglo-Dutch War on 4th April, 1654, had given the Manhattan settlement recognition. But this war was not sufficiently decisive, and the second broke out in 1664. This enabled the English to capture New Amsterdam, not merely as a hostile act but by virtue of that old-standing claim which had already been stressed. The Treaty of Breda in 1667 concluded the war and provided, *inter alia*, for the retention of New York and New Jersey by England. A patent was issued by Charles II to his brother the Duke of York granting him the New Netherlands territory, and New Amsterdam changed its name to New York. But once more hostilities occurred, and the third Anglo-Dutch War began, during which New York was in 1673 recaptured by the Dutch. Peace was restored in the following year, and New York was transferred to British rule, so to continue till the great Revolution, Major Edmund Andros (of whom more will be said presently) being appointed New York's Governor from 1674 until 1681. The earliest map of New Amsterdam, known as *The Duke's Plan*, drawn in colours and gilt, showing the " towne of Mannados " as it was in September, 1661, is now preserved in the British Museum.

We mentioned just now the serious interference with Virginia's sea-borne trade during the troublous times with Holland. Samuel Pepys reminds us that the English merchant ships did not always stop to fight, and the genial diarist records (under 16th January, 1666–67) : ". . . so away to the other Council door, and there got in and hear a piece of a cause, heard before the King, about a ship deserted by her fellows (who were bound mutually to defend each other), in their way to Virginy, and taken by the enemy." The Dutch privateers had become so dangerous that the western approaches of the British Isles made an exciting zone. In March, 1673, the

Lords of the Admiralty had to ask Prince Rupert for half a dozen of the smallest and best-sailing frigates (or, as we should to-day call them, light cruisers) from the fleet, in order to protect the " rich fleet of East India and Barbados already arrived in Kinsale, and the Virginia fleet daily expected."

At that period the ships to London from Virginia would go in convoys of six and more. Sometimes they numbered as many as fifty sail, and if they could only get into the above-mentioned Irish harbour, where their escort was awaiting them, they might reach the Downs with safety. But there were occasions—such as that brush with Evertsen—when the valuable tobacco fleet was attacked off Virginia's very shores, with the loss of seven ships. Among the old records one finds lists of the vessels entered and cleared, and whether they were " plantation built " ; and to the mother country, which was now expanding both its fighting and commercial navies, the American colonies' supplies (in respect of timber, spars, tar, hemp and other items) were now most welcome. So many local varieties of craft began to be built, that by the time the final quarrel came with Britain most of twenty distinct types were afloat in Maryland and Carolina, classed as follows : round stern, pink stern, hagboat, round pink, pink, ketch, shallop, bark, canoe, sloop, schooner, snow, brig, brigantine and big ship. They were evidences of the influence caused by navigable waters on those who had settled and remained close to the shore.

But it is possible to ruin a colony's industrious efforts by negligent, unimaginative regard at headquarters. Sir William Berkeley had done splendid work ; he had been called upon to see Virginia through great historical crises. After Virginia's enforced submission to the Commonwealth Commissioners, he had retired to his own plantation as a private person. The pity is that he ever came back to public life ; far more prudent is he who has the sense to withdraw at the height, and not on the wane, of his fame. He was now getting old, irritable, unable to adapt himself to new developments, unlikely to see another man's point of view. A younger, more pliable Governor should have been in office.

Virginia in its seventy years of colonization had now become a vast undertaking. Its white people numbered about forty thousand, who were mostly of English stock, with very few Irish and fewer Scotch. The population had increased largely by successive shiploads of emigrants, but especially by births. There were also some two thousand negro slaves. The whole colony by 1676 was still nominally a Church of England community of freeholders, living on their partly-cleared farms, ten per cent. of the people consisting of convict or indentured labour. The Indian menace was as recurring as the apples in the orchards, and always dying down again, but then once more it would blossom out into another massacre. This time the massacre was to develop into something else.

There now comes into prominence Nathaniel Bacon, Jr., cousin of the great Lord Bacon. Nathaniel had taken his degree at Cambridge, been called to the Bar, travelled widely, and had not long since settled in Virginia with his wife near to where Richmond now stands. He is to be visualized as a man of twenty-nine, dark-haired, vain, passionate, headstrong and fanatical; just the fellow who would annoy the obstinate, choleric, horse-breeding Sir William Berkeley. The trouble began when the Indians killed two of Bacon's servants. While he was a born leader, and attracted men to serve under him, Bacon was too impulsive and hot-headed, and too well-known a hater of the Indians to handle this problem reasonably. We see him this April, 1676, at the head of three hundred armed settlers going forth on a campaign against the natives, and inspired by anger as well as nervousness of the continual redskin danger. But at the back of this was a dissatisfaction with Berkeley's inertia and refusal to launch a bold anti-Indian policy. Bacon's impatience thus found a perfect excuse for direct and instant action, but Berkeley found also every cause for annoyance at this young man's daring to take such a decision into his own hands.

Without a commission from Jamestown, Bacon disregarded orders, led his forces against the Indians, slew one hundred and fifty of them, and for a time relieved the frontier of peril. Infuriated at the contempt of authority, Governor Berkeley started off westward with an armed force to arrest Bacon. But the latter was now a popular hero; the whole country was in revolt nominally because of the neglect to have protection

against the savages, but actually because this was the culmina-
tion of grievances—some real, some imaginary—which had
been for a long time collecting. Berkeley hurried back to
Jamestown, and dismissed the General Assembly which had
sat ever since the Restoration, and was popularly said to have
become the tool of the Governor and his friends.

Virginia at this time was in the hands of an oligarchy
consisting (a) of those who had survived through the hard,
unprofitable pioneering days to comfort, prosperity and
gentility ; (b) of those who had comparatively recently come
out from England with enough capital to buy lands, establish
homes and obtain trade from the first. But the plain, illiterate
farmers and tillers of the soil were in practice dumb politically ;
they could but nod their heads in acquiescence. Now there
is no more inspiring battle-cry than that which calls on the
people to demand and obtain their human rights ; the pages of
history are full of the wild actions which men and women will
perform in response to such a summons. Bacon's fluency as a
speaker, and his incendiary emotion, made democracy alive
against oligarchic rule. His head-lines were " sure-fire " ; his
speeches were the stuff of which revolutions are always
well manufactured. The unfairness of appointing one class of
society to all offices, the iniquity of the taxes, the financial
corruption at headquarters, the limitation of franchise to
freeholders, these were the topics excellently chosen by this
champion of the people's rights. The Navigation Laws of
England were a further irritation.

Bacon with his supporters reached Jamestown by water,
where he was arrested by Berkeley under the strength of the
twenty-gun, two-hundred-ton warship *Adam and Eve*. Having
been brought before the Governor in the State House, Bacon
was released on parole, pleaded guilty and received pardon.
Having been elected by Henrico to be a representative in the
new Assembly, Bacon now took his place and promptly began
revising the laws. Thus followed such radical legislation
as was afterward known as " Bacon's Laws." Berkeley's
sympathies were not in line with this reformation, and it
became known that he was about to have Bacon arrested again.
The latter, however, fled up-country, got together six hundred

raging armed men, and descended on Jamestown, where the
Governor could muster only a hundred of the train band. By
threats and armed pressure, Bacon was able next to obtain
from the Governor a commission against the Indians.

It was now midsummer. By his personality and impassioned
speeches, by his insistence on the principles of freedom and the
necessity for smashing the red peril, Bacon was able to draw to
himself enthusiastic followers. Berkeley also was gathering
troops, ostensibly to attack the Indians likewise, but actually
to rout Bacon. Taking ship to the Accomac district, the
Governor was able by means of promises to collect about a
thousand indifferent men. Bacon defeated the Accomac
rabble, captured Jamestown and burned it to the ground,
Berkeley taking refuge afloat and proceeding to Accomac.
But that autumn Bacon became sick with malaria and died
on the banks of York River. Thus, after a meteoric career
lasting less than five months, the rebel passed away and the
rebellion collapsed. Berkeley returned, many flocked to
submit, about thirty were hanged, others fled to the backwoods,
and " Bacon's Laws " were annulled. William Clayborne, who
has previously been mentioned, was one of the Court which
tried the rebels. But by January the hunt for Bacon's followers
had ended. This rising, however, caused consternation in
England, and the well - informed Samuel Pepys refers to
" Bacon's having got the mastery of all, and that not only by
land but at sea too." Sir John Berry was summoned on 30th
September, 1676, to attend on Charles II ; all merchant ships
bound to Virginia or Maryland were stopped from leaving the
Downs till eight suitable vessels had been selected for the
dispatch of soldiers. Berry took with him a force of 1,130 men,
and was given power to impress ships and seamen on arrival in
the colony. Incidentally we get a thumb-nail picture of sea-
travel this year, when the two sons of Sir Charles Wheeler were
allowed to proceed from England to Virginia in the *Bristol*
man-of-war. Each of them went aboard with his mattress on
which to sleep, a seaman's chest in which to keep his possessions,
one runlet of brandy, one hamper of wine, one firkin of butter,
one cask of cheese and biscuit, and one hamper of arms.

Before the King's men could reach Virginia the trouble was

all over. Arrangements were being made in April, 1677, for
the troops to come back, although any soldier who desired to
remain was welcome so to do as "standing security to the
colony."   These red-uniformed men were the first British
regulars ever to land in America.   In this same year sailed
Berkeley for England, where he died in July.   His departure
from the colony had removed the chief difficulty that stood in
the way of restoring peace out of discord.   Virginia settled
down again into its aristocratic autocracy, and so continued till
the Great Revolution.   Nevertheless, while this third and most
ominous rebellion had failed, the cause of freedom was by no
means abandoned ; on the contrary, from now till the accession
of William and Mary we have the continuous struggle of the
Burgesses to protect the people's rights against the royal
Governors.   And let there be no misunderstanding ; the
anxieties in England with regard to civil and religious liberties
did not fail to intensify that dangerous discontent in America,
which was now something more permanent than mere hysteria.

Thomas Penn

Son of William Penn

Thomas, with Richard Penn, was principal proprietor and hereditary Governor of Pennsylvania. After the picture painted in 1751.

CHAPTER XXIII

INDEPENDENCE

THE picture of historic Jamestown burned to ashes was symbolical of the change which had taken place ; the old order of things was gone. Virginia must be builded upon new foundations. But a fresh construction was being inaugurated to the north. Another son of Oxford's university with colonial ideas was William Penn, who during his residence at college had come under Quaker influence and was to become one of the leaders of that sect. In 1681 he obtained a grant of territory, to be called Pennsylvania, where he made a refuge for the Quaker sect, and included from 1682 till 1776 those three counties now the State of Delaware. Penn's equitable treatment of the Indians was part of the new structure that was being erected in America piece by piece.

The first New York General Assembly did not take place till 1683. Three years later the death of Charles II came as the New England charters were annulled, and the work of reorganization was being attempted. His brother, James II, came to the throne, and in 1686 appointed Sir Edmund Andros to unite New York and New England, his title being presently Governor-General. If ever a man won unpopularity and hatred it was Andros, and his attempt in 1687 to seize Connecticut's charter will never be forgotten. But Andros was unlucky to have been chosen for thankless jobs. It was a time when revolutions were becoming fashionable, and the spirit of independence was being sustained, strengthened, encouraged, by contemporary events. The " glorious Revolution " in England of 1688, and the overthrow of James II, had its counterpart the following year when the citizens of Boston rose in revolution, deposed Andros, sent him back to England, and re-established their old colonial government. So great had become the determination in the desire for freedom from mother-control.

But the new monarchs William and Mary surprised the American colonists by insisting that colonies should still be content to be governed as dependencies, and not as independent dominions. This was quite a shock to New England, a set-back to their aspirations, though not indefinitely. By the charter of 1691 William and Mary merged Plymouth, Massachusetts, Maine and Nova Scotia into the one province of Massachusetts ; and while the latter was given a liberal government, it remained a distinctly dependent one. Laws could indeed be made by a representative assembly in co-operation with the King's Governor and his Council, but within three years the King could still place his royal veto on any of them. Thus we have a ready - made spiritual alliance — waiting only to become visible in physical form at the proper opportunity—between New England, New York and Virginia for the triumph of independence against British rule identified in the persons of royal Governors. Dissatisfaction had become a habit ; rebellion, intended or perpetrated, had developed into a set policy. It was only a question of time and opportunity before the greatest of all Anglo-American revolutions would occur, and the delay was caused by the interruptions of war with the French and Indians.

When John Smith assigned to north-eastern America the name of New England, he was grafting a picturesque idea on to insular minds. History was busy in the seventeenth century as it had been in the sixteenth. So many novel thoughts, habits, institutions had already taken hold ; change had become a craze. The bait of free land, free labour, freedom in faith and politics in a new country, were irresistible to people of a certain temperament. They brought a new England into America ; they carried over the same ideals and abilities which they had respected in Europe, and transplanted them in more spacious territory. Agriculture, trading, fishing and seafaring were thus bound to have less limited possibilities than within Britain. But it is essential to emphasize that the New England policy from the first was distinctly Separatist—not merely in the restricted religious connotation, but in the widest meaning.

There was a dour determination on the part of hard-bitten Pilgrims and Puritans to inaugurate an independence from all control, and this inherited disposition was kept active till the final cleavage. Thus, through more than a hundred and fifty years all this New England struggle was not solely anti-regal, anti-Parliamentarian, anti-Cromwellian, but anti-bureaucratic and wholly self-expressionist. They were tired of the Old World; they were enjoying the novelty of the New.

But certainly religious freedom they were incapable of installing; they had neither the mentality nor the inspiration for that; so they established religious intolerance. After the Restoration the interest between England and America became more strictly commercial and less colonial. Relationship between the old mother and her rebellious daughters became strained to breaking - point, because the former could not allow for adolescence nor realize grown-up daughters prefer independent homes of their own, with their own household laws and their own selected friends. When once the wars with the French and the Indians had been ended, and the conquest of Canada completed, then the spirit of independence was advanced still further; New England had no need for a mother's help and guidance. The daughter found even the least parental control an embarrassment. Moreover, the province had been able to prove its own strength and fighting ability in actual warfare.

Down in Virginia stabilization was going on likewise. The founding of the William and Mary College at Williamsburg in 1693 was a prelude to transference of the colony's capital thither five years later; it was the final severance of the John Smith tradition and early pioneering days. When Sir Edmund Andros became Virginia's Governor there was revived that friction which was caused by the choice of unsuitable administrators, and was continued by others. But the abandonment of that initial mistake in unhealthy Jamestown was something more than a change in geographical position. There were now about sixty thousand people in Virginia, self-sustaining and developing a sense of self-determination. Jamestown has been called with much truth the cradle of the United States Republic, and its graveyard to-day contains not merely the remains of its early citizens, but the very foundations on which the greatest Western nation has been built up. All those sad fatalities through malaria, through ship-bred pestilence, through starvation, massacre and other unhappy causes, were merely the harsh events that preceded success. "Except a corn of wheat fall into the ground and die, it abideth alone; but if it die, it bringeth forth much fruit." Virginia was at length luxuriantly productive, but only because the seeds had been sown in pain and grief.

No better evidence of the security of Virginia's roots could be found than in the extension of colonization still farther south beyond that Cape Fear which had been at once a source of unhappiness to the early storm-tossed three-masters and a joyous indication that at last the long voyage to Cape Henry was ending. Georgia, like Carolina, was an expressed, active belief in the future of American settlement. Here was to be a home for the English debtor classes and oppressed, and thus from 1732 we get additional public opinion likely to unite a generation later in the final demand for national independence. The fact that Virginia was so well-established on bays and rivers induced the logical desire to explore farther inland west of the Blue Ridge and Alleghany Mountains; the aspiration was a natural pendant to the chain of explorations wrought by John Smith and his colleagues. But a royal proclamation of 1763 definitely forbade sales of land west of the Alleghanies, and thus, by practically reserving this territory to the Crown, created still another occasion for offence—just one more addition to the load of restrictions fast becoming unbearable.

The interference by the Board of Trade had also prevented a plan of confederation, which was intended in 1754 by reason of the impending French and Indian War. In its origin the Board of Trade was not a separate Government department, but acted merely as a body of advisers to the Crown. It was, however, to play a most important part in the history of American colonization. The royal Governors ever since 1670 and up till March, 1752, were under orders to send letters to the Secretary of State, whenever any colonial incidents demanded the Crown's immediate directions. Before the year

Jonathan Belcher

One of the Georgian Governors of Massachusetts Bay and New Hampshire

1696 trade had been controlled by unbusinesslike courtiers. Merchants therefore desired Parliament to take the matter in hand. The King declined to allow encroachment on his prerogative, but on 15th May, 1696, William III did bring about a special board for promoting trade and improving the American plantations.

This board used to meet every week, except during August, but confined themselves to the protection and advancement of colonial trade ; administration was outside their sphere. The work was done efficiently by competent men, who drafted the Governors' commissions and instructions, and also scrutinized all colonial laws. But from 1714 we get a modification. With the coming of the Hanoverians and establishment of the Whigs, the Board became also Whig, and not infrequently quite unequal to the duties. The Governors' correspondence from across the Atlantic remained unanswered, initiative and encouragement vanished, while political intrigue and indifferent morality were allowed full play. But in 1748 under Halifax it regained life, and four years later obtained complete control over colonial trade as well as the nominations of royal officials in the colonies. The great increase of wealth, of independence and political organization in America had presented fresh problems when (by an Order in Council) the Board of Trade's powers were curtailed on 15th May, 1761. And the matter of the westward migration over the Alleghanies was about to come into serious consideration.

After the year 1768 the Board obtained a limited power, and the Privy Council referred to it all matters connected with trade, Governors' instructions, and so on ; still, the work was of an advisory nature, with no power to carry out a definite policy. But we can immediately see that the appointment of unsuitable men to the Board must inevitably have caused their bad influence to permeate through ill-chosen Governors to a dissatisfied colony of human people. Such disgraceful bureaucratic management would nowadays be tolerated by no English political party for a week. It was bad enough that a letter would necessarily, because of sea-distance, take six or seven weeks to pass from Governor to Board of Trade, and then perhaps three months from the Board of Trade to the Governor,

U

but this period was further lengthened by having to wait till
the next ship sailed. Thus nine months was not an exaggerated
time between the asking of a question in America and the
receipt of a reply from London. In the meantime one particular
crisis had long since passed, and others of greater immediacy
had taken its place.

All this was bad enough, and calculated to bring about the
keenest annoyance, so that thousands of colonists were probing
their minds and asking themselves: " Why should we be treated
in this dilatory manner, when we could regulate our own affairs
on the spot much more ably and without all this formality ? "
Then, having so inquired of their own consciousness, they put
the question to their fellows, with only one answer to be made.
What could be more exasperating, more calculated to snap all
connections, than those occasions when as many as half a dozen
letters from one Governor remained unanswered by London for
three whole years ?

It is possible from existing data to get some mental picture
of the London office with its Board-room, Secretary 'sroom,
and old-fashioned furniture. In the anteroom would wait the
gentlemen who had called concerning plantation business. No
one hurried, there was no such thing as competition, and the
clerks in another room were slowly making their copper-plate
writing. Perhaps a ship had just arrived in the Thames and
brought correspondence from an American Governor, which
was now being considered by the Board this winter's morning.
Had we been allowed inside the Board-room we should have
noticed the painted woodwork and white plaster, the walls
covered with maps and pictures, the windows with their heavy
hangings and curtains. As we trod over the matted floor to
the cupboards and presses containing accumulated dusty
documents, or paused to examine the leather-bound books, we
should have passed a long table in the centre of the room.
Around this table, covered with green cloth, and seated in
comfortable chairs upholstered in green velvet, would have been
observed the Commissioners, and we should have heard them
speaking with deliberate, pompous and studied sentences.
Then the clock on the wall would indicate it was time for a
hearty meal ; so, after warming themselves at the coal-fire in

the wide grate, the weekly meeting would dissolve and the business be carried forward.

From this stuffy atmosphere emanated the instructions which were to guide the Governors in their administration. Into this room would come letters from Governors, sometimes holographs, but sometimes written by a Governor's secretary and only signed by the big man. The subjects would deal with pirates and prizes, statistics and social affairs, trade and politics, maps and charts, suspensions and appointments ; matters connected with the religious, military, economic or legal side of colonial life. There would be boundary disputes, ecclesiastical quarrels, and Councillors' troubles to be set forth. A Governor's letter and enclosures would make up a packet of sometimes fifty documents, which would then be placed in a box, sealed and lettered. The box was then taken down to the water-side and given into the custody of the ship's captain, who on arrival in England either delivered it personally to the Board of Trade Plantation office, or sent it by messenger through the post office. Inasmuch as there were such risks of the sea as pirates, privateers and shipwrecks, to say nothing of hostile men-of-war, the painful process had to be gone through of sending a copy of every document in another ship by a different route.

Such was the ponderous machine which was supposed to be assisting the colonial wheels to go round in the mid-eighteenth century.

We now come to the final phase in the drama of freedom, and this last act has for its leit-motif the American taxation. The contest may be summed up as that between arbitrary power on the one hand and the common rights of representation on the other. If the basis of resistance varied slightly, it was collectively this principle on which the colonies relied : " No taxation, and no legislation to be imposed on American colonies, without the latter being represented." We shall not forget that in Europe, and especially in France which was to have its own Revolution in 1789, there was (by reaction to years of oppression) growing up a body of thought concerned with human liberty and the grievances of the people. It would be some time before social reforms would so crystallize themselves in England as to manifest improvements of monstrous taxation, labour conditions, criminal laws, prison accommodation, sanitary conditions, franchise and many other much-needed alterations. But already Rousseau's writings on the origin of inequality among men had firmly established him as the champion of popular rights, and done much to influence public affairs, no less than private intellects.

In North America, we shall remind ourselves, Virginia had now for offspring Maryland, North and South Carolina, Georgia, making in all five colonies. In the North there were the four New England colonies of Massachusetts, Connecticut, Rhode Island and New Hampshire ; while situated between the North and South groups were New York, New Jersey and Pennsylvania. Thus there were no fewer than a dozen colonies, comprising such wealth and populations that they could no longer be regulated from London. In 1761 the Massachusetts lawyer James Otis, of Boston, strenuously toiled for the colonies' liberty in matters of taxation, and embodied his claim in *The Rights of the Colonies Asserted and Proved* (1764), and in *Considerations on Behalf of the Colonists* (1765).

Nothing could weld these twelve separate colonies so closely together as that series of events which began with the Stamp Act of 1765, when the British Parliament passed during Grenville's ministry the measure for the purpose of military defence in America. The colonists resented this dictation ; nine of them met in New York, and prepared their " Declaration of Rights and Grievances." The elder Pitt boldly denounced the folly of this tax, and insisted that, as regards the Americans, " as subjects they are entitled to the common rights of representation, and cannot be bound to pay taxes without their consent." In the following year this stupid Act was repealed, yet the right was at the same time declared by Parliament to tax the colonies at its pleasure. Thus there still remained, and was confirmed, a principle which caused the colonists even more indignation ; they were being bound by grievous fetters, which could cause only righteous anger. But matters went now from bad to worse, from one piece of Parliamentary foolishness to sheer lunacy. In 1767 came the Act to tax glass, paper, painter's colours, lead and tea, for the support of

New York

As seen from New Jersey at the end of the eighteenth century

Crown servants in America. These and other measures roused the colonists to determined action, and we see the employment of confederacy again invoked ; for, by mutual agreement of the colonies to avoid using the taxed articles, the iniquitous law was made unavailing.

Parliament's next move in this petty procedure was to banish the tax from everything except tea, and this was done in 1770. By slow and irritating steps the mother country had thus been driving her daughters almost to desperation, and acting in such a manner that every bond of filial sentiment must be forgotten in wrath. So-called statesmen in England could not see that the times had changed since the Middle Ages, that in the New World new thought had been developed and fresh ideals set up. Parliamentarians, secure in their own self-satisfaction and isolation, were unable to perceive that equal opportunities for all, liberty of self-government, and a big American brotherhood, were about to be established if Britain pursued its effete and fatal aim of binding the overseas people " in all cases whatsoever."

John Locke (1632–1704), the father of eighteenth-century English philosophical thought, who incidentally had once been Secretary of the Board of Trade, and in his later days became one of the Commissioners of Trade at one thousand pounds a year, had, in his writings on toleration and civil government, not merely powerfully encouraged freedom of thought but even vindicated the principles of revolution. But stubborn legislators could not be persuaded that the Great Separation was about to become a greater reality than the Separatists' departure of a century and a half ago had been to their forefathers. It was James Otis whose initiative had caused the Stamp Act Congress of 1765 to be summoned, and he led the active opposition to the Crown in resistance to the issuing of writs for compelling citizens to aid Revenue officers. The temperament at this period, both of the British Government and colonial Governors, was scarcely conciliatory or tactful, but it was in Massachusetts, with its always keener feeling for freedom, that these recent actions had brought about the most bitterness. When royal troops were sent to Boston, the populace was excited to extreme irritation ; and when in 1770

some garrison troops in self-defence shot down a few of the
Boston crowd who had attacked, there was a perfect opportunity
for exaggerated remarks on massacre and martyrdom.

It is pathetic to watch British common sense sliding down
the slippery colonial path to destruction, with a blind obstinacy
reckless of consequences. One usually finds the statement that
America renounced England, but it would be truer to say that
England made conditions of association no longer possible.
The rights of the governed were of little consideration in
London ; it was rather the question of how much were the
colonies worth commercially to the old country that really
mattered. It has been truly said that nationhood of any
community dates back just as far as its churches and the tombs
of its ancestors ; which, in plain language, signifies that after
two or three generations a new colony may have developed its
own individual ideas and ideals and begun a tradition not fully
in keeping with those of the parent stock. America by about
1763 was not merely a number of plantations but a new people,
needing only to be knit together by some formal agreement.
In speech, character, aspirations, political aims, attitude toward
England there was common gound ; there was also a mighty,
if at present invisible, unity of strength. But that essential
fact had not yet been appreciated in London.

During the agitation immediately antecedent to the
American Revolution no incident has become more famous
than that of 1773, when about fifty men disguised as Indians
boarded certain ships laden with taxed tea and threw three
hundred and fifty chests into Boston Harbour. This historic
" tea-party " induced the Parliamentary retaliation of closing
commerce by means of the Boston Port Act, and depriving
Massachusetts of her charter rights. What resulted therefrom ?
Surely it should have been obvious that in English-bred
colonists, with all their inherited hatred of oppression's heavy
hand, this would stiffen resistance and draw the colonies
together for mutual support. The truth is that another
revolution was, either in America or England, just about due,
as it was in France The attempt to regain political power for
the Crown, the personal Government of the King of England,
had to be decided on one side of the Atlantic or the other.

Had the personal rule of George III been protracted, and any longer unchecked, there would have been in England an anti-royal rebellion. But it was actually, by the chain of circumstances, America which was to be the revolutionary scene, and to expound the lessons which must follow from a certain course of conduct. The mind of the politician cannot always look ahead ; he can understand only after he has been shown concrete results. But America's colonial, stiffened resistance brought about such an independence that, in England, government by Prime Minister and Cabinet was destined to overthrow government by personal kingly power.

The Continental Congress which assembled in Philadelphia during September, 1774, and prepared its " Declaration of Rights," was a protest of unity against legislation without consent of the governed. Force always creates force, and the two together create trouble. British troops were in Boston, the citizens were organizing their own militia and collecting stores at Concord. In command of the former was General Gage, who sent an expedition to destroy the stores, and some fighting began on 19th April, 1775. In May the second Continental Congress at Philadelphia met, and next month George Washington was elected Commander-in-Chief of the colonial forces. And with the Battle of Bunker Hill we get the first big engagement in the War of Independence. When on 4th July, 1776, the Declaration of Independence was adopted, the long struggle of bygone days had taken on a new character which was to bring about the final triumph of colonial nationality. Britain was no longer to interfere with American expansion and with those ambitions which belong by right to healthy youth. The daughters, now united in one confederacy, were resolved to be guardians of their own freedom and their own honour.

Such, then, is the story of America striving for liberty ever since those remote days of ill-found ships wallowing in Atlantic waves toward an uncharted coast. It is, with all the sadness, the courage, the enterprise, the follies and disappointments, one of the most human as well as one of the most fascinating chapters in the volume of the world's records. However we study this subject—as the account of pioneering, the evolution of political autonomy, the peopling of the seaboard, or the beginnings of Western culture—we find therein the compelling qualities of an epic drama, which has for its background a tapestry of sea and ships, with rugged, sun-tanned sailors, weather-stained hulls and storm-torn canvas. For if ever a country owed its very soul to seafaring it is America.

English and American Shipping

This interesting view of Charlestown, South Carolina, shows not merely contemporary eighteenth-century English ocean-going vessels, but local-built colonial sloops with a schooner in the foreground

INDEX

w